S-Boote
German E-boats
in action
(1939-1945)

Jean-Philippe Dallies-Labourdette
Drawings by Bruno Pautigny

S-Boote
German E-boats
in action
(1939-1945)

Translated by Janice LERT

Histoire & Collections

CONTENTS

THE PRECURSORS

The first « motor boats », ancestors of the motor torpedo boats, actually made their appearance at the beginning of the 20th century with the arrival of the internal combustion engine. Several years earlier, Gottfried Daimler and Wilhelm Maybach had revolutionized the embryonic world of speed when they built the first of these engines in 1882. This new method of propulsion made its debuts in automobile racing before moving a few years later from dry land to sea where it soon equipped the first rapid vessels of Kaiser Wilhelm II's navy. After this first generation of mechanical engineers, arrived a group of young technicians specializing in naval construction. They would prove to be true precursors in this domain.

Among them, one man in particular would be responsible for both civilian and military productions that would span more than a century: Otto Lürsen. He headed a family-run company, located on the banks of the Weser River in Vegesack, on the outskirts of Bremen, that had been founded in 1875 by Friedrich Lürsen. He was a true pioneer in designing small, fast and versatile boats. In 1890 a prototype, the *Donner Wetter*, came off the drawing boards. This little boat was

Above:
The speedboat built by Otto Lürssen with which he won the world speed record in 1912. It is a small vessel, eight meters long and propelled by two Daimler Benz 102-hp engines, for a speed of more than 28 knots.

Inset:
Friedrich Lürssen, founder of the Lürssen Naval Shipyards in Bremen-Vegesack in 1875.

Below:
The Lürssen speedboat entered in the Monaco Rally in April 1912. The boat raced in the category « 8- to 12-meter-cruisers ». The Vegesack firm had built a vessel with remarkable nautical qualities t hat had won the event. 8,57-meters long, weighing 1712 kg, it could move at a speed of 58 km/h with perfect stability in calm or slightly choppy seas, thanks to its flat bottom and its streamlined shape.

powered by a 40-horsepower engine that allowed it to attain, over a short distance and time, a speed of 38 knots, a considerable feat for the time.

At the same time, the other European constructors were not just twiddling their thumbs, and they were able to try out their new boats in a whole new series of sporting events, of which the most famous remains the Monaco Rally, run for the first time in 1904. In 1905 the first Algiers-Toulon race was organized. The racers used boats measuring between 9 and 23 meters long and able to navigate in high seas. They managed to make the first lap, Algiers-Mahon in the Balearic Islands, a distance of 370 kilometers, in from 12 to 19 hours, at a top speed of 15 knots for the fastest. The Italians and French dominated the competition, however none of the competitors crossed the finish line in Toulon; weather conditions forced the last two boats left in the race to abandon.

The European military brass kept a careful and increasingly interested eye on these various competitions. In 1907 Wilhelm II's navy ordered ten 200-hp engines from Daimler-Benz, with the idea of equipping their small river surveillance boats. In the following years Monaco would again be used for trials by various constructors. In 1910 Sir John Thornycroft[1] entered a speedboat named the *Miranda IV*. She was 16,75 meters long

1 – In 1874, the Englishman John Thornycroft, who had founded a few years earlier a small naval construction firm, created for the Norwegian Navy a small torpedo boat known as the *Raps*, with a divergent torpedo in tow. This boat was directly inspired by a yacht built in 1870, the *Miranda*, 21 meters long and able to reach 18 knots at full speed, an exceptional performance for the times. In 1905, during the Russian-Japanese War, he delivered a 12-meter-long motorboat, unarmed and capable of travelling at 19 knots, to the tsarist government. In 1916 his Coastal Motor Boats entered into service in the Royal Navy. They were designed by enthousiastic young officers and the John Thornycroft shipyards. In April, 1916, three CMB s of the twelve ordered were operational in the North Sea and the English Channel.

Below:
Fern-Lenkboot (FL) built by the Lürssen company between 1915 and 1916, photographed during trials. 13 meters long, weighing 700 kg, with a 6-ton displacement, it was propelled by two Maybach 6-cylinder 210-hp engines allowing it to reach a speed of 30 knots. The FL's were drones guided by a wire connected to a ground-based operating station. They carried a heavy charge of explosives in the prow.

and capable of reaching a maximum speed of 35 knots, a prelude to the future British torpedo boats of WWI. The following year, Otto Lürsen won the « Grand Prize of the Seas » and the « Baltic Prize » with an 8-meter-long motorboat traveling at more than 28 knots and propelled by two 102-hp Daimler engines. In 1912 he won the world speed record with an identical boat.

THE FIRST OPERATIONS (1914-1918)

During World War I it was mainly the Italian and British Navies who were interested in operational development of motor torpedo boats, leaving the Germans and Austrians to take defense initiatives. The first operational units of the Royal Navy appeared in 1916. They were the result of collaboration between John Thornycroft and young Navy officers who were convinced that fast shallow-draft boats could easily reach the Belgian coast, where the Germans had positioned their fleet of surface vessels in the ports of Ostende and Zeebrugge. After torpedo attacks on these ships, they could take advantage of their speed to quickly disappear. The first three of a total of twelve «Coastal Motor Boats» were delivered to the Royal Navy in April 1916. They were 12 meters long and propelled by a 250-hp engine which allowed them to attain a speed of 33 knots over a radius of 250 kilometers. They were equipped with a single 457-mm torpedo and two 7.7-mm Lewis double machine guns. By November of 1918, eighty-three Coastal Motor Boats were in service in the Royal Navy.

Likewise the Italians, at the SVAN (*Sociéta Veneziani Automobili Navali*) shipyards in Venice, prompted by their director, Attilio Bisio, had designed the MAS or *Motoscafi Anti Sommergibili* (anti-submarine

Top left:
The coastal motor boat CMB 27 built by the Thornycroft shipyards in 1916 and in service in the Royal Navy a year later. Four anti-submarine depth charges are attached at the rear.

Right, from top to bottom:
Four *Luftschiff Motoren* (LM s) photographed in 1917 before setting out on operations. They were 17 meters long, with a 7,5 ton displacement and propelled by three Maybach 6-cylinder 210-hp engines permitting them to attain a speed of 30.7 knots.

MAS 7 snapped in 1916 as she leaves the port of Brindisi. The crew is wearing the « *combinazioni gommata* » that will reappear twenty years later in an improved version for the Decima Mas frogmen. The two 356-mm torpedoes ready for action are clearly visible on the sides. Among the powers during the First World War, only the British and the Italians used their speedboats for offensive operations.

In 1926 the Reichsmarine tested the *Bodo*, an experimental speedboat piloted by Kapitänleutnant Eduard Rabe, an officer of the old Imperial Navy. His son Günther, just a teenager, eagerly joined his father in the motor boat. We find him 14 years later among the S-Bootwaffe officers.

The *Rheinpolizei VII* built by the Lürssen company and delivered in 1926 to the *Rhine Police* created by the Weimar Republic and stationed in Köln. An identical unit was also based in Düsseldorf.

The S1 photographed in 1929 during speed trials. The boat has not yet been armed, and will not be delivered to the Reichsmarine until a year later. The Lürssen company had created an exceptional ship. 26.85 meters long, for a 39.87-ton displacement. Her three Daimler Benz 12-cylinder 2400-hp engines could propel her at a speed from 30 to 34.2 knots. The S1 was sold to the Spanish Navy on December 10, 1936.

Below right:
The Inishowen just before being delivered by the Lürssen shipyards in Bremen-Vegesack to the US Coast Guard. The general lines of the hull inspired those of the future S1, delivered to the Reichsmarine on August 7, 1930.

Below left:
The Schnellboote Lür built by the Lürssen shipyards for the Reichsmarine. She had the same characteristics as the S1 but was smaller. 21 meters long for a 23-ton displacement, she had three 450-hp Maybach gasoline engines. She was delivered to the Reichsmarine on June 14, 1930 and was later ceded to the Luftwaffe in 1938 to be used for sea search and rescue of downed pilots.

motorboats). The Italian MAS s were responsible for numerous, and often very successful, raids against the surface vessels of the Austrian Imperial Navy. On June 10, 1918, Navy Lieutenant Rizzo and his MAS 15 sank the *Szent Istvan*, an Austrian armored battleship with a 21 570-ton displacement.

The German Navy had also been busy. During the summer of 1916, German engineers perfected the FL or *Ferlenke Booten*, little boats with no pilots which could reach 30 knots. They had a unique remote control system, stationed on dry ground, using a wire unrolled at the back of the boat. There was no crew and an important charge of explosives was attached at the bow. These boats participated in numerous attacks against the Allied blockades along the Belgian coast, with little success. By January of 1917 the first German motor boats were completely operational. It was the Lürsen company, already well-known for its success in civilian competitions, which would build the LM s (*Luftschiff Motoren*), real speedboats which could reach 29 knots thanks to their three Maybach gasoline engines. Six units were delivered by the Lürsen naval shipyards in Vegesack and the Max Oerstz shipyards in Hamburg. The volatility of the gasoline, and the fact that it was dangerous when used in engines that occasionally misfired, led to explosions on two ships. This experience led the Lürsen engineers a few years later to develop a series of diesel

engines which were just as powerful but a lot safer.

The end of the production program came with the end of WWI. The 1918 armistice and the signing of the Treaty of Versailles were to have dramatic consequences for the future of the German Navy. On November 21, 1918, the German high sea fleet led by the battle cruiser *Seydlitz* surrendered to the Allies at Scapa Flow in the Orkney Islands. Seven months later, day for day, it managed, under orders from its leader, Admiral Ludwig Von Reuter, to escape the vigilance of the English squadron that was surrounding it, and blow itself up. Five battleships, nine cruisers, forty-six torpedo boats and ten other ships were scuttled. Of the seventy-four warships that the Allies thought they were going to be able to divide up among themselves, there remained only one cruiser and several destroyers.

DEVELOPMENTS BETWEEN THE TWO WORLD WARS.

The Treaty of Versailles drastically reduced the tonnage of the German Navy. The surface fleet was limited to six battleships, six cruisers, twelve destroyers and twelve torpedo boats, along with a few reserve vessels. The Weimar Republic was not allowed any submarines and the battleship tonnage was reduced to 10 000 tons. The Allies would nevertheless authorize the Reichsmarine to undertake a new construction program concerning twelve torpedo boats, displacing 200 tons each. The Germans quickly seized the opportunity of diverting this authorisation to start building speedboats. Old LM s, built by Lürsen a year before the end of the war, were rearmed from 1922 on and rebaptized UZ s (*Unterseeboote Zerstörer*, submarine destroyers).

The activity of the Lürsen shipyards at the time was not limited to orders from the Reichsmarine. For the young *Reichswasserschutz* (the Weimar Republic Maritime Guard, which became the *Rheinpolizei* in August, 1920), the Vegesack firm also built a series of small boats designed to police the Rhine River.

Top right:
The S2 was still waving the Reichsmarine flag when she was photographed in 1934. This unit was part of the S2-S5 series, 28 meters long with a 57-ton displacement and propelled by three 12-cylinder 3000-hp Mercedes Benz BFzs, for a speed of 33.8 knots. She is armed with two 533-mm torpedo tubes and a 20 mm cannon at the rear. The S2 was sold along with the S1, S3, S4 and S5 to the Spanish Navy on December 10, 1936 and renamed Falange. Using the same design, the Lürssen shipyards delivered five units to the Yugoslavian Navy in 1936 and 1937: *Velebit, Dinara, Triglav, Rudnik* and *Orjen.* These boats were seized by the Italians in April, 1941, and incorporated into the MAS flotillas of the *Regia Marina.*

Above:
The S4 flying the Reichsmarine flag. The unit, launched in June of 1932, became part of the 1st half-flotilla of the S-Bootwaffe in 1934. At that time she was commanded by Oberleutnant zur See Gottfried Pönitz. She was sold in 1937 to Franco's Navy and renamed *Requete.*

Below:
The S8, photographed in the Baltic Sea in 1935, The vessel, commanded by Oberleutnant-zur-See Eberhard von Bogen, entered service in the 1st flotilla in September, 1934. The S8 was part of the S6-S9 series, 32.4 meters long and displacing 95 tons when fully loaded. She was driven by three 1320-hp MAN LZ7 engines, permitting a maximum speed of 35 knots.

From 1926 on, two larger vessels were delivered to reinforce the existing fleet. The *Rheinpolizei VI* and *VII* were based respectively at Düsseldorf and Cologne.

Along with its dealings on the home market, the firm started to export its know-how, notably to the United States. The American Coast Guard was interested in Lürsen's little boats, and several vessels of varying tonnage were built for them. Among these was the *Inishowen*, whose form and nautical characteristics were already similar to those of the first series of S-Boote launched at the beginning of the 1930's. And then an American millionaire ordered a splendid motor yacht, the *Oheka II*[1], with remarkable nautical qualities and capable of a speed of 34 knots. This convinced the Reichsmarine in 1929 to ask the Lürsen company to develop a prototype of a rapid torpedo-launcher, using this model. After a little more than a year of work and trials, the torpedo boat was ready. It was baptized UZ 16. Its exceptional sea stability, its performances, which could approach 34 knots at full speed, outclassed all of its rivals. On August 7, 1930, the first model was delivered to the Reichsmarine as S1 or *Schnellboote 1*.

The S1 was a vessel built of mahogany and metal with a 47-ton displacement for a length of 26.8 meters. It was propelled by three Daimler-Benz V-12 gasoline engines, for a total of 900 hp, to which was added a 100-hp Maybach engine for « cruising », that is for low-speed travel (around 6 knots). Maximum speed was 34 knots. In order not to violate the clauses of the Treaty of Versailles, the boat was not armed, but it was designed to receive two 533-mm torpedo

---

1 – Equipped with 3 Maybach 550-hp gasoline engines.

Above:
The dock in front of the Lürssen factory in Bremen-Vegesack. The date is October 10, 1932 and the S6-S9 series has just finished tryouts. They will be delivered to the Reichsmarine in 1933. The dimensions of this version are slightly larger than those of the S1-S5 series. The S6 was 32.36 meters long for a 60.4-ton displacement. She was propelled by three 7-cylinder 900-hp MAN diesel engines, giving her a speed of around 30 to 32 knots. The 533-mm torpedo launching tubes and the 20-mm anti-aircraft guns at the back are still canvas-covered.

Below:
The 1st half-flotilla of S-Boote on maneuvers off Kiel in 1933. The S2, S3, S4 and S5 are visible. The half-flotilla is under the orders of Kapitänleutnant Erich Bey and has a mission of assistance to the rare surface vessels of the Reichsmarine.

Bottom:
The 1st S-Boote flotilla photographed in the fall of 1934 with the support ship Tsingtau. The S1 is visible in the picture on the right. Notice her characteristic torpedo tubes (bevelled). All of the boats are still flying the Reichsmarine flag.

tubes and a 20-mm pursuit cannon located in the stern, which gave it impressive fire power.

The auxiliary armament was to change considerably during the war as the pressure exerted by the Allied air forces grew. In 1943, the S100 series received a 37-mm anti-aircraft gun in the stern, a 20-mm two or four gun turret in the center, and a 20-mm cannon in the bow, as well as two or three 7.92-mm machine guns. The torpedos were G7As, identical to those equipping the U-Boote at the beginning of the war. In the axis of each launch tube, a second reserve torpedo could be lined up in less than forty-five seconds. Along with its offensive weapons, each vessel could transport six 500-kg anti-ship mines, which were attached to the stern and

Top left:
The S5 before she was sold the Franco's Spanish Navy in December, 1936. The S5 was part of the first series of S-Boote built for the Kriegsmarine starting in 1932 by the Lürssen company in Bremen-Vegesack. She was 28 meters long with a 57.6-ton displacement. With her three 12-cylinder Daimler Benz BFZ engines, she could reach a top speed of 33,8 knots. She was armed with two 533-mm torpedo-launching tubes and a 20-mm cannon placed in the stern.

Left:
The S12 during tryouts in the Baltic Sea in 1935. The vessel, built by the Lürssen shipyards in Bremen-Vegesack, has just been delivered to the Reichsmarine, and the torpedo-launching tubes are still covered with their protective canvases. In September, 1939, the S12 was assigned to the 2nd flotilla, and surrendered to the US Navy in January, 1946.

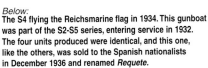

Above Left:
The support ship *Tsingtau* in the port of Swinemünde in 1937, with the S6, S8, S12 and S13 plus a fifth gunboat whose registration number cannot be seen in the photo. The *Tsingtau* participated in April of 1940 in the invasion of Norway along with her sister-ship, the *Carl Peters.*

Below:
The S4 flying the Reichsmarine flag in 1934. This gunboat was part of the S2-S5 series, entering service in 1932. The four units produced were identical, and this one, like the others, was sold to the Spanish nationalists in December 1936 and renamed *Requete.*

Above right:
The support ship *Tsingtau*, probably photographed in 1938, surrounded by units of the 1st S-Boote flotilla, at that time under the orders of Kapitänleutnant Kurt Sturm.

WORLD SPEED RECORD: AUGUST 7, 1939

On August 7, 1939, an S-Boote designed for the Bulgarian Navy and piloted by Gert Lürsen, grandson of Friedrich Lürsen, reached the speed of 68,14 km/h. This record was immediately ratified by the International Automobile Yachting Union (UIYA – Union Internationale du Yachting Automobile). In the words of Gert Lürsen:

It was stormy and weather conditions were quite bad when we left the Vegesack dock in the afternoon. Among the crew

on board were official represen-tatives of the International Yachting Union. We had to reduce speed until we reached the little river port of Brake, situated half way between Bremen and Bremerhaven. Once past that line, we could finally open up the throttle. We felt a sudden thrust as the engines reached top speed. The motorboat rose as if she was going to fly above the waves. This created a bow-wave several meters high on each side of the hull. The world speed record was certified at 36.79 knots over a distance of more than a mile.

This world record rewarded the exceptional performances of the speedboats built by the Lürsen shipyards. On March 17, 1937, the Bulgarian Navy ordered five speedboats[1] from the Vegesack company, through their Berlin intermediary, the Hapro Society. Only one boat, the F3, was built and delivered in 1939 to the Bulgarian Navy. It was this boat that won the world speed record that same year. She was 28 meters long with a 68-ton displacement, and was propelled by two 12-cylinder MB 500 diesel engines developing 950 hp. At full speed she could sustain 37 knots for a few minutes. She received two 533-mm torpedo launching tubes and a 20-mm rapid-fire cannon at the rear, just like the boats in the S1 to S5 series. In September of 1939, this boat was on a cargo ship ready to leave for Bulgaria, when the declaration of war abruptly changed things and she was requisitioned by the Kriegsmarine. The Bulgarians, allies of the Reich, finally got their boat in 1942. She was not disarmed until 1975.

1 – The four other gunboats originally ordered by the Bulgarian Navy were never built. In 1940, the F3 joined the 2nd S-Boote flotilla to participate in the June fighting. She was registered as S1.

Certificate recieved from UIYA.

Above:
The S11 training in the Baltic Sea. This snapshot, reproduced from a post card, was taken before the beginning of the war. This unit was part of the S10-S13 series, delivered in 1934. She was propelled by three 1200-hp MB 502 engines allowing her to reach a top speed of 35 knots. The S11 was turned over to the Soviet Navy in November, 1945.

Above:
The world speed record certificate presented to Gert Lürssen on August 28, 1939 by the International Automobile Yachting Union.

Right:
The support ship *Tanga* delivered to the Kriegsmarine on January 21, 1939. The picture shows the ship in the port of Rostock at the end of the year 1938. She is just about finished but her artillery had not yet been installed. The S21 is visible coupled with her on the port side.

Right:
The Lürssen company dock in Bremen-Vegesack in 1937 with six S-Boote to be delivered to the Kriegsmarine. They are probably series S14-S17.

which finally caused more losses to Allied ships during the war than the torpedo attacks. In 1931 the Reichsmarine ordered four production-line models (S2 to S5). Their motorization was changed to accommodate gasoline engines totalling 1 100 hp which propelled the boats at a speed in excess of 34 knots.

The major innovation, other than the remarkable general performances of these boats, was the positioning of the rudders, an invention of Lürsen's engineers. The main rudder was attached at the stern in the middle of the hull with, on either side, exactly in line with the screw-propellers, two small independent rudders. When the boat was launched at full speed, the two small auxiliary rudders were inclined on a 30° angle toward

The S19 pictured in 1938 shortly after entering service. She was part of the S14-S25 series, with tubes that have not yet been streamlined. On October 1, 1939, the S19, under the orders of Leutnant zur See Detlefsen, became part of the 1st flotilla. She ended the war in 1945 surrendered to the Royal Navy.

BPAUTIGNY

Schnellboote S1

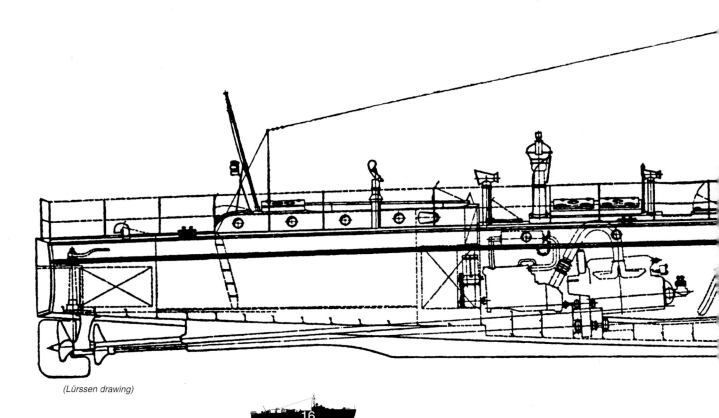

(Lürssen drawing)

The S1 in 1932 a few months before being delivered by the Lürrsen shipyards in Bremen Vegesack to the Reichsmarine. Development of the boat had started in 1929. A year later she was finished and baptized UZ16, then renamed W1 on March 31, 1931. 27.03 meters long for a 40,4–ton displacement when fully loaded, the S1 was driven by three 12-cylinder 900-hp Daimler Benz BFz gasoline engines, along with an additional 100-hp Maybach « cruise » engine. She could reach 34 knots at full speed. Her main armament was made up of two 533-mm torpedo launching tubes, with four torpedoes, and a 7.92mm-caliber machine gun. The crew was composed of an officer and 13 seamen. The above plate represents the S1 without her weapons, so as not to violate the Treaty of Versailles. On March 16, 1932, the gunboat joined the 1st S-Boote half-flotilla under the orders of Oberleutnant zur See Klaus Ewerth, with an enlarged crew of 25 men. The S1 was sold on December 10, 1936 to the Spanish Navy and became the *Badajoz*.

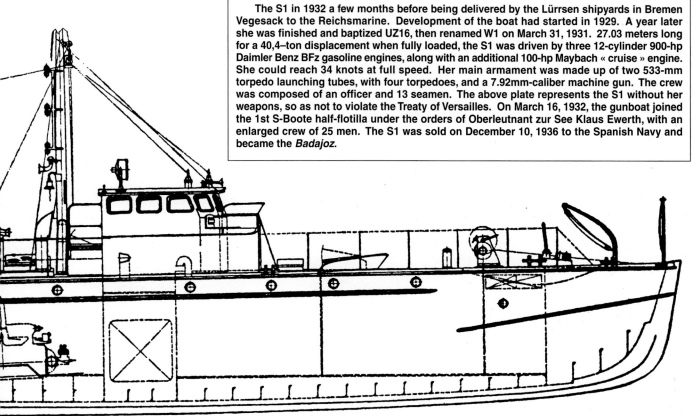

S-BOOTE DESIGN

The S-Boote built by the Lürsen shipyards were remarkably stable even in bad weather. To approach their target during night attacks their 100-hp auxiliary engine could propel them almost silently at a speed of 6 knots. The secret of the nautical performances of the S-Boote also lay in the conception of their diesel engines. The German engineers had not forgotten their bitter experiences of WWI with gasoline engines, and threw all their weight behind diesel propulsion. In 1935, the Navy adopted the MB 502, a 16-cylinder 1 320-hp Mercedes[1] engine. Lightweight, compact, repair-friendly, it satisfied all the requirements of the S-Boote crews. But it was actually the use of the MB 501, another Mercedes engine, which gave the German rapid fleets the tool they needed to meet the challenge of the coming conflict. The MB 501 developed 2 000 horsepower and its twenty cylinders allowed it to easily exceed 40 knots at top speed. The S-Boote received three engines of this type each, bringing their total strength to 6 000 hp. From 1943 on, the S100 series received the 2 500-hp MB 511, and at the end of the war the Mercedes engineers developed an even more powerful engine, the MB 518[2], which, with its 3 000 hp, could propel the German ships at 43,5 knots.

1 – Between September 1,1939 and October 1, 1944, the Mercedes factories delivered a total of 756 engines of various types. This represented an average of 12.3 engines per month. 856 engines were produced during the war, including 109 MB 512s, 741 MB 511s and 6 MB 518s.
2 – The first trials of the MB 518 took place in October, 1942. In view of the incredible performances of the prototype, production was immediately launched. The engines started being delivered to the Lürsen shipyards in December, 1943, and in February, 1944, the brand new S170 with three MB 518 engines developing 3000-hp each was operational. American bombing raids on factories during the months of September and October prevented assembly-line production.

The other factor in the astonishingly successful S-Boote conception was the internal structure of the boats, made from different types of wood associated with metal parts. For body parts, the German engineers were able to create lightweight structures made of various types of wood, reinforced with pieces of metal, thus insuring better protection for the vessel and for her crew.

Throughout the war years, combat experience would lead the German engineers, in collaboration with Petersen's headquarters, to continually modify the structure of these boats. After 1943, the command bridge was replaced by an armored cabin, the *Kalottenbrücke*, round-shaped and stream-lined to insure better protection for part of the crew. Likewise the gunners fore and aft were well protected inside their low-lying combat stations, from which it was easy to fire on enemy ships. The crews of the British MTB s were comparatively more exposed than their Kriegsmarine counterparts during cannon fighting, and often sustained heavier losses. During the first two years of the war, the British Admiralty admitted in private that the operational qualities of the German gunboats were clearly superior to those of their Royal Navy counterparts.

Previous page:
Different phases of S-Boote hull assembly in the Lürssen shipyards in Bremen-Vegesack.

Top left:
Workers in a Lürssen plant in Bremen-Vegesack assembling an S-Boote fusebox.

Top right:
An S-Boote pilot's bridge being assembled at the Lürssen shipyards in Bremen-Vegesack.

Above:
The Lürssen naval shipyards in Bremen-Vegesack. The pieces of a hull are being assembled in a plant under the watchful eye of a Kriegsmarine officer.

Top right: The MB 518 was developed from 1944 on for the S170 series. Only six copies ever came off the assembly lines: Allied bombing raids over factories in 1944 prevented further production. With 3000 hp, the boats that it equipped could reach 43.5 knots.

Top left:
The 6-cylinder 1600-hp M.B. type 512 diesel engine used from 1939 on for models S30 and S31.

Below:
1320-hp Mercedes Benz type MB 502 diesel engine.

Below:
The M.B. 501. Several hundred of these 2000-hp engines were produced from 1938 on. They equipped 65% of the S-Bootwaffe units.

Bottom:
The machine room inside an S-Boote.

Top:
Different phases of S-Boote hull
assembly in the Lürssen shipyards
in Bremen-Vegesack.

Above:
Assembling a propeller shaft housing.

Above:
Schnellboote under construction
in the Lürssen naval shipyards
in Bremen-Vegesack.

Left:
February, 1940: launching an S30-type S-Boote
at the Lürssen shipyards in Bremen-Vegesack.

the exterior, creating a water flow around the screws which diminished the bow-wave. This created the *Lürsen Effekt*, adding two or three additional knots to the speed. At full speed the S-Boote had an autonomy of 400 nautical miles, which increased to 800 miles at a speed of 20 knots. The structure of these vessels employed several different types of wood, making them particularly robust and flexible. The keel and the hull were made of oak. Eight waterproof compartments were created inside, containing 6 tanks with a maximum capacity of 7 500 liters of fuel. The outer shell of the hull was made of mahogany and the upper and lower decks and intermediate sections of the ship were of cedar. The 25-man crew, unlike their colleagues working on the U-Boote, had living space that could be qualified as almost comfortable. The twelve bunks on board were used alternatively by shifts.

In November of 1932 the German Navy possessed a half-flotilla of S-Boote, that is four boats (S2 to S5), which could become 8 in time of war. At that time the flotilla was under the orders of Kapitänleutnant Erich Bey with the mission of supporting the few remaining surface vessels in service in the Reichsmarine.

When the Nazis took over, a major remilitarization effort followed. At that time the leaders of the new Kriegsmarine spent much time discussing the future construction programs and the tactical use of ships. The question came up of the true operational utility of the S-Boote. If war were to break out, Germany would once again be confronting its traditional enemy, France. But the French coasts were much further away from the German ports than the 700 nautical miles of autonomy of the S-Boote. This autonomy

would thus be totally insufficient if the ships were to be used to launch full-speed raids against French targets and then return to their bases.

On August 28, 1936, the Lürsen firm received a new order for four more S-Boote, series S6 to S9, to be equipped with three Man L7 diesel engines for a total of 1 300 hp. From then on, new boats would be ordered regularly. Series S10 to S13, then S14 to S25, were lengthened by 4,50 meters in order to take the new V-16 Daimler-Benz MB 502 diesel engines, which allowed a fully-loaded ship to make 38 knots for a 92-ton displacement and a length of 35 meters. The S10 series had an autonomy of 878 miles at a speed of 20 knots. The S14s were able to cover 1000 miles at the same speed.

In 1937, the Kriegsmarine had at its disposal the following units: S1 to S5[1], propelled by delicate gasoline engines, and S6 to S16 equipped with much more rugged Man diesels. This represented barely two operational half-flotillas of 6 gunboats plus two reserve vessels each. These 16 ships were relatively few considering the needs of the reorganized German fleet and the increasingly persistent threat of war.

A major construction effort was undertaken during the year 1938, and at the beginning of the hostilities the Kriegsmarine was able to line up two S-Boote flotillas comprising 17 units, with 10 more vessels under construction. The first flotilla was commanded by Kapitänleutnant Sturm.

Kapitän Zur See Walter Lohmann

One of the most important naval figures during the post-WWI period in Germany corresponding to the birth of the Weimar Republic was Kapitän zur See Walter Lohmann. First, as an administrative officer in the Kaiser's Navy, he was tapped at the end of the war to try to facilitate the Armistice negociations with the officers of the Royal Navy. The restrictions contained in the Treaty of Versailles deprived the future Weimar navy of large warships. Thus Lohmann insisted on developing construction programs for small, rapid, heavily-armed boats, and elaborating new tactics for using them. As a result of his determination, during the summer of 1925 a group of reserve officers, under the orders of Kapitänleutnant Eduard Rabe and Leutnant Friedrich Ruge, started refurbishing some of the old LM speedboats which had been used during the last year of the war. These boats were discreetly reequiped with the help of the Lürsen shipyards.

During the numerous exercises that took place during this period, the bases for the future S-Boote offensive tactics were laid. Units grouped together by twos or threes at night, when the sea was calm, were remarkably effective in simulated attacks against old warships of the ex-Imperial Navy which had somehow managed to escape the tragedy of Scapa Flow. Their low profil, and their light grey camouflage paint, permitted them to melt into the surface of the Baltic or North Sea. The British and Italian naval experiences of the Great War were studied and improved upon. By the end of the 1920s, the only thing needed for the German coastal forces to be completely operational were the boats themselves. It was during this period that young officers like Petersen, Birnbacher, Fimmen, Opdenhoff, Johansen, Von Mirbach, Zymalkowski were learning the trade. They were to make names for themselves several years later as flotilla commanders.

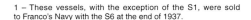

1 – These vessels, with the exception of the S1, were sold to Franco's Navy with the S6 at the end of 1937.

Top left: **The S9 photographed in the Baltic in 1938. The vessel was part of the S7-S13 series delivered to the Reichsmarine in 1935. Oberleutnant zur See Rudolf Petersen was named commander in September, 1935. After the declaration of war, history repeated itself and the S9 became part of the 2nd flotilla under the orders of Kapitänleutnant Rudolf Petersen.**

Top right: **The S13 after colliding with the laboratory-ship** *Meteor* **on June 14, 1939. The front of the boat is completely bashed in, but she unexpectedly remains afloat. She was taken in tow and repaired at the Kiel naval shipyards, and in September, 1940, was back at work with the 3rd flotilla in Rotterdam.**

Left: **The S10, part of the S7-S13 series, launched in March, 1935. This photo was taken before the war. At that time she was commanded by Oberleutnant zur See Hans Henning von Salisch. The S10 was turned over to the US Navy in 1945.**

It was made up of the S11, S12, S18, S19, S20, S21, S22, S23 and for logistic support the surface ship *Tsingtau*. It was based in Kiel. The second flotilla, commanded by Kapitän-leutnant Petersen was positioned in Heligo-land. It was composed of the S9, S10, S14, S15, S16, S17 and the support ship *Tanga*.

On June 14, 1939, the S13, while participating in a series of exercises in the Baltic Sea, smashed into the *Meteor*. She was towed back to Kiel, where she stayed in dry dock for several months. On September 4, 1939, it was the S17 that ran into trouble in the North Sea. Her keel broke during a storm; she nevertheless made it alone back to her base in Heligoland.

Above:
The S14 photographed before the beginning of the war. This boat was never used on operations during the war, but served in the Baltic Sea for crew training.

Following pages:
An S-Boote of the S101-S133 series, from one of the training flotillas, photographed here in the Baltic Sea at the end of 1944. Crew training was carried out up to the end of the war by three training flotillas based in Swinemünde. These flotillas also participated in the last battles in the Baltic Sea.

Below:
The support ship *Tsingtau* in the port of Kiel during the summer of 1938, surrounded by several units of the 1st flotilla under the orders of Kapitänleutnant Kurt Sturm.

Right:
A first-generation S-Boote, probably from the S14-S17 series, speeds over the water somewhere in the North Sea.

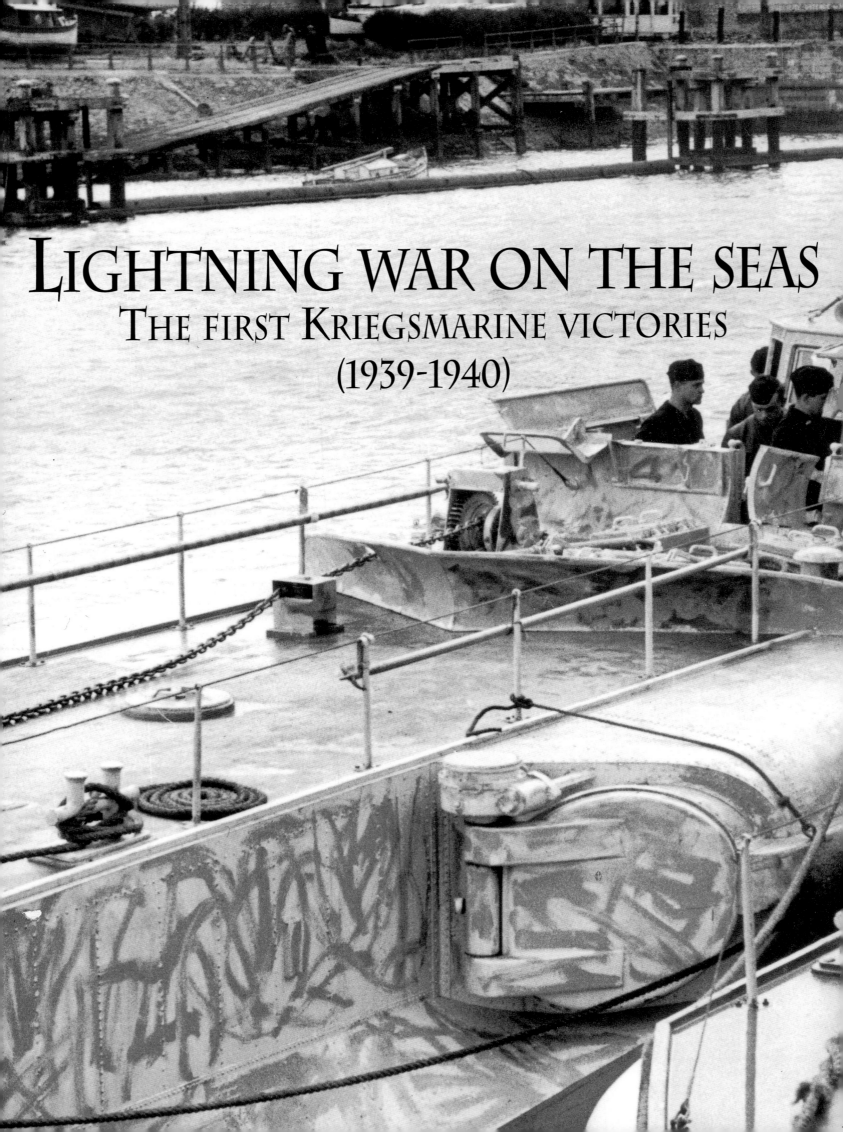

Lightning war on the seas
The first Kriegsmarine victories
(1939-1940)

The lightning attack on Poland wasover before the S-Boote got a chance to intervene. Certain units participated symbolically around Dantzig during the last days of August 1939 helping to prevent ships fromleaving the Polish port. During the first days of autumn, weather conditions were so difficult that the S-Boote were often unable to leave their bases to accomplish their missions. That *drôle de guerre* was to continue in the North and Baltic Seas during the winter of 1940. The main ports of Germany were iced over and because of the poor weather, no major operations were undertaken by any of the powers. Considering the meager results of the two S-Boote flotillas during the first six months of the war, the Kriegsmarine headquarters, which had grouped the T-Boote and S-Boote under a unified command, decided to reduce the number of new units. Originally five flotillas of eight S-Boote each (plus 2 reserve boats) were to have been created at the beginning of 1940. This would have meant a total of 50 operational vessels. But the construction programs were stopped and replaced by new U-Boote construction, as these boats were starting to intervene more and more frequently against the Royal Navy in the Atlantic.

Previous page, left:
Kapitänleutnant Heinz Birnbacher probably snapped in 1939 just after taking over command of the 1st S-Boote flotilla, a job he kept until September, 1942 (4th from the left in the middle row).

Previous page, centre:
The S9 and S11 paired side by side before the declaration of war. In the background notice four U-Boote, probably type IIs.

Previous page, bottom:
An S30-type S-Boote enters the port of Kiel on April 1, 1940, returning home after a mission.

Above:
An S14-S25-type S-Boote returning to the German port of Kiel during the winter of 1939.

Centre:
An S14-S25 type S-Boote stuck in the ice in the port of Kiel in December, 1939. That winter was particularly harsh, and the crew are doing their best to try to break the ice. The 20-mm gun located in the stern has been dismounted to protect it from the freezing weather.

Below:
The S11 photographed in 1939 in the Baltic Sea. At that time she was commanded by Oberleutnant zur See Fro Harmsen and was part of the 1st flotilla under the orders of Kapitänleutnant Kurt Sturm.

THE INVASION OF NORWAY.

In March of 1940, on the eve of Operation *Weserübung*[1], the Kriegsmarine still had only two operational flotillas. The first, even though its composition remained the same, received a second support ship, the *Carl Peters*[2]. The second flotilla had just received the S30, S31 and S32, equipped with new 1 600-hp Mercedes MB 512 diesel engines. The naval force put together by the Kriegsmarine commanders for the invasion of Norway and Denmark was composed of eleven groups of surface vessels and nine U-Boote groups. The main mission of these German boats during Operation *Weserübung* was to protect the invasion sites where troops would be landing against any possible counter-attack by the Royal Navy. The first S-Boote flotilla, including S19, S20, S21, S22, S23, S24, was part of « Gruppe 3 ». The backbone of this group was composed of the cruisers *Königsberg* and *Köln*,

1 – Code name for the invasion of Norway.
2 – As well as a new commander, Kapitänleutnant Heinz Birnbacher..

Above:
Two 2nd flotilla S-Boote escorting small German ships preparing to land troops near the Norwegian *city of Kristiansand.*

Left:
A unit from the 2nd S-Boote flotilla passing in front of the cruiser *Karlsruhe off Kristiansand* during Operation *Weserübung.* The mission of the gunboats was to protect the larger Kriegsmarine surface vessels and also carry assault troops ashore.

Below:
A unit from the 1st flotilla checks a Norwegian steamerduring Operation Weserübung.

Below:
2nd S-Boote flotilla at sea during the invasion of Norway. Six anti-submarine DM11-type depth charges are attached to the rear of the boat because British submersibles were present in the German landing zones. The British submarine *HMS Truant* torpedoed the German cruiser Karlsruhe off Kristiansand on April 9. The ship sank within a few hours.

Above:
An unidentified S14-type S-Boote from the 2nd flotilla under the orders of Kapitänleutnant Rudolf Petersen, patrolling along the Norwegian coast.

Right:
A 2nd S-Boote flotilla along side a German transport ship in the Norwegian port of Kristiansand several days after the fall of the city.

Below:
S30-type S-Boote from the 2nd flotilla on April 9, 1940 embarking Wehrmacht troops to be landed near the city of Kristiansand.

Bottom:
The support ship Tsingtau at dock in the port of Kristiansand with units of the 2nd flotilla. The relaxed attitude of the crew would tend to indicate that the photo was taken several days after the fall of the Norwegian city.

as well as two Leopard-class destroyers, and the *Carl Peters*, a support ship. This group was under the orders of Rear Admiral Hubert Schmundt, with the mission of landing troops who were to establish a foothold for occupying the city of Bergen.

The 2nd S-Boote flotilla, with S7, S8, S17, S30, S31 and S33, was attached to « Gruppe 4 ». This flotilla supported the cruiser *Karlsruhe* and three torpedo boats, with the mission of taking *the city of Kristiansand*. In this plan, the S-Boote were to be used basically as landing vessels to allow the larger Kriegsmarine troop transport ships to get their soldiers onto dry land as quickly as possible,

B.PAUTIGNY

Schnellboote S7

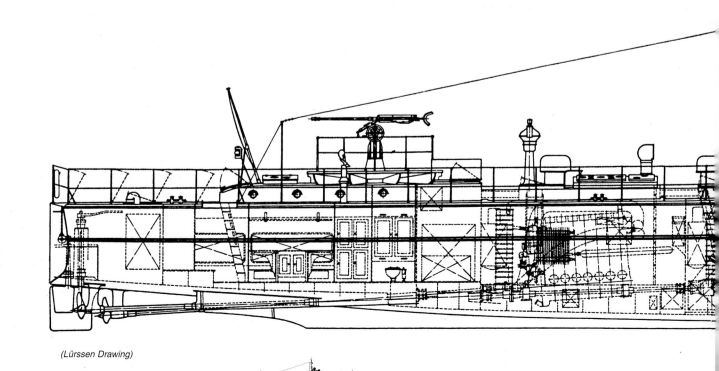

(Lürssen Drawing)

The S7 shown in 1935 at a time when the boat was still part of the 1st half-flotilla and was commanded by Oberleutnant zur See Kurt Sturm. This unit was part of the S7-S9 series, launched in 1933 and entering service in the Reichsmarine in 1934. Her dimensions were quite different from those of the S1. The S7 measured 32,30 meters long for an 86-ton displacement. Her three 1320-hp MAN L7 diesel engines allowed her to reach a top speed of 36,5 knots and gave her a radius of 600 miles. Her armament was also improved, including a 20-mm rapid-fire anti-aircraft piece installed in the stern. The crew was made up of 23 men. The S7 was surredered to the Royal Navy in 1945.

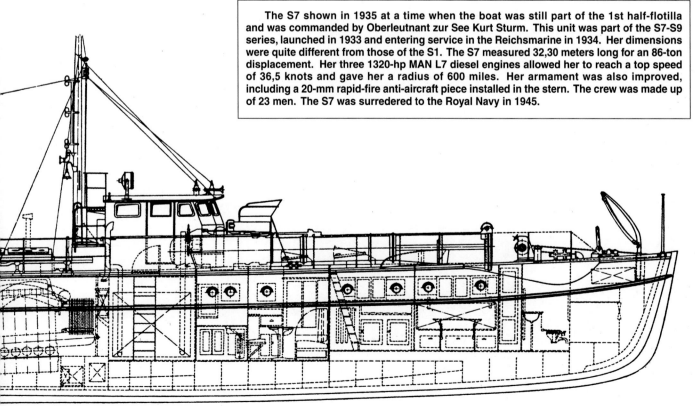

while at the same time insuring their protection with their auxiliary weapons[1]. Right from the beginning of operations the S19 and S21 collided, thus reducing the number of boats in the first flotilla to four. The landing of the troops from the cruisers *Köln* and *Königsberg* began on the morning of April 9. The S-Boote moved back and forth along the sides of the large surface vessels without running into any real reaction from the Norwegian defense forces. By noon the city was in the hands of the Germans. The second flotilla was used in the same way at Kristiansand without any major problems. On April 10, before Hitler, Goering and the generals of the *OberKommando der Wehrmacht*[2], Admiral Raeder announced that the first landing operations had been carried out as planned in spite of the loss of the cruisers *Blücher* and *Karlsruhe*. However the presence of the Royal Navy created a real threat of which the Germans were well aware. The two S-Boote flotillas, stationed in the ports of Bergen and Kristiansand, were ordered to remain on location with their support ships.

The last S-Boote participation in the Norwegian campaign took place on April 23 at the entrance to the Skagerrak Gulf. Three French destroyers, the *Indomptable*, the *Triomphant* and the *Malin*, belonging to the 8th DCT (*Division de contre-torpilleurs*: torpedo-boat destroyers), were taking part in a night raid as part of Operation *Rake*

---

1 – The British used an early version of the LCM s to transport their troops during the Norwegian campaign, but the Germans had no such craft. It wasn't until August, 1940, when the Kriegsmarine was preparing the invasion of England, that they finally received flat-bottomed landing barges, which would never be used.
2 – The Wehrmacht High Command

Top left: An S30-S37-type S-Boote in the port of Wilhelmshaven in February, 1939. The boat has just been launched and is not yet armed. The S30-S37 series was the first to be equiped with streamlined torpedo tubes.
At the beginning of the war, four units were operational within the 2nd flotilla commanded by Kapitänleutnant Petersen.

Centre left: The S30 in the port of Wilhelmshaven in February, 1940. The vessel was delivered to the Kriegsmarine in November, 1939, and was operating in the 2nd flotilla. She was under the orders of Oberleutnant zur See Wilhelm Zimmermann. The S30 was scuttled on May 3, 1945 with the S36 and the S61, off Ancône.

Left: An S30-S37-type S-Boote in the port of Wilhelmshaven in February, 1939. The boat has just been launched and is not yet armed. The S30-S37 series was the first to be equiped with streamlined torpedo tubes.
At the beginning of the war, four units were operational within the 2nd flotilla commanded by Kapitänleutnant Petersen.

in the waters around southern Norway. Their mission was to destroy the German anti-submarine chasers, which represented an increasing threat to the Royal Navy. A brief engagement took place around 3: 00 AM opposing the *Indomptable* and the *Malin* to several S-Boote which fired their torpedos at the French ships without striking them.

THE CAMPAIGN IN FRANCE.

The 2nd S-Boote flotilla was the first to be engaged on May 9, 1940. Its units were at that time divided among two ports: the S30, S32 and S33 were in Wilhelmshaven, and the S34 and S36 at Stavanger, Norway. The Royal Navy had taken back the initiative in this part of the North Sea by using one of its submarines, the *HMS Taku*, to torpedo the destroyer *Möwe* as she was heading out to meet the *Scharnhorst* to escort her back to her base. The German ship was badly damaged but did not sink, and all units of the 2nd S-Boote flotilla were sent out to get her back to Wilhelmshaven. The British immediately reacted to the presence of Kriegsmarine

Top right:
The French squadron torpedo ship *Bourrasque* capsizing on her port side on May 30, 1940, after hitting a mine.

surface craft in this zone and hustled over the heavy cruiser *Birmingham* along with a group of 4 destroyers[1]. At the same time, a second group of British ships belonging to the Fifth Destroyer Division commanded by Captain Lord Louis Mountbatten, including the *Kelly* (F01), the *Kandahar* (F28), the *Kimberly* (F50), and the *Hostile* (H55), raced North. And around noon a third group of destroyer [2] left the port of Scapa Flow in the Orkney Islands.

Mountbatten's group met the *Birmingham* and its escort in late afternoon. At 19: 00 a patrolling Dornier 18 spotted the converging British warships and alerted the units of the 2nd S-Boote flotilla, which were only 80 nautical miles from there. A half hour later, contact was made between the S30, S31, S32, S33 and two destroyers of the *Birmingham* group. There was strong fire from both sides without any real damage to any of the ships involved.

At nightfall the S-Boote launched a second attack. At 23: 30 the S31, commanded by Oberleutnant zur See

1 – *HMS Janis* (F53), *HMS Hyperion* (H97), *HMS Hereward* (H93) and *HMS Havock* (H43).
2 – *HMS Fury* (H76), *HMS Mowhawk* (F31), *HMS Foresight* (H68), *HMS Bulldog* (H51) and *HMS Gallant* (H59).

Right:
Crewmembers from the torpedo ship Bourrasque rescued by a British ship off Nieuport on May 30, 1940.

Left:
The support ship *Tanga* coupled with an unidentified S-Boote in the spring of 1940. Along with the *Tsingtau*, the *Tanga* supported the units of the 2nd flotilla at the beginning of the war. She was launched on January 21, 1939, and had a mission of supplying and servicing the S-Boote outside their home bases. With a 2600-ton displacement for a length of 90 meters, the *Tanga* could reach a top speed of 17,5 knots. She was armed with two main 105-mm pieces, two 37-mm cannons and four 20-mm guns in the anti-aircraft version. She was turned over the the US Navy after the war, then sold to the Danish Navy in 1948. She was rebaptized *Aegir* and finally disarmed in 1967.

Left:
Oberleutnant zur See Fimmen has just received the Knight's Iron Cross from Korvetten Kapitän Hans Bütow on August 14, 1940, for his heroic action during the attack of the French torpedo-ship *Sirocco* on May 31 off Dunkerque. On his left Oberleutnant zur See Götz Friedrich von Mirbach has just received the same decoration for attacking and sinking, with his S21, the French torpedo-boat destroyer *Jaguar* on May 23 off Malo-les-Bains.

Above:
Korvetten Kapitän Hans Bütow in front of the S26 crew giving the habitual speech before pinning on the medals. On his right stands Oberleutnant zur See Kurt Fimmen.

S-BOOTE LIFE AS EXPLAINED BY OBERLEUTNANT ZUR SEE FIMMEN, COMMANDER OF THE S26 (AUGUST 1940)

When port activity in the Channel ports is just starting in the early morning, we are usually on our way back from an expedition against England. Generally we are a small flotilla of three or four boats, changing bases regularly so as not to attract the attention of the enemy aviation. Before leaving the boat, the crew covers her with camouflage nets so that she looks like a simple fishing boat. Once on dry land, daytime is used for rest, and the men split up among the different hotels that have been requisitioned. Early in the afternoon we start preparing our missions; there is nothing improvised about night operations against the English. This is the job of the flotilla leader and the officers. Meamwhile the crews are getting the boats shipshape for the coming combats. Some are in the machine room, others on deck checking the weapons one last time. The engines are turned on two hours before departure time. They have to run perfectly, which means that the mechanics have to check every detail. Then it's « Anchors a-weigh! », with that second of anxiety which comes with every departure on mission. And suddenly we melt into the night and the only thing existing for us is the boat and the surrounding sea. You don't actually realize the terrible power of the S-Boote until you come in contact with an enemy ship. During the attack, the boat is litterally one with her torpedo. That moment lasts for only a few seconds, until the torpedo leaves the tube. Then the boat whirls around to the port or starboard side at top speed. The maneuver leaves us just enough time to observe the impact of the shot and test the enemy's reactions. If a destroyer comes near, we open up our smoke pots, and a protective screen of smoke soon separates us from the English.

Right:
The crew of the S26 assembled in Boulogne in June of 1940. On May 31 the gunboat, under the orders of Oberleutnant zur See Kurt Fimmen, attacked and sank, with the help of the S23, the French torpedo ship *Sirocco*, on her way to England. For this feat, the entire crew were decorated by Korvetten Kapitän Bütow, Commander in Chief of the torpedo units of which the S-Boote flotillas were a part.

Opdenhoff, and in spite of strong fire coming from the destroyers *HMS Kelly* and *Kandahar*, managed to fire two torpedos from a distance of 750 meters. The *Kelly* took a straight hit on the level of boiler room N°1 and sustained major damage up to and including the upper deck. The vessel stayed afloat nevertheless and the British were able to have her towed. It would take the crew 91 hours to get her back to England[1]. Around 1:30 AM the S33 was rammed by a British destroyer. The entire bow was torn off along a length of 9 meters, and compartments VIII and IX were completely submerged. In spite of this damage, and also of the order to scuttle her sent out by Oberleutnant zur See Schultze-Jena, the vessel managed to stay afloat and was able to get back to her base in Wilhelmshaven at the extraordinary speed of 20 knots.

Thus within 90 minutes the S-Boote had had four contacts with units of the Royal Navy. The offensive tactics that the Germans had perfected between the two wars had proved their worth: a surprise attack involving several aligned units, and then, once the torpedos had left their tubes, an immediate withdrawal at top speed and under cover of a smoke screen.

The lightning offensive of May 10, 1940 would force the French and British to try to destroy the installations of the Dutch and Belgian ports before they fell into the hands of the Germans. The mission of the Royal Navy was to plant mines around the Dutch ports. An identical mission was assigned to

Top:
S18-type S-Boote patrolling in the North Sea in September, 1940.

Right:
Artist's rendering of an S-Boote travelling at top speed.

Previous page, top:
The S33 back in Wilhelmshaven on May 10, 1940. The gunboat had left the German port the evening before with the S30 and S32, while the S34 and S31 left from Stavanger in Norway. This group of S-Boote from the 2nd flotilla later encountered a British formation composed of the light cruiser *Birmingham* and seven destroyers. During the fighting, the *HMS Kelly*, commanded by Lord Louis Mountbatten, was hit by the S31. The S33, commanded by Oberleutnant zur See Hans Schultze Jena, was violently smashed by the *HMS Bulldog*.

Previous page, inset:
The back of the S19 after hitting a mine on August 28, 1940. During the night of the 28th, the 1st S-Boote flotilla left Rotterdam heading for Great Yarmouth where a British convoy composed of 14 freighters escorted by two destroyers had been observed. The S19 and S22, part of the 3rd flotilla, left Hoek van Holland, heading in the same direction, to join them. Along the way the S19, commanded by Leutnant zur See Detlefsen, hit a mine. In spite of the damage, the S-Boote was taken in tow by the S22 and brought to Calais.

the French Navy, with the help of British warships, around Antwerp, Ostende and Zeebrugge. The operation was only partially successful because of the action of the Luftwaffe which had total mastery of the skies. Only the use of the port of Zeebrugge was impaired.

During this period the 1st and 2nd S-Boote flotillas were preparing to participate in the westward offensive from their new base in Borkum which was not yet completely operational. On May 19, the Kriegsmarine headquarters sent the two flotillas[2] around Nieuport with the mission of intercepting the Allied ships which were beginning to evacuate the ports of Calais and Boulogne. By May 20 the Germans were in position around the Channel ports and tightening their stranglehold around the British and French hemmed in at Dunkerque. During this first fighting, the S-Boote were attacked by the twin-engine Avro-Ansons of the Coastal Command. The S30 was assailed simultaneously by three planes, and a bomb fell less than 20 meters from her.

During the night of May 20-21, the S32, commanded by Oberleutnant zur See Carl

Eberhard, attacked a 2 000-ton transport ship in front of Nieuport. The first torpedo missed, but the second hit the middle of the ship, creating a giant explosion that turned the vessel into a fireworks display. The next day, at nightfall, the two flotillas again left their base in Borkum. The 1st S-Boote flotilla was assigned to attack the Allied ships gathering around Dunkerque. The 2nd flotilla took up position along the coasts of Britain to intercept the boats that were starting to evacuate the troops waiting on the beaches.

Once again the Germans were lucky. The Kreigsmarine radio-listening services were able to intercept Allied messages about the positions of their boats. This information was immediately relayed to the units of the 1st S-Boote flotilla, and the S21 and S23[3] positioned themselves in wait in the west

---

1 – On May 22, 1941, the *Kelly* was participating in the defense of Crete in the eastern Mediterranean, when she was attacked by several Stukas. A 450-kilogram bomb hit the front of the ship and she sank within a few minutes. 128 crew members, including Lord Louis Mountbatten, were saved.
2 – 9 S-Boote took to sea: S30, S31, S32, S34, S13, S22, S23, S24, S25, accompanied by the support ship *Tanga*.
3 – S21, commanded by Oberleutnant zur See von Mirbach, and S23, commanded by Oberleutnant zur See Christiansen.

Dunkerque channel. The *Jaguar*, a French Navy torpedo-boat destroyer, was unaware of the German presence in the sector. She headed slowly into the channel, her clearly visible silhouette outlined on the surface of the water. A few seconds later two torpedos coming out of nowhere ripped through the bridge on the port-side. The explosion shattered the night, and even though she was listing dangerously, the Jaguar was towed to the beach in Malo-les-Bains where she was grounded.

From May 24 on, the two flotillas operated directly out of the base of Hoek-van-Holland in the Netherlands, giving them a considerably increased radius of action. On the afternoon of May 26, the Allies launched

Previous page:
Loading a G7a-type torpedo on an S-Boote of the S30 type in the port of Ostende in September, 1940. The vessel was part of the 2nd flotilla, under the orders of Korvetten Kapitän Rudolf Petersen.

Top:
Loading a G7a-type torpedo on an S30-type gunboat from the 2nd flotilla in the port of Ostende in September, 1940. The G7as and G7es were the standard torpedoes used by the Kriegsmarine ships at that period. During the invasion of Norway, many problems with these torpedoes occurred during attacks against Allied ships; the detonating system was particularly trouble-prone.

Right:
Two S14-type S-Boote leaving Ostende in September, 1940, heading out on patrol in the North Sea. The S14 series, produced from 1934 on, would be replaced little by little, from the end of the year on, by boats of the S30 series, with a more modern design and streamlined tubes.

Operation *Dynamo*, the evacuation of the British Expeditionary Corps from the beaches of Dunkerque. On the night of May 29-30, the S30 under the orders of Oberleutnant zur See Wilhelm Zimmerman, made contact with a British destroyer, the *HMS Wakeful,* returning to England along the Y route[1]. From 600 meters away, two torpedoes whooshed out of their tubes and disappeared into

the night. The British ship was much too close, had no time to maneuver, and was broken in two by the explosion. She capsized within a few minutes, carrying with her several

1 –The British Admiralty had imagined three routes for the evacuation of Dunkerque. Route Z, the shortest, went from the south side of Dunkerque to Dover. Route X went through the middle, avoiding the Goodwin sand banks. Finally route Y, the longest of the three, went from the north side of Dunkerque to Dover.

hundred British soldiers who had been evacuated from Dunkerque. At about the same time, the S34, commanded by Oberleutnant zur See Obermaier, out on patrol with other units of the 2nd S-Boote flotilla off the coast of Britain, sank a freighter, the SS Aboukir.

On May 31 the torpedo boat *Sirocco* was attacked by the S-Boote as she was heading for England with British and French soldiers on board. Taking advantage of the total obscurity on the surface of the waves, the S26 and the S23[1] launched their attack at 1: 00 AM. Two torpedos grazed the bow of the ship and disappeared into the darkness, while at almost precisely the same moment, two others hit the starboard stern. The roof was partly torn off and the machine room was submerged. Two minutes later the boat pitched over onto the starboard side and disappeared with 480 soldiers and part of the crew. At about the same time, Oberleutnant zur See Detlefsen's S24, patrolling along the British coast, surprised the torpedo-boat *Cyclone* heading for Calais. The French boat was able to avoid the first torpedo, but couldn't get out of the way of the second, which came ripping through her prow right next to her 130-mm double cannon. Even though the damage was serious, the crew managed to keep the boat afloat and get her back to Brest[2]. The 2nd S-Boote flotilla would continue operations until June 1. The S34 managed to sink the Stella Dorado, an armed trawler, and the S35[3] did the same to the trawler *Argyllshire*.

---

1 – S26, commanded by Obezrleutnant-zur-See Fimmen, and S23, commanded by Oberleutnant zur See Christiansen.
2 – The *Cyclone* was scuttled in dry dock before the German troops took Brest.
3 – S35, commanded by Oberleutnant zur See Keecke; S34, commanded by Oberleutnant zur See Albrecht Obermaier.

Right:
2nd flotilla S30-type S-Boote leaving the port of Ostende to patrol the North Sea in 1940. Dark grey camouflage paint will start appearing in the fall of 1940 on certain units. The pilot's bridge is not yet armored, and the auxiliary armament is still composed of a single 20-mm rapid-fire piece.

Before heading out for a mission, the flotilla commanders had to determine the precise routes followed by the Allied convoys and estimate their passage times at different pre-selected points on the maps. Once the speed and the direction of the convoy had been calculated, the eight or ten S-Boote participating in the operation positioned themselves in a single moving line, at a distance of 20 or 30 miles from their target. As they approached, the flotilla divided itself into two groups composed of several pairs, or *Rotten*, which advanced at top speed on two parallel lines. In order to prevent the convoy escort vessels from identifying them until the last minute, the two half-flotillas were separated from each other by a distance of about 3 miles. Each *Rotte* within the group kept about a mile away from the two other boats participating in the attack. During the whole operation, the S-Boote maintained contact with each other by VHF radio, and every unit had to work in tight collaboration with his « buddy » to

Advance stage.

The *Lauertaktik*
S-Boote attack technique

Attack exercise with units from a training flotilla in the Baltic Sea in 1945.

be as effective as possible. The last part of the procedure was the most delicate, because the boats had to reduce their speed to 10 knots to be able to launch their torpedoes in the best possible conditions. Too much speed would have destabilized the trajectory of the G7As, which came out of the mouth of the tube at a speed of more than 44 knots. Chances of destroying enemy targets were much greater if the two groups managed to fire their torpedoes at the same convoy at the same time. Their low profil and their light grey color made the S-Boote particularly difficult to identify. If the first attack failed, their rapidity permitted them to come back for a second try once the crew had reloaded the tubes. The Royal Navy escorters had a good deal of trouble intercepting these enemy boats, moving at a top speed of 42 knots. They had to wait for delivery of new MTB s and MGB s with high speed gasoline engines before they could hope to regain the upper hand.

Approach of the convoy.

Attack stage.

High speed withdrawal using smoke screen.

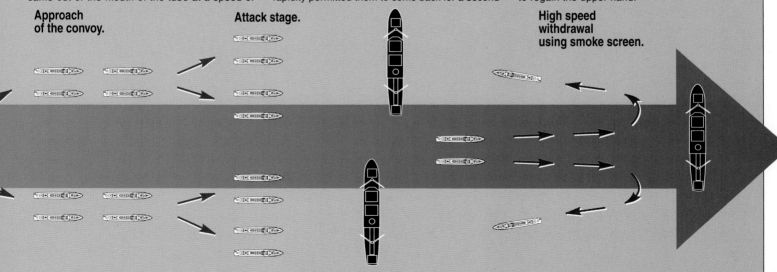

OPEN SEAS FOR THE GERMANS.

Previous page and above:
Loading an EMC-type mine on board an S-Boote in 1940 in a North Sea port. Six devices of this type could be loaded onto the back of the boat. Along with their traditional attack missions, the S-Boote flotillas were regularly involved in mine-laying operations in the Thames River estuary, resulting in considerable disruption of British maritime traffic in the year 1940.

At the beginning of June 1940, the Germans had the upper hand and were finally in possession of ports giving them direct access to the Atlantic Ocean. Once the Kriegsmarine had taken the Dutch, Belgian and certain French ports on the English Channel, they had offensive bases which would be particularly useful for harassing British sea traffic. All of the convoys along the south and the northeast

coasts of England were now within the reach of German surface vessels[1]. Starting on June 6, the 1st, 2nd and 3rd S-Boote flotillas tried to attack British ships leaving ports in the south of England[2], but without much success. There were many problems with the G7a magnetically-activated electric torpedoes; sometimes they even refused to explode on impact. These attacks were repeated during the nights of June 9, 10 and 11, with the same results.

On June 11, during the day, the S30, S31, S34, S35 and S1 arrived in Boulogne, moving closer to the British ports. The English reacted immediately and the Royal Air Force, with a half-dozen Blackburn Skuas, attacked the S-Boote which had grouped in the Loubet basin. The crews fired back as best they could with their 20-mm guns. In the face of this British action, the German command decided to pull the torpedo boats back to Rotterdam. They finally returned to the French port after June 16, once units of the Luftwaffe had established effective anti-aircraft cover around the basins.

The S19 and S26[3] joined the flotilla two days later, and during the night of June 19-20 were able to sink the Roseburn, a British freighter with a 3 103-ton displacement, off Dungeness. Weather conditions were excellent for continuing operations, but at dawn on June 22, 30 miles west of Boulogne, the S32 hit a floating mine, probably dropped from a Coastal Command plane several hours earlier. The explosion ripped off the front of the ship and seven men were killed including the commander, Oberleutnant zur See Eberhard. On June 23, a new convoy was reported south of Dungeness. Five S-Boote divided into two groups went after it[4]. The tanker *Albuera* (3 474 tons) was hit twice by the brand new S36 commanded by Oberleutnant zur See Wolf Dietrich Babel, while the S19 sank the armed packet boat *Kingfisher*.

The collapse of the French army, within the space of less than 4 weeks, resulting in the signing of the armistice of June 25, 1940, allowed the Germans to take over all of the French ports on the English Channel and the Atlantic Ocean. On June 27, the 1st S-Boote flotilla[5] arrived in the port of Cherbourg, with the mission of intercepting British traffic in an area stretching from the Isle of Wight to east of Brighton. At the same time the port of Boulogne was also equipped to receive S-Boote. The 2nd S-Boote flotilla[6] was based in Ostende, meaning that it could intervene rapidly against any convoys along the southeast coast of England. And the port of Rotterdam housed the 3rd S-Boote flotilla.

During the night of July 4-5, convoy OA 178, which had already come under fire from the Luftwaffe squadrons, was attacked by two groups of S-Boote from the 1st flotilla[7] working

---

1 – The 3rd S-Boote flotilla was based in Rotterdam from June 1, 1940 on, with the S1, S10, S11, S12, S13 and S54.
2 – 40 000 tons of coal were transported every week from the mines around Newcastle to supply southern England.
3 – S19 commanded by Oberleutnant zur See Toniges; S26 commanded by Oberleutnant zur See Fimmen.
4 – S35, S36, S31 and S19, S26.
5 – Including the S20, S21, S22, S25, S26, S27, and S28.
6 – The S18 was under repair in Wilhelmshaven and the S19 under repair in Kiel after hitting a mine on August 28, 1940. Including the S30, S33, S34, S36, S37, S55 and S56.
7 – The S19, S26, S20 and S24.
8 – Or in pairs: *die Rotte* in German means « gang ».

in *Rotten*[8] out of Cherbourg. The attack was only partially successful. Two English boats were damaged by the S20 and S26, the 4 343-ton *Emcrest*, and the 6 972-ton *British Corporal*. The S19 sank a 6 000-ton freighter. This type of operation, harassing the British convoys, would continue on throughout the month of July. On July 24, at nightfall, convoy CW 8 was attacked by the S19, S20, S21, S25 and S27, and three freighters were sunk. A little later, off the Isle of Wight, the same S27 torpedoed the French liner *Meknes*. The brightly lighted vessel had been travelling unescorted, with 1 100 soldiers on board, coming home following the armistice agreements. The torpedo hit the back of the ship and she sank immediately. Three hundred seventy-four men disappeared with her. On August 7, the S20, S21, S25 and S26, under the orders of Kapitänleutnant Birnbacher, attacked convoy CW 9 southwest of Dungeness and sank two freighters and a 4 000-ton tanker. The Germans had to retreat after the arrival of the destroyer *HMS Bulldog*[1].

MINE WARFARE.

After the beginning of the Battle of England, operations directed against convoys would take a back seat, since the S-Boote of the 1st flotilla were needed to give assistance to the Luftwaffe pilots shot down over the Channel. Offensive operations began again in September. On the 5th, the S18, S21, S22 and S54 came into contact with convoy CW 12. Five freighters were sunk and a sixth ship was badly damaged. On October 1, the 1st S-Boote flotilla left Cherbourg for the port of Rotterdam, and on the 26th, it moved to Kiel. The 2nd S-Boote flotilla, under the orders of Kapitänleutnant Rudolph Petersen, continued its activities. Beginning in July, the gunboats started laying mines at the entry to the estuary of the Thames River[2]. These operations would continue on through September with significant results. Mines that were laid during the night were often more effective than torpedo attacks. In face of the threat represented by the S-Boote attacks on their system of coastal convoys in southern England, the British were determined to react. Two air raids launched within several days

1 – After the losses incurred by the German attacks in July, the British decided in August to reorganize their system of coastal convoys. The number of ships was reduced to twelve and protection was reinforced by *Hunt*-class escorters.
2 – Mine-laying would begin in this zone on June 6.

Top left, and left:
The results of a Coastal Command air raid on the port of Ostende in September, 1940. The vessel hasn't been seriously damaged and is still afloat. Allied air raids on S-Bootwaffe units intensified considerably from 1943 on and reached a climax a year later with the raids on Le Havre, Boulogne and Ijmuiden.

Following page, on top:
2nd flotilla S30-type S-Boote leaving the port of Ostende to patrol the North Sea in 1940. Dark grey camouflage paint will start appearing in the fall of 1940 on certain units. The pilot's bridge is not yet armored, and the auxiliary armament is still composed of a single 20-mm rapid-fire piece.

Following page, on bottom
Detailed view of the pilot's bridge on this boat. After taking part in operations against Dunkerque in June and rescue missions for Luftwaffe pilots shot down over the Channel during the Battle of England, the 2nd flotilla units, during the first two months of autumn in 1940, were used for mine-laying operations along the east coast of England.

Left:
An S-Boote maneuvering near Lorient
in 1940. The photo was taken from a
third boat of the S26-S29 type,
more recently built, with streamlined
torpedo tubes. The three units were
part of the 1st flotilla.

of each other over Ostende and Vlissingen destroyed two German gunboats and damaged five others[1].

In October, the weather in the English Channel started to deteriorate, which meant that attacks against the convoys slowed down.

The 2nd and 3rd flotillas, because of losses sustained during the previous months[2], had only seven operational boats left, and the expected new units had not yet been delivered[3]. On November 20, in a stormy sea with visibility close to zero, the brand new S38, commanded by Oberleutnant zur See Hans Detlefsen, was sunk by the destroyers *HMS Garth* and *HMS Campbell.*

Weather conditions in December prevented any form of offensive action by the S-Boote. It was only at the end of the month that the three flotillas with eleven boats[4] could finally take to sea. Two convoys (FN 366 and FN 367) were reported by the Luftwaffe reconnaissance observers during the night of December 23-24. After two failed attacks against a 1 600-ton tanker and a small freighter, the S28, commanded by Oberleutnant zur See Klug, managed to sink a 2 500-ton transport ship, while in a different sector Oberleutnant zur See Albrecht Muller (S29) sent to the bottom a Dutch ship, the *City of Maastricht,* displacing 6 552 tons. The force-6 wind and the 4-meter swell were considerable handicaps for the S-Boote during this operation, as well as the presence of an increased number of British escort ships protecting the convoys.

The year 1940 ended on the positive side for the Germans. The S-Boote had sunk 26 Allied commercial vessels for a total of 49 985 tons, to which should be added ten destroyers either sunk or badly damaged. Their proximity after the occupation of the French ports on the Channel and the Atlantic Ocean represented a real danger for commercial traffic on the south and east coasts of England. At the end of the year the English actually over-estimated the operational capacities of their enemies: they were persuaded that the Kriegsmarine had a particularly formidable force of fifty units in three operational flotillas. Real strength was actually quite different. In the following year the British would react and the balance of power would tilt in the opposite direction.

1 – The S1 and S10 were destroyed, the S11, S13, S33, S36 and S37 damaged.
2 – On July 12 the S23 hit a floating mine and blew up. On August 15 the torpedo depot in Ostende accidentally exploded, partly destroying the S24, S31, S34 and S37.
3 – The S38, S54, S56, S57, S58, and S59.
4 – The 1st flotilla was made up of the S26, S27, S28, S29 and S101; the 2nd flotilla: the S34, and S56; the 3rd flotilla: the S54, S57, S58, and S59.

Left:
An unidentified S-Boote in the port of Lorient,
France, in 1940. This unit belonged to the 1st flotilla
and appears to be a type S26-S29.

Next page:
A watchman on board a gunboat in November, 1940,
somewhere in the English Channel. The photograph appeared
in the magazine *Signal* in the first week in November.
To protect himself from the spray during these last days
of autumn, the sailor is wearing a thick leather suit
and cap that were also part of the gear of the U-Boote crews.

N0. 15

fr.

Belgique fr. 2.— / Bahama· Moravie Kr. 2.50 / Bulgarie leva 10.— / Danemark 50 øre / Estonie 40 sent / Finlande mk. 4.50 / France fr. 3.— / Grèce drachmes 15.— / Italia lire 2.— / Yougoslavie dinars 5.— / Norvège... / Pays-Bas cents 20 / Portugal esc. 2.50 / Roumanie lei 16.— / Suède 50 øre / Suisse 45 centimes / Slovaquie cour. 2.50 / Espagne pes. 1.50 / Turquie kuruş 15.— / Hongrie 36 fillér / États-Unis 10 cts

Signal

Vigie
sur une vedette
rapide, l'unité
la plus moderne
de la marine
de guerre
allemande

THE ALLIES
EVEN UP THE SCORE
(1941)

THE BRITISH RESPONSE.

The British reacted at the beginning of 1941 by reorganizing their Coastal Force and speeding up their new ship constructionprograms. British shipyards like British Power Boat or Vosper which had received government orders before the declaration of war, were beginning to deliver their vessels to the different fleets. The convoys were now accompanied not only by destroyers and corvettes, but also by MTBs and MGBs which were altogether as good as their Kriegsmarine counterparts. Using German tactics, the British started to use MTBs and MGBs together in combined operations designed to destroy enemy coastal traffic going through the Straits of Dover. Along with the new ships, the British, after the beginning of 1941, developed a series of measures designed to eliminate the threat to their maritime traffic represented by the S-Boote. The situation started to change when the British introduced squadrons of night pursuit planes specialized in fighting coastal forces. The Coastal Command and the Fighter Command launched 187 attacks against S-Boote units during the winter of 1942, without, however, managing to sink a single ship. The German boats were extremelydifficult targets because of their rapidity and their low profile on the water. In June of 1942, dismayed by these poor results, the British Admiralty decided to transfer to the Coastal Command a squadron of Fairey Albacores equipped with night radars. They were grouped with two squadrons of antique Fairey Swordfish to track the Germans.

During the winter of 1942 the British raids after each attack on a convoy became more

Top:
In an S-Boote machine room during operations in the English Channel in March, 1941.

Left:
A 2nd S-Boote flotilla on a night sortie leaving Ostende in 1941.

Right:
In an S-Boote machine room in February, 1941.

Previous pages:
Ostende, February, 1941. An S30-type S-Boote leaves the Belgian port to join up with other units of the 2nd flotilla on the east coast of England in search of a convoy to raid.

and more intense, a fact that considerably hindered the S-Boote during their night operations. In January of 1941, the *Schnellbootwaffe* could theoretically line up 40 units against England. However in reality there were only 21 boats that were actually

Top:
Ostende, winter of 1941. 2nd flotilla gunboats are covered with camouflage tarpaulins, changing their shapes in the hopes of escaping identification by British planes. Raids were starting to intensify over the ports housing the three flotillas operating against England and her maritime commerce.

Left:
The S57 leaving the port of Rotterdam in February, 1941. This S30-type gunboat was launched in October 1940, when she joined the 3rd flotilla, commanded by Kapitänleutnant Friedrich Kemnade, operating on the western front. Then in June, 1941, she was transferred with the rest of the flotilla to the Baltic Sea. In December,1941, she was sent to the Mediterranean and participated in the blockade of Malta and attacks on British convoys from her base in Porto Empedocle, Sicily. The S57 was sunk on August 19, 1944 off Dubrovnik during a dogfight with three British MGBs.

Composition of the flotillas (1941)

1st S-Boote flotilla

Fleet leader:	Kptlt.	Heinz Birnbacher
S26	Oblt. z. S.	Kurt Fimmen
S27	Oblt. z. S.	Hermann Büchting
S28	Oblt. z. S.	Bernd Klug
S29	Oblt. z. S.	Götz Friedrich Götz von Mirbach
S101	Oblt. z. S.	Georg-Stuhr Christiansen
S102	Oblt. z. S.	Werner Toniges

2nd S-Boote flotilla

Fleet leader:	Korv. kpt.	Rudolph Petersen
S30	Oblt. z. S.	Klaus Feldt
S33	Lt. z. S.	Paul Popp
S34	Oblt. z. S.	Albrecht Obermaier
S36	Oblt. z. S.	Wolf-Dietrich Babbel
S55	Oblt. z. S.	Hermann Opdenhoff
S56	Oblt. z. S.	Wilhelm Meentzen
S201	Oblt.z. S.	Ullrich Roeder

3rd S-Boote flotilla

Fleet leader:	Kptlt.	Friedrich Kemnade
S54	Lt. z. S.	Herbert Wagner
S57	Lt. z. S.	Güntger Erdmann
S58	Lt. z. S.	Eberhard Geiger
S59	Lt. z. S.	Heinz Haag
S60	Oblt. z. S.	Siegfried Wuppermann

4th S-Boote flotilla
(still training in Germany)

Fleet leader:	Kptlt.	Niels Bätge
S11	Lt. z. S.	Erwin Lüders
S22	Oblt. z. S.	Bogislav Priebe
S24	Lt. z. S.	Hans Joachim Stöve
S25	Oblt. z. S.	Karl Schneider

sea-worthy; the other 19 were immobilized for either repairs, maintenance or training[1].

At the beginning of the year German operations slowed down once again, because of the difficult weather conditions that considerably handicapped sea sorties.

As quoted by Henri le Masson in his book *Guérilla sur mer* (*Guerilla Warfare at Sea*), Oberleutnant zur See Friedrich Karl Künzel, commander of the S103, described the difficulties:

When we left our base at Ijmuiden, it was – 16 °C. This was on January 28, 1941. We had received orders to intercept an enemy convoy in the sector around the Brown Ridge tun-buoy[2], between Great Yarmouth and West Hartlepool, half way between Ijmuiden and the English coast. The flotilla[3] was advancing at a speed of 20 knots in a calm sea. The moonlight seemed to us a bit indiscreet. It was so cold that the spray froze immediately, covering the boat with a layer of ice from prow to stern. Two hours later, the temperature unexpectedly rose above 0 °C. As we were about to establish contact with the convoy, we realized that the starboard torpedo was covered with ice inside the tube, meaning that it was impossible to fire it. We turned back bitterly. Once back at our base, we found the answer to the problem: for some reason the starboard tube had not thawed. We had to use a blow-torch to free that torpedo.

1 – From May, 1940 on, either one or two new S-Boote were launched every month. In November, they were increased to 5 per month.
2 – To mark the channel which had been dredged through the shallows, the English had placed buoys known as *tuns*. The Germans, on patrol, had spotted them, and the S-Boote commanders had got into the habit of stopping their boats in the vicinity of these buoys to wait for passing convoys.
3 – The 1 st S-Boote flotilla was under the orders of Kapitänleutnant Heinz Birnbacher.

Above: A 2nd flotilla S-Boote getting ready to leave on mission in the port of Ostende in February, 1941.

Right: Two S26-type S-Boote at dock in an unidentified port.

Above: A 1942 Kriegsmarine propaganda poster illustrated by S-Boote in operation.

Several operations took place in February. On the 19 th, in spite of the terrible weather, and as a result of information gathered from two shipwrecked Englishmen, the vessels of the 1st flotilla took up position opposite the east coast of England. At 1:00 AM the S-Boote located convoy FN 411 and headed toward it. The S102, commanded by Oberleutnant zur See Werner Toniges, sank the British freighter *Algarve* (1 355 tons). On February 26 the three flotillas took to the sea in several groups, with 15 gunboats in all. Around 21:00 elements of the 2nd S-Boote flotilla spotted a convoy heading north. At the same time the S30, commanded by Oberleutnant zur See Feldt, saw the outline of a destroyer about 1 200 meters away. He identified her as a Hunt class. The gunboat, with the S33 at her side, raced straight toward the British ship and sent two torpedoes at her from a distance of 700 meters. The *HMS Exmoor* (L61) took a direct hit at the rear and was cut in two, disappearing in just a few minutes. A little further north, the 1st S-Boote flotilla was busy attacking convoy FN 417. At 3 : 20 AM the S28, commanded by Oberleutnant zur See Klug, sank the 1 123-ton British freighter *Minorca*.

Above and Right:
S30-type S-Boote belonging to the 2nd flotilla getting ready to leave on operations from the Belgian port of Ostende during the spring of 1941. The auxiliary weapons of these boats have not been modified and for a few more months the Germans will still control the English Channel. The crews don't seem to be worried about British air attacks : the gunboats aren't camouflaged.

B.PAUTIGNY

Schnellboote S26

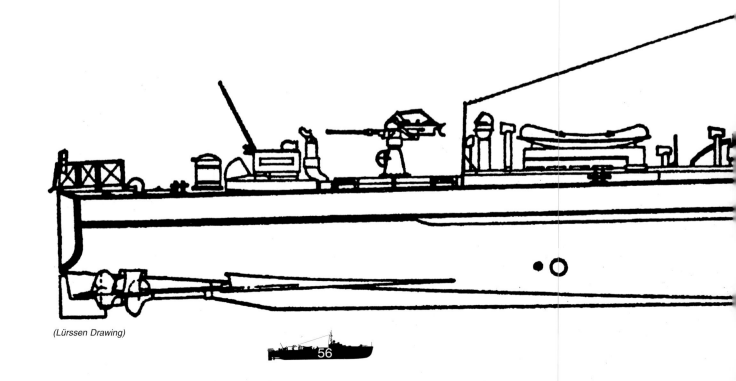

(Lürssen Drawing)

The S26 in March, 1941. The boat was commanded at that time by Oberleutnant zur See Kurt Fimmen and operating with the 1st S-Boote flotilla based in Ijmuiden, Holland. The S26-S29 series was a follow-up to the S30-S37s. The torpedo launching tubes were streamlined and the weight of the boat now exceeded 100 tons. The S26 was 34,94 meters long and driven by three 2000-hp 20-cylinder Mercedes Benz MB 501 diesel engines, giving her a maximum speed of 39.9 knots and a 700-mile radius of action. The main armament was composed of two 533-mm torpedo launching tubes with four G7a-type torpedoes. A 20-mm rapid-fire cannon was placed in the rear. The prow of the boat was equipped with a 7.92mm MG 34 machine gun. Smoke pots completed the defensive equipment. Six EMC-type anti-ship contact mines were attached to the stern. The S26 was sunk along with the S40 and S72 by Soviet fighter-bombers on August 19, 1944 in the Romanian port of Sulina. At the time she was commanded by Leutnant zur See Carl Silies.

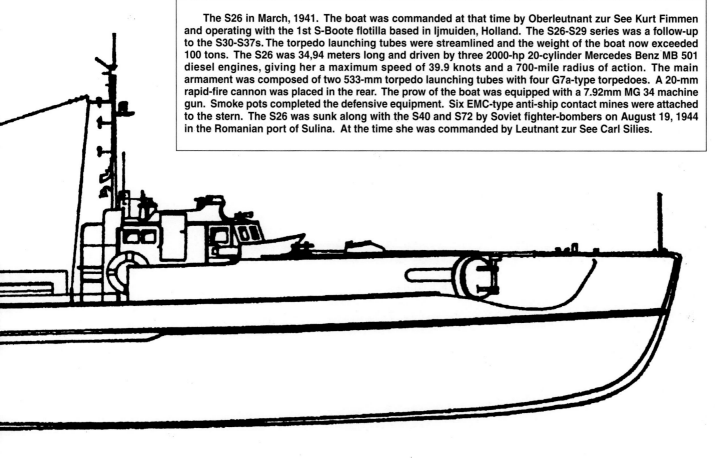

During the night of March 7-8, the three flotillas were once again sent into action after Luftwaffe planes spied convoys FN 26 and FN 29 off Cromer and Southwold. During that night, seven merchant ships were sunk by the Germans representing a total of 13 134 tons[1]. However no British destroyer was hit during the fighting, as was erroneously mentioned in the victory bulletin which was later put out by the Kriegsmarine head-quarters. Until mid-April operations were again interrrupted because of weather condi-tions, and the rare sorties of the S-Boote were basically devoted to mine-laying[2].

On April 17, during one of these night operations, the vessels of the 2nd S-Boote flotilla came upon convoy FS 64 travelling northeast of Great Yarmouth. Two freighters were sunk: the 1 446-ton *Effra*, and the *Nerens*, a Dutch vessel displacing 1 298 tons which had taken refuge in England in June, 1940. Meanwhile, the 3rd S-Boote flotilla was operating near the Haisborough Sand zone where a convoy had been spotted. As the S57 and S58, paired, were starting their approach, three British MTBs suddenly appeared beside the Germans, firing with everything they had. The S58 received several direct hits on the hull and the machi-ne room, but was able to get safely back to her base. During this operation, the English showed that they were capable of responding to German attacks, even if they caused little serious damage to enemy boats. At the end of the year, encounters with the more heavily armed MGBs obliged Petersen and his com-manders to react by reinforcing weapons and protection on their units.

THE NEW KRIEGSMARINE UNITS

In 1941 on the western front, between the Channel and the North Sea, the Germans started deploying a series of vessels capable

Above:
An S26-type S-Boote photographed in the Dutch port of Hoofden in May, 1941.

Left:
Kriegsmarine recruiting poster.

Below:
The S111 after being captured by MGBs 87, 88 and 91 off the coast of Holland in the early morning of March 15, 1941. The fight with His Majesty's gunboats had been particularly violent : notice the holes made by the 20-mm guns that go right through the hull and the upper structure. The S-Boote was part of the 2nd flotilla which had attacked convoy FN 55 the night before. The British boarded the boat and took her in tow to try to get her back to England.

1 – The S101 with Oberleutnant zur See Christiansen sank the 957-ton freighter *Norman Queen* east of Crown. The S28 with Oberleutnant zur See Klug sank the 2 345-ton freighter *Corduff*. The S27 with Oberleutnant zur See Buchting sank the 1,049-ton freighter *Rye*. The S31 with Oberleutnant zur See Hans Jürgen Meyer sank the 1 047-ton *Kenton*. The S61 with Oberleutnant zur See Gerner sank the 4 805-ton *Boulderpool*. The S102 with Oberleutnant zur See Werner Toniges sank the 1 547-ton *Togstone*. The S29 with Oberleutnant zur See Friedrich Götz von Mirbach sank the 1 048-ton freighter *Dotterel*.
2 – Allied ships totalling 230,000 tons were sunk or damaged in 1941 on the east coast of England by mines.

of insuring their supremacy not only in fire power, but also in speed and radius of action. Even though their displacements were superior to those of the previous models, these new series of S-Boote were propelled at a speed of 42 knots with a stability that allowed them to navigate even under the worst weather conditions. With a 92,5-ton displacement and a length of 34,94 meters, models S38-S53 would allow the Kriegsmarine fleets to deal a deadly blow to commerce along the coasts of Britain

Top and Bottom:
The S106 photographed in June, 1941. The S-Boote had just joined the 2nd flotilla and was to head into the Baltic Sea under the orders of Korvetten Kapitän Petersen. Coming back from a mine-laying operation on the night of June 27, the boat hit a Soviet mine and was completely destroyed along with the S43. A few days before the accident, two crew members requisitioned *local facilities* to get fresh milk.

Centre:
German propaganda postcard with an illustration of an S-Boote.

Above:
On the bridge of an S38-type S-Boote operating somewhere in the English Channel in January 1941. Notice the ship's commander (actually an ensign in training) on the right-hand side of the photo, beside him the pilot, behind him the signalman, and on the left the torpedo officer standing beside the sighting instrument.

Right:
A *Fähnrich* or ensign learning the difficult art of navigation on an operating S-Boote. The speaker that he is holding in his left hand connects him directly to the ship's radioman, giving him up-to-the-minute information.

Above:
The chief machinist raises his right hand to show that he has understood.

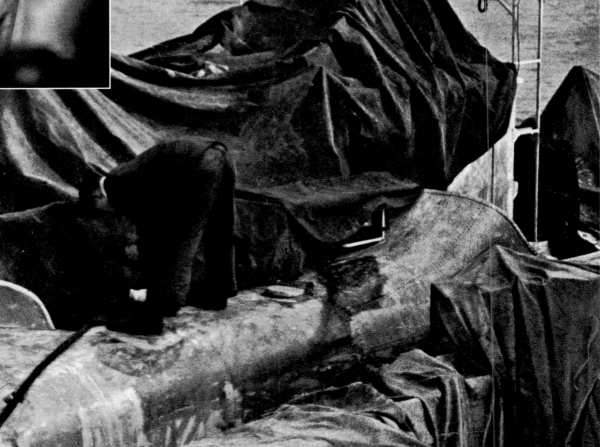

Right:
January, 1942, in a port on the North Sea. Two carefully camouflaged S-Boote under their tarpaulins are preparing to go out on operations. At the beginning of the year 1942 the British air threat was starting to worry the Germans, and the vessels were disguised to make them look like ordinary fishing boats.

Left:
The cook makes coffee in the galley. At this time of year temperature in the Channel goes down to zero Celsius, and the men are soon frozen stiff by the spray when the boat is travelling at full speed. A good hot drink is always welcome.

Below:
In the machine room with the engines turning at full speed, the chief machinist has to use sign language to communicate. The thumb and index finger spread apart tell the men to check the temperature of the radiators.

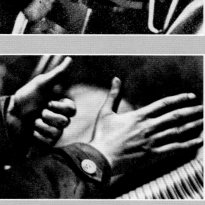

Left:
The answer comes back : 6 fingers raised (each one represents 10 degrees) means that the radiator temperature is 60° C.

Above: The torpedo officer awaits the order to fire ; his hand is on the ignition switch. Once the commander has given the order, the torpedo leaves the tube and hits the water at a speed in excess of 44 knots. At that moment the S-Boote spins around at full speed to move out of the contact zone as rapidly as possible to escape enemy fire.

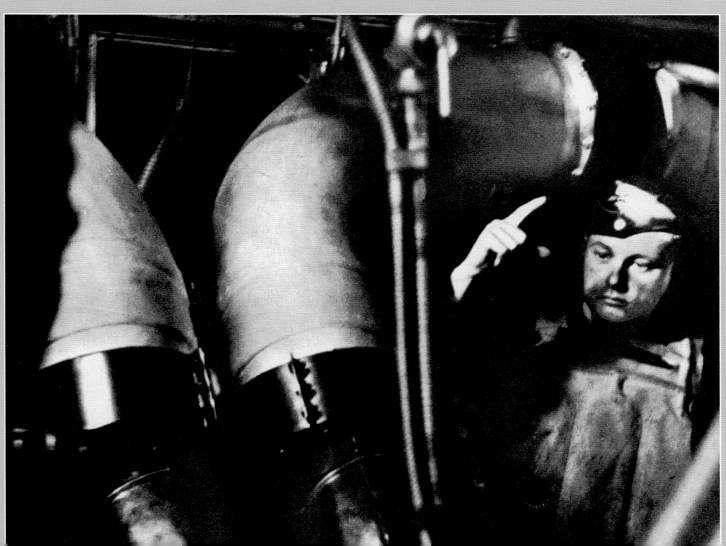

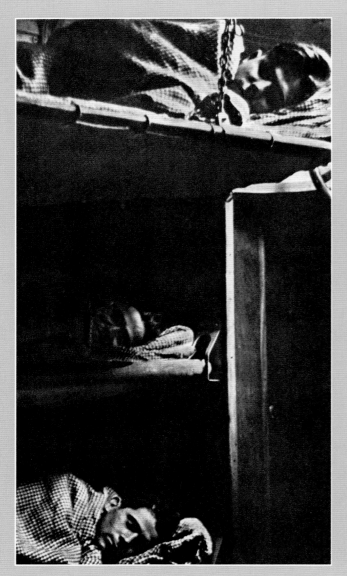

Left: The crew's cabin inside an S-Boote. This view was taken by a German war correspondant and is not exactly true to reality : as was often the case for this type of picture, the scene was set up. Operational sorties left very little time for the men to relax ; each one had an important job to do on board, especially when the vessel came in contact with enemy ships.

Above:
Checking the temperature of the diesel engine exhaust pipes in the machine room. Half of the S-Boote crew works underneath the deck. It is difficult for these men to move around in this over-heated crowded space where they must constantly keep an eye on the three engines.

Above:
Just before nightfall the S-Boote start out on a new mission. The commander is the only person who knows the direction the boat will take and the type of mission assigned.

Left:
As it approaches the enemy escort ships, the S-Boote produces a screen of grey-white smoke from two tanks placed at the back of the boat.

right up until the Allied invasion of June, 1944. The S38 was equipped with three 2 000-hp MB 501 diesel engines and could sustain a top speed of 44 knots for several minutes, with its diesel engines wide open. She was armed with two 533-mm torpedo launching-tubes, and two 20-mm guns placed fore and aft, reinforced in 1943 by a 37-mm Bofors cannon. From the end of 1942 on, the captain's bridge was modified and its entire structure was armored. These vessels, which were constantly undergoing improvements, were able to defy the Allies on all theaters of operations during World War II.

On April 29, a new mine-laying operation offered a chance for the three flotillas to work together. The 1st and 2nd flotillas were operating north of Cromer. At 1:15 AM, the *HMS Worcester* and the *HMS Cotswold*, part of the 16th destroyer fleet, were able to identify units of the 1st flotilla and unsuccessfully tried to attack them. Their little game of hide-and-seek was to last until 4:00 AM, when the S-Boote came upon the 57 ships of convoy EC 13. The S26 and S29[1] launched torpedoes against three English freighters, but only one was sent to the bottom: the 1 555-ton *Ambrose Fleming*. Meanwhile the gunboats of the 3rd S-Boote flotilla[2] were laying their mines in the zone between Haisborough Tail and Hammond Knoll in the estuary of the Thames. The Germans were surprised to find themselves nose-to-nose with MGBs 61 and 59, part of the 6th MGB flotilla based in Portsmouth. The combat between the S-Boote and the British MGBs was to last 25 minutes. During the fray, the S61 fired 800 20-mm shells without seriously damaging any of the enemy boats. Along with the April 17 fight, this was the second direct confron-

1 – The S26 was commanded by Oberleutnant zur See Fimmen, and the S29 by Oberleutnant zur See Von Mirbach.
2 – The S61 and S58.

Top:
An S38-type S-Boote in the North Sea in 1941. With streamlined tubes and three 2000-hp MB 501 engines, her top speed approached 42 knots, far outclassing equivalent Allied units.

Right:
2nd S-Boote flotilla in the port of Ostende in 1941. At the back of the two craft can be seen DM 11-type hydrostatic anti-submarine grenades. The pressure exerted by the sea water will trigger the explosion of the device, preset on the surface. This type of grenade could be used up to a depth of 125 meters.

tation between the German and British coastal forces. At the end of May, the three German flotillas left the western sector for Swinemünde to be reorganized in preparation for Operation *Barbarossa*.

Excerpts from the ship's log of Oberleutnant zur See Hans Weber, commander of the S35[1]: May 19, 1941.

In the evening of May 18, the weather finally started to improve. No sorties for two weeks because of terrible weather: we were all anxious to take to sea. 10:00 Met with flotilla leader, departure set for 21:00. Five vessels are to participate in the operations, and will be met by two other units belonging to Petersen's flotilla that will join up with us in our contact zone. It is a routine mission, one which we have accomplished dozens of times: mine-laying along the coast of Britain or in the Thames estuary. Until recently the English hadn't been reacting to our night

incursions, but for the last two months their coastal forces have become more and more agressive and we have had to return their attacks. Each gunboat carries three ordinary EMC-type mines, which seem to cause our neighbors on the other side of the Channel serious problems. Mine-sweeping takes a lot of men and material, beyond the damage done to surface vessels. The weather is calm, we approach the enemy coastline at reduced speed; it is 22:30-23:00, the wind is coming up and the sea is getting heavier. The calm didn't last. We now have a 3-meter swell and a good force-6 back wind: our target is still a long way away. Wagner's S54 has lost two mines when their cables broke; our crew is in the stern checking our EMC cables. They appear to be holding good. The weather is against us and getting worse by the hour. 1:30. Orders to all boats to change direction. Return to base.

On June 1, 1941, the 4th S-Boote flotilla arrived in Rotterdam with the S19, 320, S22, S24 and S25[2]. A new encounter would take place between the S-Boote and the MGBs of the 6th fleet during the night of June 20-21 during a mine-laying mission. Three MGBs, the 58, 59 and 65, surprised the S20, S22 and S24 and attacked them from a distance of between 1 500 and 600 meters. The Germans fired back with their 20-mm cannons and their MG 34 machine guns without doing serious damage to the enemy boats, which broke off the fight after only a few

1 – The S35 was part of the 3rd S-Boote flotilla.
2 – At the beginning of July three new boats were added to the flotilla: the S107, S49 and S50; the S63 arrived in October.

minutes. On June 24, the flotilla left the North Sea and took up quarters at Cherbourg. For two months most of the missions would involve nighttime mine-laying around the Isle of Wight and the Portland peninsula. Only one boat[1] was sunk during this period, on August 11 off Dover by the S49. As often happened, during this attack the arrival of a British destroyer was to prevent the S-Boote from further harassing the convoy. At the beginning of October, the 2nd S-Boote flotilla[2], with the exception of 4 boats, was sent to the western front. The S42, S44, S45 and S46 were sent into the Arctic Ocean with the mission of protecting the German ships cruising near Nord Kapp, a zone where there was a lot of Soviet activity. These vessels would form the embryon of the 8th S-Boote flotilla.

THE RAIDS CONTINUE

Operations continued on the western front. During the night of November 19-20, the 2nd and 4th flotillas took to sea with the mission of intercepting an important convoy spotted near tun 56. At 00 :20 several British freighters appeared at the entrance to the channel. The Germans reacted immediately and sped toward the English, who had no escort ships. The S105[3] sank the 1 159-ton steamer *Aruba*. Then the S41[4] sent down the freighter *Waldinge* (2 462 tons). A 5 502-ton tanker, the *War Mehtar*, was targetted by the S104[5], which literally broke her in two thanks to a direct hit from a torpedo that transformed her into a ball of fire.

During this time a second group of S-Boote had taken up position at the entrance to the channel marked by tun 54, waiting for a second convoy, but the arrival of a British destroyer forced them to hastily abandon their position. When the first group of S-Boote had finished their attack at tun 56, not far from there, they hurriedly left the zone, moving at top speed to avoid the enemy destroyers. Suddenly the S62 commander, Oberleutnant zur See Hermann Opdenhoff, probably as a result of a misunderstood order, turned sharply to the starboard side. The S47, travelling beside her, was obliged to change her course to avoid a collision. With this sudden change in direction, she cut right in front of the S41, which was heading straight ahead at top speed in back of the other two boats. There was a violent crash. The S41 was seriously damaged and water started flooding into the machine room. Her crew had a hard time keeping her afloat. The S47 was not as hard-hit. She was taken into tow by the S62 and, under protection of the S104, the three boats tried to make their way slowly back to their base in Rotterdam.

1 – The *Sir Russel* (1 548 tons) by Leutnant zur See Max Günther.
2 – That is, the S41, S47, S53, S62, and S105.
3 –The S105 was commanded by Leutnant zur See Howaldt.
4 –The S41, commanded by Oberleutnant zur See Paul Popp.
5 –The S104, commanded by Oberleutnant zur See Rebensburg.

Left:
Guard duty on board an S-Boote operating in the English Channel. The sailor is wearing the leather suit designed to protect the crew members from the cold and spray.

Above:
On the command bridge of the S105 when she was operating on the Western front in the 2nd S-Boote flotilla. The officer on the right may be the commander, Leutnant zur See Hans Victor Howaldt.

Below:
An S-Boote *Signalmeister* preparing to communicate with another boat by flags. This method of signals was only used during exercises and in calm seas. As soon as the S-Boote started moving fast, communication between units was carried out by VHF radio liaisons or Scotte projectors.

Meanwhile the S53 and S105 had moved in to try to save the S41. As soon as the English had news of the German attack, they sent out 4 MGBs from the 6 th fleet under the orders of Lieutenant Commander Hitchens[1]. Two boats ran into engine trouble on the way, so that only MGBs 64 and 67[2] were able to take on the Germans to cut off their retreat. To the west of Hoek-van-Holland Hitchens suddenly noticed a group of three boats with their engines stopped. Since they did not answer reconnaissance signals, the English decided to attack these S-Boote. From 300 meters away, the MGBs sped toward their opponents, firing for all they were worth. The Germans managed to get into position to face the MGBs. They charged each other three times, in parallel lines, with an explosion of fire power remniscent of the great man-o'-wars of the old days when European sailing ships paired off in merciless duels. The S62 alone fired 600 20-mm shells. MGB 64 was hit and her 20-mm Oerlikon cannon destroyed. But MGB 63 was practically untouched. So the Germans decided to pull back, abandoning the S41[3], riddled with holes, on the spot. As Hitchens was heading back to England he spotted the silhouette of the S41 half-submerged. Once they had made sure that the Germans had left no booby-traps, the English decided to go on board. However they were unable to tow the boat back to England and the S-Boote sank a little later.

At the end of November, the units of the 4th S-Boote flotilla undertook a number of successful attacks around tuns 55A and 56. On the night of November 23, the S109[4] sank the tanker Virgilia, the S51[5], the British freighter *Blairnevis* (4 155 tons), and the S52[6], the Dutch steamship *Groenlo* (1 984 tons). On November 28, the S64, S50, S51 and S52 travelled to the vicinity of tun 58 north of Cromer where they sat in wait for a convoy. The S51 attacked and sank the coal ship Cormash (2 848 tons) after having missed a 7 000-ton tanker. At the same time, from a distance of 1 500 meters, the S52 sent the 2 840-ton British freighter Empire Newcommener to the bottom.

Operations continued at the beginning of December with the 2nd S-Boote flotilla engaged in a mission of mine-laying in the zones around tuns 54B and 57 east of Orford Ness. In the period from December 2-25, 1941, twelve commercial vessels were destroyed

1 – Robert P. Hitchens was born in Cornwall in 1909 and was attracted to the sea at an early age, as is often the case along this part of the English coast which is the natural continuation of French Brittany. He was fond of sailing but also of speed, and was able to participate in the Le Mans 24-hour automobile race, where he finished in an honorable position. In 1941 he was 32 and a member of the Royal Naval Volunteer Reserve. He was the brain behind the idea of combining MTBs and MGBs during operations against the Germans. It was also thanks to him that, after the first duels with the S-Boote, the weapons on the MGBs were upgraded. *Hitch* was awarded two DSOs and three DSCs, and disappeared tragically, killed in action during an operation on April 13, 1943, after having carried out 148 missions and participated in 14 combats. In 1944 the posthumous book *We Fought with Gunboats* was published, in which he recalled his war experiences.
2 – MGB 67 commanded by Leiutenant GR Campbell.
3 – The crew of the S41 was picked up a few hours before by the S53 and S105, after its collision with the S47.
4 – The S109, commanded by Leutnant zur See Bosse.
5 – The S51, commanded by Oberleutnant zur See Hans Günter Jürgenmeyer.
6 – The S52, commanded by Oberleutnant zur See Karl Müller.

by cable mines for a total of 50 396 tons. The German results at the end of 1941 were more than satisfactory. The S-Boote had sunk 29 commercial ships for a total of 58 854 tons, not counting the boats damaged or destroyed by mines.

The new models, types S38 and S100, starting to come off the production lines, had stream-lined tubes and new 20-mm high speed guns which could be used both in sea warfare and as anti-aircraft weapons. The British, on the other hand, were fully aware of the danger to their trade routes resulting from the incessant German raids, and decided to make an unprecedented effort to increase the power of their coastal forces. By the beginning of 1942 they were able to line up 7 flotillas of MTBs, 9 of MGBs and 18 flotillas of MLs based in the North Sea or the English Channel[1]. In this same zone the Germans had only 12 operational vessels[2].

1 – The first 14-ton Fairmile type C MGBs were armed with a 37-mm gun up front and could reach a speed of 25 knots. 24 boats of this type were delivered to the Royal Navy in 1941.
2 – The 1 st S-Boote flotilla was in Kiel for repairs. The 2nd S-Boote flotilla had 4 vessels + 1 extra from the 1st flotilla based in Rotterdam. The 4th S-Boote flotilla had 6 operational vessels based in Rotterdam. The 6th S-Boote flotilla had 1 operational boat stationed in Rotterdam.

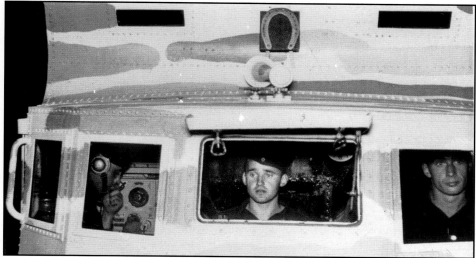

Below:
Crew members on the S105 check the Scotte projector used to send Morse Code light signals from one boat to another.

Top:
Part of the crew of the S47 on the command bridge searching the horizon. This gunboat belonged to the S38 series and entered the Kriegsmarine 5th flotilla in June of 1941, to be engaged aganist the Russians in the Baltic under the orders of Leutnant zur See Hans Joachim Stöve. The S47 later participated in fighting in the Black Sea in 1943 and 1944. She was scuttled by her commander, Leutnant-zur-See Gerhard Behrens, with the S45, S49 and S51,on August 29, 1944 off the port of Varna.

Above:
On the command bridge of the S105 when she was operating on the western front in the 2nd S-Boote flotilla. The officer on the right may be the commander, Leutnant zur See Hans Victor Howaldt.

CREWS AT WORKS

S-Boote in service in the Kriegsmarine had 24- to 30-man crews, depending on the series type of boat on which they served. Their missions usually lasted less than 48 hours, because their radius of action was limited to between 500 and 700 miles, and their bases, spread out from the coast of Holland to the southern end of the English Channel, were generally close to their targets. During the first two years of the war, missions often took place in broad daylight, since the Channel and the North Sea were still controlled by the Luftwaffe aircraft. Starting at the end of 1941, the flotillas began heading out on missions at twilight, taking advantage of the dark to move in on their targets and attack without risking being intercepted by Coastal Command planes. Transferring of gunboats between ports in Norway, Holland, Belgium and France also became standard practice at this time, in order to outwit the RAF reconnaissance pilots.

Before leaving on a mission, the boat commanders met with the flotilla leader to determine the day's target and the attack tactics to be used. During this time, the crews got the boats ready for the coming fight. Everything had to be carefully checked four hours before setting out. The diesel engines were especially important, since the success of the mission and the survival of the crew depended on their performance. After early skirmishes with the British escort ships and especially the MTBs, the S-Boote often limped back to their bases with only one or two engines running.

At sea the sailors had little time to relax. Every station on the boat required a constant presence and uninterrupted attention. Night navigating conditions involved serious risks of collision during convoy attacks when gunboats travelled at top speed close to each other. Stress and fatigue were the daily lot of the German sailors. Standing on the bridge or beside the deck guns, at a speed in excess of 30 knots, the cold and spray paralyzed them in less than 30 minutes.

Combats with units of the Royal Navy were often fatal. Sometimes the boats fighting each other were less than five meters apart, and when they ran out of ammunition one boat might ram into the other to prevent her from escaping. Wounds from the small- or medium-caliber guns at that distance were devastating, and crew members who could not get immediate medical attention died on the spot. The men of the S-Bootwaffe were particularly obsessed by air raids and mines. Even though their anti-aircraft weapons had been upgraded, gunboats attacked by Coastal Command planes had very little chance of escape. When a mine exploded as a gunboat went by, it was « double or nothing » depending on which parts of the boat were hit and the importance of the damage.

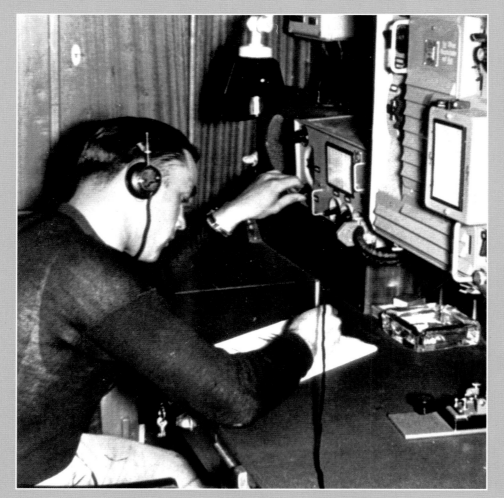

Top:
In an S-Boote machine room in February, 1941.
A young mechanic is checking the diesel engines
under the watchful eye of a Chief Machinist.
The success of the mission and the survival of the crew
depend on keeping the engines in good running order ;
the vessel can only count on the excellent performances
of her engines to escape the British escort ships once
her torpedoes have been launched.

Left:
In the radio room of the S105 on operations.
The *Funkmaat* or radio operator plays a major role on board.
He is in permanent liaison by VHF with the other units
of the flotilla, and he receives coded messages
from the S-Bootwaffe headquarters through
the *Enigma* machine.

Left:
Two mechanics doing maintenance work on the S-Boote diesel engines. The engines were subject to hard use because of the wide variations in speed during sorties, so they had to be permanently maintained in good working condition : the survival of the crew and the boat depended on it.

Below, and next page:
In the machine room of an S-Boote on operations. The speed of the three diesel engines was under constant surveillance throughout the mission. If one engine broke down, the two other working engines were capable of getting the boat back to her home base.

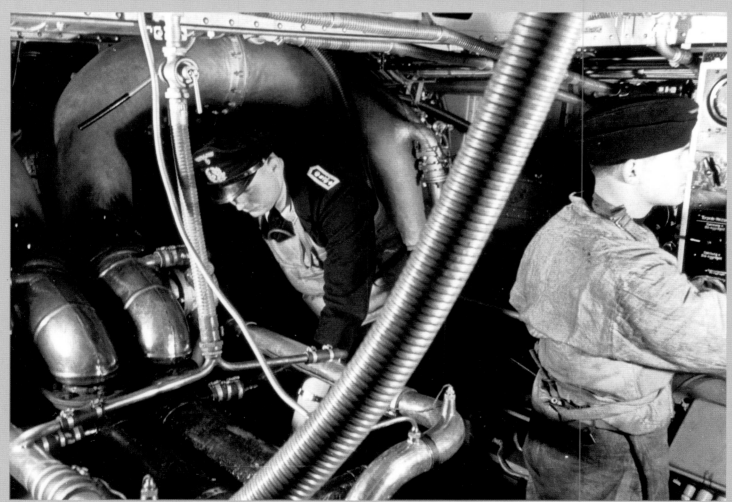

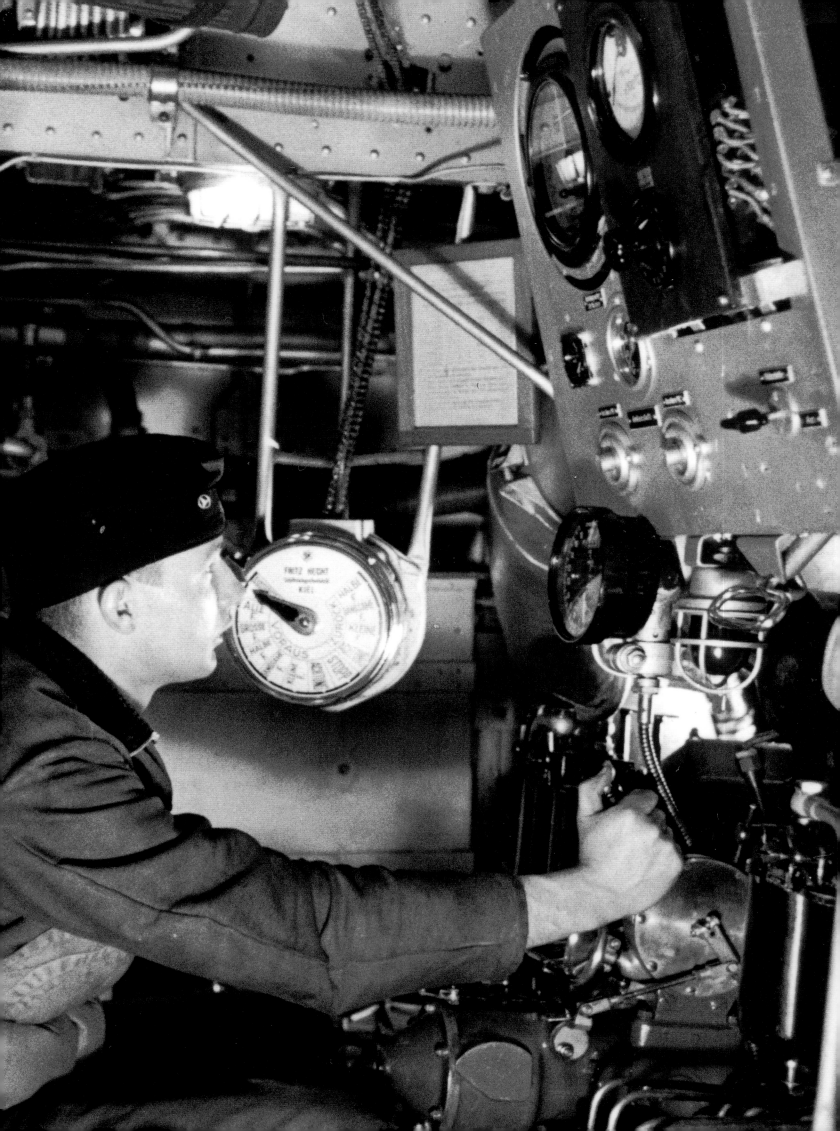

THE *S*-BOOTE
IN THE MEDITERRANEAN
(1941-1945)

In the evening on October 7, 1941, the S33, S31, S34, S61 and S35 left their Wilhelmshaven base for Rotterdam. This first group of S-Boote from the 3rd flotilla were heading for the Mediterranean to reinforce the units of the *Regia Marina* operating off Tripolitania. The Italians were having more and more trouble with the Royal Navy ships. On land the military situation of the Italian expeditionary corps was also becoming increasingly alarming.

The twelve gunboats travelled up the Rhine to Mannheim and by the 14 th had reached Strasbourg. It would take them more than a month longer to reach Port-Saint-Louis-du-Rhone and the blue waters of Mare Nostrum[1]. On November 18, the vessels arrived in Spezia where they spent a week being reequipped. Finally on December 1, they reached the port of Augusta on the east coast of Sicily which would be their first operational base.

1– The units of the 3rd S-Boote flotilla were carefully camouflaged during their transfer to the Mediterranean, especially going through the Rhine-Rhone Canal and down the Rhone River. Fake structures were added to the tops of the boats to make them look like simple towboats.

Top:
The S35 photographed in October, 1941, leaving the port of Wilhelmshaven for the Mediterranean with the first units of the 3rd flotilla. The boat is coming out of dry dock to take to the sea again. She was commanded at that time by Leutnant zur See Horst Weber. The S35 disappeared on February 28, 1943, after hitting a mine northwest of Bizerte.

Above and right:
A 3rd S-Boote flotilla transformed into an ordinary civilian vessel going through a lock on its way to the Mediterranean in October, 1941. The torpedo tube holes have been blocked and the general silhouette of the boat has been modified. All exterior weapons have been dismounted.

THE BLOCKADE OF MALTA

Their first sortie took place on December 12, 1941. Five gunboats laid mines around Malta. Operations against Malta and its port would continue almost daily throughout December and up to February, 1942. The result would be increased difficulties for Royal Navy comings and goings. The British Navy had suffered heavy losses in 1941[1] but continued to try as it might, and in spite of intense German bombing, to get supplies through once a week to the island and its capital city. On February 5, 1942, the eight flotilla gunboats[2] left Augusta and moved to Porto Empedocle on the south side of the island. From this new operational base, the S-Boote would continue their daily mission of mine-laying off Malta or Tripolitania (the region around Tripoli), where a large number of British ships passed regularly, bringing in supplies for the units of the 8 th Army. On March 24, off the coast of the island, the destroyer *HMS Southwold* hit a German mine and capsized. And on May 10, the S31 also was hit and sank.

On the morning of June 14, Luftwaffe reconnaissance planes reported the presence of several convoys heading for Malta. Five freighters and a tanker, escorted by the anti-aircraft cruiser *Cairo*, nine destroyers and four mine-sweepers, had left Gibraltar heading out into the Mediterranean. These ships were later-

---

1 –On November 13, 1941, the U81 sank the aircraft carrier *Ark Royal*. On November 25, 1941, the U331 sank the battleship *Barham*. On December 15, 1941, the U557 sank the cruiser *Galatea*. On December 18, 1941, the cruiser *Neptune* and the destroyer *Kandahar* blew up on a barrage of mines placed by the Italians off Tripoli. Cruisers *Penelope* and *Aurora* were also damaged. On December 19, 1941, three teams of Italian frogmen from the 10 th MAS flotilla, under the orders of Lieutenant Commander Luigi Durand de la Penne, managed to sneak into the port of Alexandria and, using underwater explosives, blow up the battleships Queen *Elisabeth* and *Valiant*, as well as a tanker, the *Sagona*. The attack team was transported on board the submarine *Scire*, specially equipped for the occasion and commanded by Prince Valerio Boghess
2 – Including the S33, S54, S57, S35, S34, S59, S56, and S61.

Top:
The S58 photographed in October 1943 in the port of Toulon. The boat was commanded at that time by Oberleutnant zur See Günther Schutz and had left her Italian base in mid-September after the American and British invasion of the south of the Italian peninsula, to take shelter in a more secure port.

Right:
The S31, S33, S34, S35 and S61 in dry dock in the Italian port of Spezia in November, 1941. These gunboats were part of the 3rd flotilla. They left their base in Wilhelmshaven at the beginning of October and took more than a month to reach the Mediterranean, where they were operational out of the port of Augusta, in Sicily, on December 1.

Above: An S54-S61-type S-Boote photographed in an unidentified port somewhere in the Mediterranean in 1942. This could be the S54, commanded by Oberleutnant zur See Klaus Degenhard Schmidt, identified with the help of her flotilla insignia : an wide-mouthed crocodile.

Wuppermann, again launched an attack against a large cruiser. The S56 managed to squeeze through a gap in the British defense forces and approach the Newcastle. From 400 meters away, and in spite of the wall of fire coming from the escort vessels, she managed to launch her torpedo, and hit the front of the cruiser. Fifteen meters of the prow of the ship were ripped off by the explosion, but she was able to stay afloat and be towed back to Alexandria.

The S55, part of the first group, commanded by Oberleutnant zur See Horst Weber, added another trophy by torpedoing the destroyer *HMS Hasty* (1 340 t.) which was finished off by the Royal Navy ships themselves. The convoy coming from Gibraltar also ran into serious trouble as it approached Malta. The mines which had been laid during the previous week by the 3rd flotilla did a good deal of damage to the English ships. Three destroyers were sunk, along with a mine-sweeper and a large freighter[3].

Rommel's victories in March, 1941, and his rapid break-through toward Egypt, after only a few months' fighting, were to completely reverse the military situation on the North African theater of operations. Tripolitania and Cyrenaica were now entirely under German control, and the siege of Tobruk, where it was now England's turn to be surrounded, was organized. It would last 242 days. In less than 10 days, the Afrika Korps had pushed the boundaries of the territory controled by the Axis

joined by two aircraft carriers, the *Eagle* and the *Argus*, the battleship *Malaya*, the cruisers *Liverpool* and *Charybdis*, and a group of eight destroyers. Operation *Harpoon* had begun. The forces leaving Alexandria were just as impressive. Under the code name Operation *Vigorous* they included eleven transport ships protected by twelve destroyers, two mine-sweepers and four corvettes. Once out to sea they were reinforced by eight cruisers[1] and fourteen destroyers. Between June 14 and 16, the English would come under repeated attacks by the *Regia Aeronautica* and the Luftwaffe[2].

At this time, the 3rd S-Boote flotilla was operating out of the little Italian island of Pantellaria, located between Sicily and Malta, as

well as out of the port of Derna in Cyrenaica, North Africa. The S-Boote were alerted on June 14 th about the presence of the convoys, and the S54, S58, S55, S56, S36, and S59 took to sea under the orders of Korvettenkapitän Wuppermann, heading out to meet the ships coming from Alexandria. The Germans divided into two attack groups with the idea of intercepting the convoy simultaneously from the north and the south. However the gunboats found it extreemly hard to penetrate the protective barrier created by the Royal Navy forces. On every attempt they were repulsed by heavy fire from the destroyers.

At 3 : 00 AM, after several unsuccessful incursions, the second group, commanded by

1 – The eight cruisers were *HMS Cleopatra, Dido, Hermione, Arethusa, Coventry, Birmingham, Newcastle* and *Euryalus*
2 – The cruiser *Birmingham* and the transport ships *City of Calcutta* (8 063 t.) and *Potaro* (5 410 t.) were hit several times by bombs from the planes of the 10 th *Flieger Korps.* Two freighters were sunk : the *Bhutan* (6 100 t.) and the Dutch steamship *Aagterek* (6 811 t.). Finally on June 16, the U205 sent down t he cruiser *HMS Hermione.*
3 – The ships destroyed were the destroyers *HMS Matchless* (1 920 t.) and *Badsworth* (1 050 t.), the Polish destroyer *Kujawiak* (1 050 t.), the mine-sweeper *Hebe* (820 t.), and the transport ship *Orari* (10,350 t.).

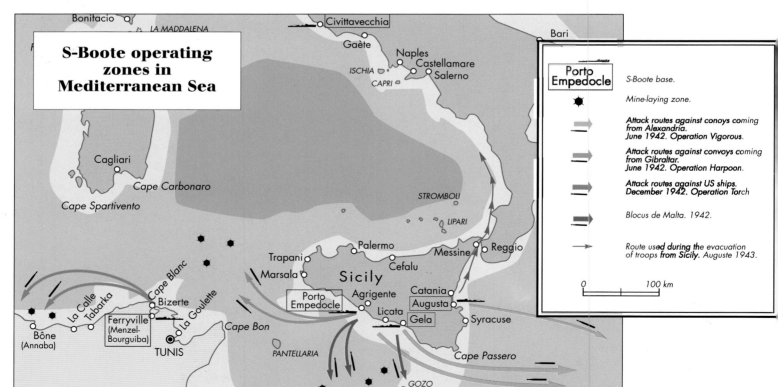

S-Boote operating zones in Mediterranean Sea

Porto Empedocle	S-Boote base.
	Mine-laying zone.
	Attack routes against conoys coming from Alexandria. June 1942. Operation Vigorous.
	Attack routes against convoys coming from Gibraltar. June 1942. Operation Harpoon.
	Attack routes against US ships. December 1942. Operation Torch.
	Blocus de Malta. 1942.
	Route used during the evacuation of troops from Sicily. Auguste 1943.

0   100 km

powers out to the Egyptian border. The 36 000 British soldiers, dependent on supplies brought in by sea, held a space surrounded by a 48-kilometer perimeter that the Germans would continually try to penetrate during the coming months.

CHECKMATING BRITISH CONVOYS

Accompanying the German land operations, the 3rd S-Boote flotilla was mobilized to intercept off Tobruk any British ships trying to get supplies through to the besieged garrison, and participated in numerous operations involving mine-laying and convoy attacks. On June 22, the S54 and S56 sank the 1 225-ton steamship *Brook*. The next day the S36 and S55 attacked and sent down two new British freighters near the besieged city. On June 30, the Axis forces were within 100 kilometers of Alexandria. On August 11 a large convoy left Gibraltar for Malta. Operation *Pedestal* had started. Once again the British Admiralty had decided to mobilize a large number of vessels to bring assistance to the martyred island. Fourteen merchant ships were escorted by four cruisers[1] and eleven destroyers. Half way there, they were met by Force H, including two battleships, the *Rodney* and the *Nelson*, the aircraft carriers *Furious, Indomitable, Eagle* and *Victorious*, along with three cruisers[2] and thirteen destroyers.

On August 11, 12 and 13, the German and Italian forces submitted the British ships to continuous attacks. The U73 sank the *HMS Eagle*, while the Italian bombers struck the *Victorious* and the *Indomitable* several times.

1 – The cruisers were *HMS Nigeria, Kenya, Manchester* and the anti-aircraft cruiser *Cairo*.
2 – The cruisers were *HMS Phoebe, Sirius* and *Charybdis*.

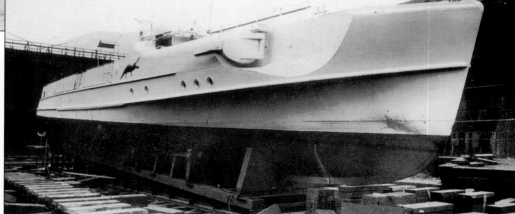

Top : The S35 photographed in 1942 when she was operating under the orders of Leutnant zur See Horst Weber with the 3rd flotilla in the Mediterranean. The gunboat can be identified thanks to her flotilla insignia representing a lobster. The S35 sank on February 28, 1943, after hitting a mine north-west of Bizerte.

Above: The S54 in dry dock in the port of Spezia in 1942. This unit was part of the 3rd flotilla operating in the Mediterranean since December of 1941. She was under the orders of Oberleutnant zur See Klaus Degenhard Schmidt, who won fame a year later on the S61 by taking Venice without a shot being fired.

Below: An S-Boote from the 3rd flotilla photographed somewhere in the Mediterranean. The gunboat can be identified by its flotilla insignia.

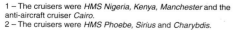

Above:
MTB 655 going through the Straits of Gibraltar in 1942 heading out to defend the island of Malta.

Left:
The chief torpedo officer *Torpedomaat* has his finger on the torpedo-launching switch, waiting for the order to fire from the commander of the gunboat. After the G7a leaves the tube, the crew needs only 45 seconds to reload.

Below:
A *Fährprahm* pictured in the Mediterranean in 1942. The ship had a large transportation capacity, and three 88-mm cannon and several vehicules are visible on board. Even though they travelled at a speed of between 10 and 12 knots, they were heavily armed. A 20-mm 4-gun Flakvierling turret was installed on the superstructure.

Cruisers *Cairo, Nigeria* and *Kenya* were torpedoed by Italian submarines, which also finished off two large freighters, the *Empire Hope* (12 688 t.) and the *Glenorchy* (8 982 t.), a job that the Luftwaffe planes had started. On August 13, the units of the 3rd flotilla[1], working with the Italian MAS, got their turn at the ships which had escaped the aviation and the submarines. This time it was the Italian teams who beat their Kriegsmarine counterparts to the stake. The heavy cruiser *Manchester* was torpedoed by MAS 15, MAS 16 and MAS 22[2]. On August 12, the S58, S59, S30 and S36 worked off Cape Bon. The S-Boote were joined by MAS 554 and 557[3] and they spent the night attacking the Allied convoys, inflicting heavy losses[4] in spite of the intense fire coming from the British destroyers. On October 8, the brand new 7th flotilla[5], under the orders of Kapitänleutnant Hans Trumer, arrived in the Mediterranean, and by December 15th all of the units were operational at the Augusta port. At the same time the 3rd flotilla had moved to Porto Empedocle, where it was being reorganized in order to again take up position near Malta and continue mine-laying and attacks on Allied convoys. Thus 22 S-Boote were now operational in the Mediterranean.

1 – Composed of the S30, S36, and S59.
2 – MAS 16, commanded by Corvette Captain Giorgio Manuti; MAS 22, commanded by Corvette Captain Franco Hezzadaa.
3 – MAS 554, commanded by Lieutenant Calcagno; MAS 557, commanded by Second Lieutenant Cafiero.
4 – Four transport ships were sent down: the Wairangi (12,436 t.), the Rochester Castle (7 795 t.), the American freighters Alméria Lykes (7 723 t.) and Santa Eliza (8 379 t.). Five other ships were sunk by the Luftwaffe.
5 – Originally formed in Swinemünde on October 1, 1941: composed of the S151, S152, S153, S154, S155, S156, S157, S158, S159, and S166.

Insigna of the 3rd S-Boote flotilla operating in Mediterranean Sea

B.PAUTIGNY

MAS 554

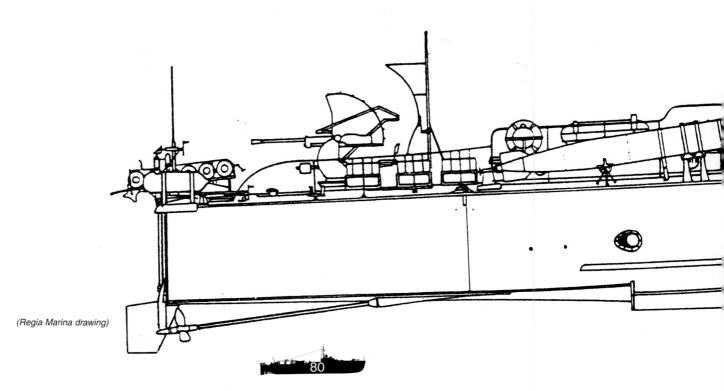

(Regia Marina drawing)

80

MAS 554 shown here at work with the 20th squadron of the 4th MAS flotilla in the Mediterranean and about to participate with units of the 3rd S-Boote flotilla in the attack of a British convoy heading for Malta on August 12, 1942. At that time the gunboat was commanded by First Lieutenant Calcagno. The Italian MAS were much smaller than their S-Bootwaffe counterparts. The 500 series was ordered by the Regia Marina in May of 1940 and delivered at the beginning of 1941. MAS 554 measured 18.7 meters long for a 28.3-ton displacement. Two Isotta Fraschini engines with a total of 2300 hp allowed her to reach a speed of 43 knots. In case of engine trouble, a 140-hp Alfa Romeo auxiliary engine could propel the boat at 8.5 knots. She had a 350-mile radius of action at full speed with her main engines and a 850-mile radius with the auxiliary engine. Her fuel tanks could hold 3.8 tons.

This MAS series was armed with two 450-mm lateral-thrust torpedo tubes and a 20-mm Breda 20/65 rapid-fire cannon. Six 50-kg anti-submarine charges could be attached to the back of the boat. The crew was made up of 13 men. MAS 554 was seized by the Germans in September, 1943, in the Venice Arsenal after the capture of the city by Oberleutnant zur See Klaus Degenhard Schmidt and his S54. She was rebaptized S623 and finally scuttled in April, 1945, in the port of Monfalcone.

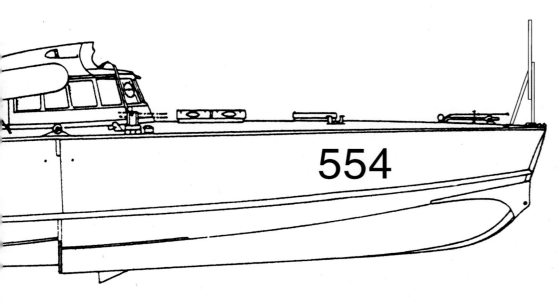

Retreat to Tunisia

The defeat of El Alamein, resulting in the retreat of the *Afrika Korps* back to Libya, and the American invasion of Algeria, forced the 3rd flotilla to leave Cyrenaica at the beginning of November to take up quarters at a new base at Ferryville, Tunisia, on the Lake of Bizerte. This new position would allow the S-Boote to easily lay mines along the North African coast, and to hinder movements of American ships as much as possible with their daily sorties.

The Allies reacted by launching bombing raids over the Tunisian port, without, however, managing to do much real damage to the carefully camouflaged German vessels. The 3rd flotilla S-Boote would also participate in operations designed to get supplies through to the Axis troops fighting the Americans in Tunisia. On December 13, the S58, S57, S61 and S33 left Trapani with the Italian destroyer *Freccia* and the transport ship *Foscolo*, carrying fuel and ammunition for Tripoli. At 22 : 00 the little group was spotted by British aircraft and they started torpedoing the German and Italian ships. After the first passage the *Foscolo* was hit ; she capsized twenty minutes later. The other boats changed directions and headed back to Trapani.

On March 12 the two flotillas moved out with six boats[1] for a mine-laying mission off the port of Bône. They had barely arrived within sight of the Algerian coast, when the six S-Boote were attacked by three destroyers. The S55 and S60 immediately fought back ; two torpedoes flew out toward the Allied ships located 1 500 meters from the Germans. The first blast went off one minute fifteen seconds later ; then two seconds after a second explosion shattered the night. Realizing that the destroyers would soon be on them, the S-Boote opened up their smoke screens and zoomed away from the combat zone. The *HMS Lightning* (1 920 tons) was sunk during the fighting, literally cut in two by the shot from the S55 commanded by Oberleutnant zur See Horst Weber[2].

Between December 16, 1942 and March 12, 1943, the 3rd flotilla undertook twenty-two mine-laying operations from the port of Bizerte. But the success of Operation *Torch* would allow the

---

1 – From the 3rd flotilla, the S55, S60, and S54.From the 7th flotilla, the S158, S156, and S157
2 – The second explosion probably came from the boat itself.

Top:
A tanker approaching Malta has been hit by one or several torpedoes.

Centre:
Attacking a convoy on its way to Malta.

Left:
A Higgins PT boat, built in November, 1942, belonging to the US Navy, photographed in the Mediterranean several months after the American invasion of Algeria. The US engaged its PT boats in the Mediterranean from April of 1943 on. The one in the photo is a Higgins type 78, displacing 43 tons for a length of 23,7 meters and a speed of 40 knots. Its principal armament was composed of four 533-mm torpedo tubes, a 40-mm Bofors cannon, one or two 20-mm cannon, and four 12.7-mm machine guns.

Following page:
The tanker Ohio under attacked by Luftwaffe planes during Operation Pedestal off Malta in August, 1942.

S-Boote Torpedoes

On September 1, 1939, all Kriegsmarine units, including the S-Boote, were equipped with two types of torpedoes: the thermic-proplusion model G7a and the electric-propulsion model G7e. Each type contained a 280-kg charge of explosives, which was ignited during flight either by a contact rocket or by a magnetic field rocket. Type G7a was designed to reach a speed of 40 knots with a 7.5 km-radius of action. The torpedo was propelled by a heat-triggering device using parafin as combustion fuel. The problem with this type of device lay in the engine exhaust, which, when it reached the surface, spread out in the form of bubbles that left a track making it easy to pick up the trail of the torpedo.

The G7e was of quite a different design. It was not as fast as the G7a, reaching 30 knots for a 5-km radius of action. The disadvantage of this type of torpedo was the batteries which had to be recharged every five days if the operational capacity of the device was to be maintained. Moreover the magnetic rocket which triggered the explosives was trouble-prone[1]. During the Norwegian campaign, many French and

1 -Many torpedoes exploded at the end of their paths without meeting their target. The system regulating the depth of the torpedo was also often defective. The G7es and G7as travelled at a depth of two meters below the draught of the ships they had targetted, which allowed them to avoid any drag.

British ships escaped the G7es: their rate of failure on impact was 65%. In November, 1942, the German technicians created a new model: the G7a Fat [1]. It was a torpedo with a programmable guidance system. It could start out on a straight path then circle to the left or right. At a speed of around 30 knots, this type of device was able to cause major damage in a convoy travelling between 10 and 12 knots, with the added advantage of being able to lock on to the tail of its target. In 1943 the G7as and G7es were equipped with a new guidance system called LUT[2]. The torpedoes could henceforth be programmed to follow a zigzagging path after heading straight for around 300 meters after leaving the tube, and at a speed of between 5 and 20 knots. The first LUTs, known as G7e T3as, equipped theU-Boote and the S-Boote starting in February 1944. A month later the same guidance system was introduced on the G7as.

After ten years of research, the German engineers in 1942 invented a new type of torpedo, with a completely revolutionary method of finding its target. It was the acoustical torpedo model G7es T IV Falke[3]. The model was first tested at the beginning of 1943 and by July it was completely operational. Propelled by a 32-hp electric motor

1 – *Fat* : *Flächen Absuchender Torpedo* (circular search torpedo).
2 – *Lut: Lageunabhängiger Torpedo* : torpille à évolution en zig-zag.
3 – *Falke* : falcon

Left:
The S105 torpedo officer checking the detonator
on the boat's port side tube.

Below:
Loading a G7a-type torpedo on an S-Boote.
7,16 meters long, and 533 mm in diameter,
this torpedo, along with the G7e, was the standard
torpedo used by the S-Bootwaffe during the war.

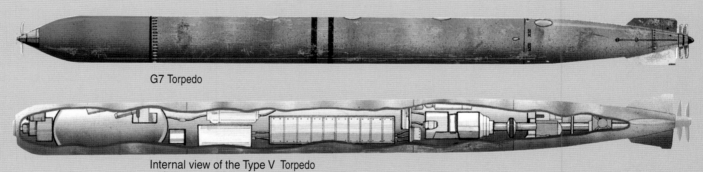

G7 Torpedo

Internal view of the Type V Torpedo

THE DIFFERENT TYPES OF TORPEDOES

	Model T1 G7a Type	Model T2 G7e Type	Model T3 G7e Type	Model T4 G7es Falke Type	Model T5 G7es Zaunkönig Type	Model T8 G7ut Steinbutt Type	Model T1 G7ut K. But Type	Model T1 G7a Type
Diameter	53,34 cm	53,34 cm	53,34 cm	53,34 cm	53,34 cm	53,34 cm	53,34 cm	53,34 cm
Length	716,3 cm	716,3 cm	716,3 cm	716,3 cm	716,3 cm	716,3 cm	716,3 cm	716,3 cm
Weight	1 538 kg	1 608 kg	1 608 kg	1 400 kg	1 495 kg	1 730 kg	1 309 kg	1 352 kg
Propulsion system	Thermic energy	Electric	Electric	Electric	Electric	Walteer turbine	Walteer turbine	Thermic energy
Power	350 hp	100 hp	100 hp	32 hp	55 hp	430 hp	425 hp	165 hp
Speed	40 N	30 N	30 N	20 N	24 N	45 N	45 N	34 N
Weight of charge	280 kg	280 kg	280 kg	274 kg	274 kg	280 kg	280 kg	280 kg
Guidance system	Direct firing Fat or LUT	Direct firing	Direct firing or Fat	Acoustical self-guidance	Acoustical self-guidance	LUT	Direct firing	Direct firing
Radius of action	7,5 km	5 km	5 km	7,5 km	5,7 km	8 km	2,8 km	2,5 km

reaching a speed of 30 knots, it weighed
almost 200 kgs less than the traditional G7e.
It was improved in October, 1943, to create
the new *G7es T V Zaunkönig*[1], which worked the same way as type IV.

An acoustical rod and 16 tubes with
amplifiers automatically guided the torpedo
toward the noise created by the propellers
of enemy ships. If the cavitation created by
the propellers deflected the torpedo, it was
able to find its path again and lock on tigh-
tly to the direction where the noise was
coming from. The Zaunkönigs were designed
for a speed of 24 knots and a 6-km radius
of action. During attacks the acoustical guidance system was often defective, and of
700 Falke and Zaunkönig torpedoes used
during the last two years of the war, only
10% hit their targets[2].

---

1 – *Zaunkönig* : wren
2 – The British immediately reacted to the use of acoustical
torpedoes by equipping their boats with a buoy carrying one
or several noisemakers : the Foxer. It was attached to the boat
by a 300-meter-long line. Once the acoustical torpedo was
launched, it frequently headed straight for the noisiest sound
and exploded against the Foxer.

Right:
A G7a-type torpedo
about to be loaded
into the port tube
of an S-Boote under
the watchful eye
of a member of the crew.
Once this operation
is finished, a second
torpedo will be placed
on stand-by behind
the tube. After the initial
firing, the two tubes
can be reloaded in less
than 45 seconds,
allowing the gunboat
to launch a second attack.

Left:
Close-up of the trap door
closing the torpedo tube situated
on the port side of an S30-type
gunboat. Streamlined tubes
will start appearing
on the S30-S37 types in 1939.

Below:
The three phases of the opening
of the trap door of the streamlined
S-Boote torpedo tube. The modification
of the tube design appeared
in 1938 on the S30-S37 series.

Above: S-Boote crew members decorating a torpedo about to be loaded on a boat heading out for a mission along the English coast. A sailor outside the range of the camera is finishing his drawing by adding the traditional words *Mit Liebe* : with love .

Below: Close-up view of a non-streamlined 533-mm torpedo launching tube on an S14-S25-type S-Boote.

Allies to take over port installations in excellent shape, which would be used over the coming months to ship in troops and material for the Tunisian campaign. By April 27, PTs 201 to 208 had arruved in the Bône port, along with MTBs 265, 316, 317, 61 and 77. At the beginning of May the Germans were trapped in Tunisia, and on May 5, as the Allies continued their advance, the S-Boote began to evacuate men and material to Porto Empedocle. By May 7, the situation of the Axis forces in North Africa had become desperate, and the S-Boote left Ferryville for one last crossing. Several officers from the Tunisia zone headquarters, as well as a hundred men and their material, were evacuated to Sicily. After the loss of Tunisia, the S-Bootwaffe was no longer able to operate out of North African ports, and all the units had to retreat to bases in Sicily[1] or go to Toulon for repairs.

THE FALL OF SICILY
AND THE INVASION OF SALERNO

The Anglo-American invasion of the coasts of Sicily[2] in July, 1943, resulting in the destitution and arrest of Mussolini, was a tough setback for the Axis forces. In spite of massive trooops sent over from the mainland, the Allies took the island in 38 days. On August 17, a few days before their retreat, the Germans launched Operation *Lehrgang*:

101 569 men (39 569 Germans, 62 000 Italians), 9 832 vehicles and 190 tanks were evacuated onto the mainland, in spite of nonstop air raids and an American invasion on

August 10[3], in a vain attempt to block the last German and Italian units. The S153 and S154 of the 7th flotilla participated in the evacuation of the German troops. During the night

---

1 – The last mine-laying operation in Tunisian waters would cost the Allies four vessels : on May 12, the British mine-sweeper HMS 89 (240 t.), on May 14, M.L. 1 154 (40 t.), on May 30, the mine-sweeper *Fantoune* (850 t.) and on August 3 the American tanker *Yankee Arrow* (8 046 t.).
2 – For Operation *Husky*, 280 boats were engaged by the Allies : 2 aircraft carriers, 18 cruisers, 130 destroyers, 6 frigates and various landing vessels, with air support furnished by 4 000 planes.
3 –The Italian Navy had sustained heavy losses, especially in transport ships, during the Tripolitania campaign. So the Germans decided to seize, in Tunisia and in the other French ports that they controlled, 128 commercial vessels of various sizes in order to bring in supplies and evacuate their troops. Many of these boats were turned over to the Italians, who gave them new names.

Top: **The S630, ex-Italian MAS 75, in the Yugoslavian port of Pola on the Adriatic Sea in November, 1943. This boat was seized by the Germans and integrated into the 3rd S-Boote flotilla, part of the 3rd assault group commanded by Oberleutnant zur See Hermann Bollenhagen. The S630 kept her Italian crew, under the orders of Lieutenant Commander Cartagna, until 1945. A Barchino assault craft, its prow loaded with dynamite and covered by a tarpaulin, can be seen behind the boat.**

Below: **Three S30-type S-Boote in the port of Gaeta in March, 1943. These boats are from the 3rd flotilla, operating in the Mediterranean since December of 1942. On the lefthand side of the S54 notice the flotilla insignia representing a crocodile with its mouth wide open. This unit was commanded by Oberleutnant zur See Klaus Degenhard Schmidt, who became a hero in September, 1943, when he took Venice with his S61. On April 22, 1944, the S54 hit a mine near the Greek port of Salonica and was seriously damaged.**

The situation in the Mediterrean at the beginning of june

Unité	Port d'attache
La 3rd S-Boote flotilla :	
• S30, S55, S57, S59, S54, S58, S60, S61	Toulon
• S36	Augusta
• S56	Palerme
La 7th S-Boote flotilla :	
• S152, S155, S156, S157, S158	Augusta
• S153, S154	
• S151	Toulon

of August 16, they were fought by PTs 205, 215 and 216. The American boats managed to hit the S-Boote several times, but when it came to speed, they couldn't compete[1]. On July 24, two weeks after the invasion of Sicily, King Victor Emmanuel «offered the government» to Marshall Badoglio. Mussolini was taken into custody the following day and imme-

diately placed under house arrest on the Lipari Islands. Several days later he was transferred to a hotel in the Apenines[2]. During the night of September 8-9, the English and Americans invaded Salerno, south of Naples. In reaction, the Germans took Rome. The invasion of the southern part of the Italian peninsula would allow the Allies to get hold of a hundred

vessels belonging to the *Regia Marina*[3].

After the loss of Sicily, Marshall Badoglio's troops also tried to take over the Kriegsmarine units stationed in the ports of southern Italy. To avoid being captured, several S-Boote took refuge in the French port of Toulon. Others went to Spain where they were boarded and seized by the Spanish authorities[4]. The S55, for her part, went through the Canal of Corinth to the port of Salamis, which was still under German control. At the same time, about 40 MAS were integrated into the Kriegsmarine units. Even though the English and Americans were far superior in numbers, the German forces nevertheless tried to oppose the invasion of Salerno. On September 11, the S57, S158, S151 and S152 left their base in Civitavecchia and patrolled along the Italian coastline, looking for Allied transport ships to destroy. Around midnight they were able to spot a group of eleven freighters protected by four destroyers, and decided to attack. The *USS Rowan* had discovered the group of S-Boote on its radar and headed

1 - PT 216 was also hit during the S-Boote fighting.
2 -On September 12, 1943, Operation *Eiche* was launched. 120 men in three gliders, led by Hauptsturmführer Otto Skorzeny, landed near the Albergo Hotel on the Grand Sasso plateau, 2100 meters up in the Apenines. The only way of reaching the spot was by cable car. Within twelve minutes Mussolini was freed by the commando. He took off for Rome aboard a Fieseler Storch 156.
3 - These included 5 ocean liners, 8 cruisers, 33 destroyers, 20 escorters, 39 submarines, 12 MAS and 16 other boats.
4 - The boats were the S73, S78, S124, S126, and S145. They later became part of the Spanish Navy.

straight toward them full speed ahead. Within a few seconds, the S57[1] found herself in good firing position and, at about 1 800 meters from her target, sent two G7as whooshing out of their tubes. Travelling at a speed of more than 44 knots, they struck the ammunition bay of the American ship, creating an explosion that destroyed the vessel almost instantly.

From November on, the military situation on the Italian front was completely blocked. The 23 German divisions led by Marshall Kesselring faced the British and Americans across the Gustav line, preventing them from breaking through to Rome. The Allies would have to wait five months before their offensive against the *Eternal City* would finally succeed. On June 5, the troops of Patton and Montgomery, and the units of the First French Army,

1 - The S57 was commanded by Oberleutnant zur See Günther Erdman

Top:
The crew of the MTB 262, part of the 10th MTB flotilla, practicising anti-aircraft firing in the eastern Mediterranean.

Above:
Four S-Boote of the S38 type, apparently intact, were captured in the Italian port of Ancône by the Allies in 1943. These units may have been part of the 3rd flotilla, which was operating in the Mediterranean from December 1941 on. The boat on the right in the photo has a 20-mm 3-gun turret.

Left:
American PT boat of the ELCO 80 type. As you can see in the photo, in spite of a length of 24 meters and a 51-ton displacement, the ELCO 80 was heavily armed. Along with her four 533-mm torpedoes, she has a 37-mm cannon, a 20-mm piece and four 12.7-caliber machine guns visible behind the second torpedo, as well as two 5-inch (127-mm) rocket launchers. An additional turret with two 7.62-mm machine guns has also been installed on the front righthand side of the boat.

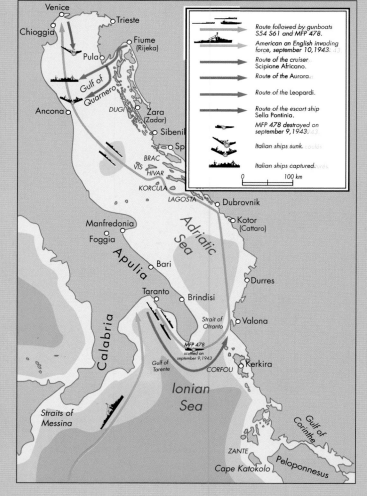

The day the S54 took Venice

At the beginning of September 1943, a few Kriegsmarine units were still stationed in Italian ports, but since Marshall Badoglio had replaced Mussolini the relationship between the former allies was tense. Many of the crews of the Regia Marina had gone over to the Allies with their ships, and the Germans had received orders to evacuate the ports which were no longer secure in order to avoid any fighting. On September 8 the S54 and S61[1], along with the *Fährpram MFP 478*[2], transporting 30 type-TMA and -TMB magnetic mines, left Tarente on a mission of mine-laying to be carried out the next day in the lagoon beside the port. The operation was designed to prevent the Italian ships from leaving their bases and also to keep any Allied ships from approaching. When they had finished their job, the little group of boats received orders to head north toward Venice. The German officials feared an English and American invasion of the city of the Doges, so the S-Boote were to try to get there first and take the city, after testing the reaction of the Italian troops present and requesting their surrender if necessary. On September 9, the German boats travelled up the Dalmatian coast toward Raguse, but the *Fährpram 478* moved so slowly that Schmidt was forced to leave her behind[3].

During the night, the two S-Boote left Raguse and slowly continued north. Considering the large number of mines scattered along the Dalmatian coast, Schmidt decided to move out into the center of the Adriatic to proceed with his mission. Off Ancone the two gunboats sank a 935-ton armed yacht, the *Aurora*. Her 62 crew members were taken aboard the two boats which continued their route. After travelling along slowly for half an hour, the S54 and S61 met a 4572-ton transport ship, the *Leopardi*, which had left *Fiume* carrying civilians and Italian soldiers who favored Badoglio's provisional government, about 1500 people. Fearing that his ship would be sunk, the captain[4] decided to negociate with the Germans. After an hour's discussion, a boarding crew came aboard the Leopardi to disarm the Italians and capture the ship, which was immediately integrated into the German formation.

At the end of the afternoon on September 11, this strange convoy had arrived thirty miles south of Venice. As he studied the horizon through his binoculars, Oberleutnant zur See Schmidt suddenly noticed the silhouette of a warship two miles away and coming slowly towards him. It was the Italian torpedo boat *Quintino Sella*, which had been under repair at the Venice shipyards since the armistice proclamation, and had left the city of the Doges in the middle of the morning to undertake machine trials, heading toward Tarente. Her meeting with the S-Boote would be fatal. The S54 decided to attack her, and rushed in at top speed. The engine problems of the unfortunate torpedo ship kept her from effectively fighting off her agressors, and although the Italian

commander tried a last-ditch maneuver, he was unable to keep his ship out of the path of the S-Boote torpedoes. She took two direct strikes and sank within a few minutes[5].

Thus the Germans had almost reached their goal, and they were ready to play dangerously. On the S54 Schmidt, with a beefed-up crew, decided to leave the other boats behind and head out alone to conquer the prestigious city, His plan was simple : land near St. Mark's, in the historical center of the city, contact the Italian military authorities, and request the unconditional surrender of the city and its garrison. Under a deep blue sunny Mediterranean sky, the S54 slowly drew into the old city. The Germans, even though determined, were tense. They didn't know what kind of reaction to expect from the Italians nor how motivated the forces defending the city might be. After several long minutes moving in through the harbor, the gunboat landed at mid-afternoon at the Venice shipyards. Schmidt disembarked immediately and, surrounded by half of his heavily-armed crew, asked the Italians who had come to meet him to lead him to the commander of the city.

Negociations between the German officer and Admiral Emilio Brenta, commander-in-chief of the North Adriatic sector, accompanied by Admiral Brenta e Zanoni, who controlled the Italian military forces in Venice, were long. Schmidt's ultimatum was simple : the city garrison must surrender its weapons and the naval units present

in Venice must not attempt to leave the port. Otherwise the Luftwaffe was prepared to bomb the city. In this little poker game, Schmidt[6] was bold enough to add that a large fleet of German ships was anchored just off Lido, awaiting his orders to intervene against the city. The ensuing hail of bombs just might destroy the lovely old Venetian palaces. The Italians didn't quite know what to make of this, and were so impressed that they accepted an unconditional surrender. Thus Venice was captured within a few hours by 40 men with one gunboat and without firing a single shot. 5000 Italiens had laid down their weapons.

On October 31, 1944, the S54 sank off *Salonica* after hitting a mine.

---

1 - S54 : Oberleutnant zur See Klaus Degenhard Schmidt ; S 61 : Obersteuermaat Friedel Blömkert. Her official commander, Oberleutnant zur See Axel von Gernet was hospitalized in Germany with yellow fever.

2 - The Fährprams first appeared in the Mediterranean in 1942. They were large-capacity multi-purpose shallow-draft boats displacing 350-400 tons. Even though their speed did not exceed 10-12 knots, their weaponry made them dangerous opponents for the British Coastal Forces. They could receive two 88-mm pieces, several 20-mm quadruple gun turrets and 37-mm cannon.

3 - On that same day, the Allies with several large ships tried to approach the port of Tarente. The H.M.S. Abdiel hit a mine which had been laid that very morning by the German boats, and capsized, carrying down members of the 1st Airborne Division of the British Army who had been picked up at Bizerte the day before.

4 - Corvette Captain Bariche.

5 - 4 officers and 27 sailors died in the attack by the S54.

6 - Afterwards Klaus Degenhard Schmidt took over as commander of the S185, in the 10th flotilla, in December, 1944. On December 23 the S185 was working with the S192 off Ostende when the two boats were intercepted and sunk by four British destroyers.

Top:
The S61 photographed on September 11, 1943. The S-Boote left the port of Tarente on September 8, with the S54 and the *Fährprahm 478*. The three boats were heading north toward Venice. This view of the S54 was taken just after the two gunboats had attacked and destroyed an Italian armed yacht, the *Aurora*, of which part of the crew, visible on the deck, was rescued by the two German vessels.

Below:
The S61 going by St. Mark's Square heading toward the Venice Arsenal on September 12, 1943. The city had been taken a few hours earlier by the S54 without the Germans firing a single shot. 5000 Italian soldiers surrendered and forty ships were seized.

Above : The S626, part of the S621-S630 series. These boats were built by the Lürssen shipyards along the lines of the S2 and delivered in 1943 to the elements of the Italian Navy that had remained loyal to Mussolini. They served in the 24th S-Boote flotilla and were later grouped together with units of the 3rd flotilla. This snapshot was taken on April 14, 1944, after the American air raid on the port of Montfalcone. The S622 and S624 were sunk and the S623 and S626 badly damaged.

Below: Aircraft carriers *HMS Eagle* and *Indomitable*, part of H Force, escorting a convoy of 14 ships toward Malta on August 12, 1942 during Operation *Pedestal*. On August 13, the 3rd flotilla S-Boote attacked the English ships. They were assisted by the Italian MAS gunboats which sank the heavy cruiser Manchester.

paraded through the capital. On November 1, 1943, a new S-Bootwaffe unit was created in the Aegean Sea, the 24th flotilla, equipped with the Italian MAS gunboats that had been seized by the Kriegsmarine. It was placed under the orders of Kapitänleutnant Hans Jürgen Meyer. The boats making up this flotilla had actually been built by the Lürsen shipyards in Vegesack, Bremen, between 1936 and 1938 to be delivered to the Yugoslavian Navy. The Italians seized them in 1941[1] and incorporated them into the MAS flotillas.

The 24th flotilla was made up of the following units :

The 24th flotilla

S601 ex MAS 42 (ex *Velebit*)
S602 ex MAS 43 (ex *Dinora*)
S603 ex MAS 44 (ex *Triglav*)
S604 ex MAS 46 (ex *Rudnik*)
S511 ex MAS 522 (ex *Orgen*)
S512 ex MAS 542 (ex *Suvobur*)
S621 à **S630** Italian MAS seize by the Kriegsmarine.

---

1 – After the fall of Yugoslavia, the Italians seized 4 destroyers, 2 submarines, 6 gunboats and 7 mine-sweepers.

Above: The S601 and S603 in the Greek port of Phaleron in March, 1944. These two S-Boote were actually the Yugoslavian gunboats *Velebit* and *Triglav* seized by the Italians in April, 1941, during the Yugoslavian campaign. They were originally built by the Lürssen shipyards and delivered to the Yugoslavian Navy between 1936 and 1938.

Right: MTB 422 speeding along the Ligurian coast in 1945. Italian waters had been deserted by Kriegsmarine ships with the exception of the eastern Adriatic where small German ships were still fighting the British coastal forces. MTB 422 was an American-designed gunboat of the Higgins type, delivered to the Royal Navy starting in 1941.

Right: ML 340 weighing anchor in the waters of the Greek island of Skiathos in 1944. This type of boat was the Royal Navy's all-purpose vessel. It was used for convoy escorts, anti-submarine fighting, as well as in mine-sweeping operations. The MLs were the same size as the MGBs, with a 60-ton displacement and a speed varying between 22 and 25 knots. Their armament was constantly being improved during the war and consisted of a 40-mm piece, two 20-mm cannons and several 7.7-mm machine guns, as well as depth charges.

This flotilla was operational in the Adriatic Sea from December 1943 on. On April 14, 1944, an American air raid on the port of Montefalcone sank the S622 and S624, and damaged the S623 and S626. We will not enumerate the combats that took place in the Adriatic and the Aegean Sea, right up until May, 1945, between the various Kriegsmarine units[1], and the Royal Navy ships operating out of the Greek islands.

Fighting remained intense, and the Germans were able to recapture certain islands along the Dalmatian coast, which would furnish the bases they needed to supply their troops combating in Yugoslavia against Tito's guerilla fighters. During one of these operations, on June 12, 1944, the S153 was intercepted by a group of British ships and sunk by the destroyer *Eggesford* north of Hvar Island[2]. On September 1, 1944, the three flotillas fighting in the Adriatic were reorganized into a single large unit, the 3rd S-Boote flotilla, placed under the orders of Kapitänleutnant Albert Müller. It was divided into three groups:

• **1st group:** the 3rd flotilla commanded by Oberleutnant zur See Johannes Backhaus: S30, S33, S36, S58, S60, S61.

• **2nd group:** the 7th flotilla, commanded by Oberleutnant Hans Georg Buschmann: S151, S152, S154, S155, S156, S157, S158.

• **3rd group:** the 24 th flotilla, commanded by Oberleutnant zur See Hermann Bollenhagen: S621, S623, S626, S627, S628, S629, S630.

Between September 1, 1944 and May 8, 1945, 2 500 mines were laid in the Adriatic by units of the 3rd flotilla along the Albanian, Yugoslavian and Italian coasts. They resulted in the loss of two destroyers, the *Aldenham* and the *Atherstone* during December, a mine-sweeper, the *Waterwitch*, and 5 MTBs (287, 371, 710, 697, 705), ML 558 and MGB 663. At the beginning of 1945, the activities of the Kriegsmarine in the Mediterranean had been reduced basically to defensive operations in the Aegean Sea along the Dalmatian coast.

1 – Including the Italian ships requisitioned after Mussolini's arrest.
2 – The S153 was commanded by Oberleutnant zur See Sven Rautenberg.

Top:
MTB 422 photographed in the port of Livorno in 1945. The boat has a 43-ton displacement for a length of 23,7 meters. Even though she can reach a speed of 40 knots, thanks to her three Packard M 2500 gasoline engines, her armament, including two 533-mm torpedo launching tubes, a 40-mm Bofors cannon and four 12.7-mm machine guns, was not sufficient to allow her to compete with the ast-generation S-Boote.

Above:
MTB 705 going down after hitting a German mine in the Adriatic on March 23, 1945. This boat was part of the 59th MTB flotilla.

Left:
Replacing a 457-mm Mark 15 type torpedo on board a British MTB stationed in an Italian port in March, 1945. Fighting in the western Mediterranean had practically ceased in the last months and many Allied units were waiting to be transferred to the North Sea sector.

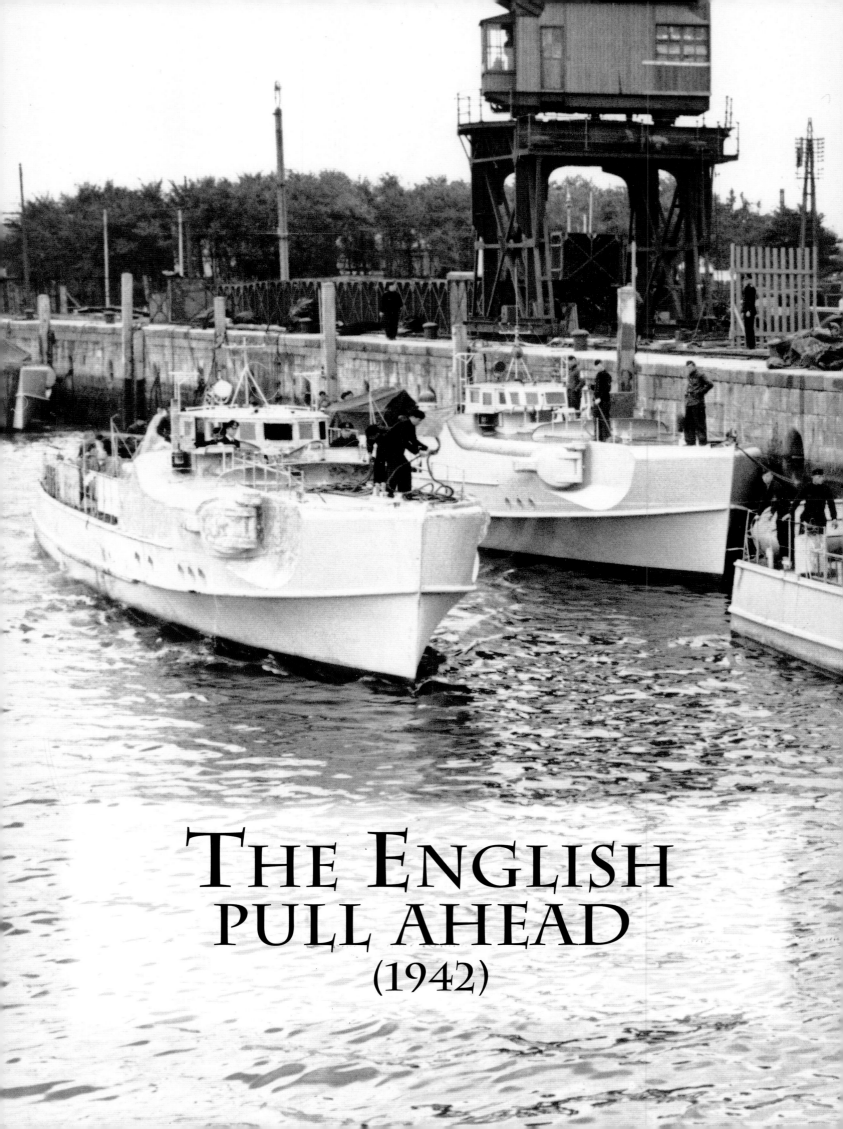

The English PULL AHEAD
(1942)

1942 would be a turning point in this period of « guerilla war at sea », since, after taking a back seat for the last two years, the Royal Navy would finally be in a position to seize the initiative over its Kriegsmarine adversaries in a whole series of operations. The English had learned their lesson during the first fights with the S-Boote and started by improving the speed and fire power of their gunboats. New types of MTBs started coming off the production lines at the beginning of 1942, including the Fairmile type D, which could reach 31 knots with her four 1,250-hp Packard engines. These vessels were equipped with two 533-mm torpedo launching tubes, which completed their initial weapons, usually including a 57-mm piece, two 20-mm Oerlikons and two double 12.7-mm and 7.7-mm machine guns. These new boats were much stabler than their predecessors.

On the German side, operational activity was quite slow at the beginning of the year. Only three new S-Boote left the naval shipyards each month. This was not enough to replace lost and damaged boats. With the opening up of new battle fronts, the flotillas were dispersed among the Baltic Sea, the Channel zone, the North Sea and the Mediterranean [1].

---

1 – At the beginning of October, 1941, the 3rd S-Boote flotilla left the Baltic for the Mediterranean. It was operational from December on, participating in the blockade of Malta.

Previous pages:
Three S26-type gunboats from the 2nd flotilla preparing to leave the Belgian port of Ostende in November, 1942. Operations against British commercial traffic had slowed down and the S-Boote were being used essentially for mine-laying along the east coast of England.

Right:
An artillery radio operator on an S-Boote in the North Sea in October, 1944. Notice in the background the 4-gun 20-mm *Flakvierling* turret whose firepower was particularly dangerous for low-flying aircraft.

Below:
An unidentified S101-type S-Boote photographed in the Channel in 1942. The pilot's bridge is not yet armored but the vessel has a 20-mm piece up front and a Bofors 40-mm cannon in the stern, giving her impressive fire power to be used against her Royal Navy adversaries.

Above:
The S39 on operations in the Channel in 1942. She is an S38-type gunboat, launched in January, 1941.
At the beginning of 1942 she was commanded by Kapitänleutnant Felix Zymalkowski and fought in the
2nd flotilla against British maritime traffic. From 1943 on she was assigned to the 6th flotilla.
On August 2, 1944, 54 Lancastars from the 1st and 8th groups of the Bomber Command
attacked Le Havre. The S39, commanded by Leutnant-zur-See Enno Brandi, was at the dock
and went down under the rain of British bombs along with the S114.

Inset:
Transfering an S-Boote into the Black Sea at the beginning of 1942.
Notice that all the weapons and the superstructure of the boat have
been dismounted to facilitate transportation.

Right:
The Semske Fjord in the north of Norway in January, 1942.
The S-Boote visible in the background are part of the 8th flotilla,
formed in October, 1941, with the S42, S43, S45 and S46, boats taken
from Petersen's flotilla and placed under the orders
of Kapitänleutnant Georg-Stuhr Christiansen.

Below:
S38-type S-Boote coming home after a mission.

German battle order on the Western Front (1942)

• 2nd S-Boote Flotilla	Kptlt. Feldt	• 4th S-Boote Flotilla	Kptlt. Niels Bätge	• 6th S-Boote Flotilla	Kptlt. Albrecht Obermaier
S 29	Kptlt. Manfred Schmidt	S 48	Oblt. z. S. Götz Friedrich von Mirbach	S 18	Oblt. z. S. Heinz-Friedrich Nitsche
S 39	Kptlt. Felix Zymalkowski	S 49	Oblt. z. S. Max Günther	S 19	Lt. z. S. Wolfgang Höming
S 53	Oblt. z. Peter Block	S 50	Oblt. z. S. Karl-Eberhard Karcher	S 20	Oblt. z. Gerhard Meyering
S 62	Oblt. z. S. Hermann Opdenhoff	S 51	Oblt. z. S. Hans Jürgen Meyer	S 22	Oblt. z. S. Herbert Witt
S 70	Oblt. z. S. Hans Helmut Klose	S 52	Oblt. z. S. Karl Müller	S 24	Oblt. z. S. Heinz Nolte
S 103	Pas de commandant en titre	S 64	Oblt. z. S. Friedrich Wihelm Wilcke	S 69	Oblt.z.S. August Licht
S 104	Oblt. z. S. Ulrich Roeder	S 109	Oblt. z. S. Helmut Dross	S 71	Oblt. z. S. Friedrich Wihelm Joppig
S 105	Lt. z. S. Künzel	S 110	Oblt. z. S. Albert Causemann	S 101	Lt. z. S. Jürgen Goetschke
	(and later Hans-Joachim Wrampe)	S 107	(not yet in service)		
S 111	Oblt. z. S. Paul Popp				

OPERATION CERBERUS.

On January 15, under orders from the Kriegsmarine west group headquarters, the 2nd, 4th and 6th fleets were transferred respectively to the ports of Ijmuiden, Boulogne and Ostende, in order to participate in a vast operation involving other German surface units[1]. The mission involved bringing back to Germany through the English Channel the battleships *Scharnhorst* and *Gneisenau*, and the heavy cruiser *Prinz Eugen*, which had been stationed in the Atlantic port of Brest. The German plan was simple: using abundant air and naval cover, get the boats out to sea and whisk them through the Straits of Dover under the nose of the English, to get them into a more secure port closer to home[2]. According to this plan, the 6th flotilla[3] with its eight gunboats, was to undertake a diversionary attack in the zone around Dungeness-Beachy Head, while the 2nd and 4th flotillas[4] assisted the destroyers in escorting the large surface vessels.

On February 11 at 23:30, under the protection of a thick fog, the German ships crossed the Brest passage, undetected by the British submarine *HMS Sealion* which had been standing guard in the zone for several days. On February 12, at the end of the morning, a British reconnaissance flight finally spotted the Kriegsmarine vessels off *Le Touquet*, escorted by the S-Boote of the 2nd

1 – About ten destroyers and 27 S-Boote.
2 – In 1941, the Kriegsmarine headquarters decided to use its large surface vessels to attack convoys in the Atlantic, as the U-Boote had been doing. Between January 22 and March 22, 1941, the *Scharnhorst* and the *Gneisenau* destroyed or captured 22 ships for a total of 115 622 tons. Since 1942 the two battleships had been stationed in the port of Brest, where they had been joined by the heavy cruiser *Prinz Eugen*. In spite of extreemly violent bombing raids, the British hd not been able to damage them. It was then that Hitler decided to pull the ships back to Germany to shelter them in a port better protected from RAF attacks. Operation *Cerberus* was launched, and the three large surface vessels left the port of Brest on February 11 at 23 : 30.
3 – The 6th S-Boote flotilla under the orders of Kapitänleutnant Albrecht Obermaier was composed of the S18, S19, S20, S22, S24, S69, S71, and S101.
4 – The 4th S-Boote flotilla under the orders of Kapitänleutnant Niels Bätge was composed of the S48, S49, S50, S51, S52, S64, S109, S110, and S107. The 2nd S-Boote flotilla under the orders of Kapitänleutnant Feldt was composed of the S29, S39, S53, S62, S70, S103, S111, S108, S105, and S104.

Inset:
The *Scharnhorst* and the *Gneisenau* accompanied by the heavy cruiser *Prinz-Eugen* going through the Straits of Dover on February 12, 1942, under the nose of the English. British torpedo boats tried to intercept the German ships but were held off by the S-Boote of the 2nd, 4th and 6th flotillas.

Top:
The 203-mm main guns on the heavy cruiser *Prinz-Eugen* firing at the Dover coastal batteries. The Luftwaffe also intervened massively from French, Belgian and Dutch bases to escort the large Kriegsmarine surface vessels back to Germany. The planes notably bombed the British coastal artillery installations.

Left:
An S-Boote crew member checking the gunboat's course.

Admiral Rudolf Petersen

Rudolf Petersen was born on June 15, 1905. His father was a pastor on the island of Als. By the Treaty of Versailles, this northern part of Schleswig was ceded to Denmark in 1918, and the family was obliged to move to Berlin. The shock of the German defeat and the Diktat imposed on Germany by the Allies led the young man to choose a military career. In 1925 he joined the new Reichsmarine and on October 1, 1929 was promoted to Leutnant zur See. From 1935 to 1936 he served as commander of the S9, and participated with his fellow officers in the elaboration of new offensive tactics for using the S-Boote. In August, 1939, at the age of 34, he was named Kapitänleutnant, taking command of the 2nd S-Boote flotilla. On October 1, 1940 he was promoted to the rank of Korvettenkapitän, and continued to command the flotilla until October, 1941, when he became an administrative officer at the torpedo boat headquarters. On April 20, 1942, he was named Führer des S-Boote, commander of all the flotillas. A year later, on March 1, 1943, he received his Fregattenkapitän's braid. He continued to rise in rank during 1944, and was promoted to Kapitän-zur-See on October 1st, then Admiral a few months later.

During the war, Petersen's relationships with Dönitz, Raeder and certain other commanding officers attached to the « Navy Group West » were cordial at best. He refused to sacrifice his units in poorly prepared offensives, in spite of Dönitz'repeated requests to undertake large operations with a maximum number of boat. Petersen never failed to use his forces efficiently, calculating the potential risk to his men of the enemy threat. He was never one to favor the idea of fanatical resistance to the dead end. He even ran into trouble from some of his flotilla commanders in the days following D-Day in June, 1944, when they wanted to attack the Allied ships non-stop day and night. The Kriegsmarine officers and Dönitz in particular criticized him for four things:

1° - During their sorties, the S-Boote did not use a sufficient number of boats against the Allied ships.

2° - Individual operations should have lasted longer, with more flexibility in boat use.

3° - Dönitz found it inconceivable that a single Allied destroyer could, by her simple presence, prevent four or five S-Boote from attacking a convoy.

4° - Finally, too many sorties were cancelled because of engine failure. (With only two diesels working, as was often the case, it was impossible for the S-Bootwaffe boats to attack the ships of the Allies.)

Petersen's men were experienced and knew that the criticism coming from the Kriegsmarine headquarters was unfounded, and that Dönitz himself was in no position to appreciate the reality of the operational situation of the flotillas. The Allied escort ships possessed displacements far superior to those of their adversaries, their structures were much more resistant, their main weapons were coupled with firing radars which meant that they were much more likely to hit their targets. Finally the combined use of Coastal Command planes and MTB and MGB flotillas, along with larger ships, made the missions of the S-Boote more and more difficult.

In spite of internal dissensions within the Kriegsmarine commandment on the western front, the S-Bootwaffe continued to be a particularly useful operational tool, even into the last months preceding the fall of Germany. Petersen was an officer with too much experience to be replaced, in spite of Dönitz'criticism. The boats and the crews remained at a high level of operational efficiency, even if difficulties concerning fuel and ammunition supplies kept them from carrying out all their missions.

In 1945, young officers of the S-Bootwaffe took Petersen's side when they learned that Dönitz, to his staff, had accused him of « half-heartedness in the face of the enemy », blaming him for hesitating to send his units into battle.

and 4th flotillas as well as several destroyers that had joined them. The British reacted first by several air attacks[1], ineffective because of the particularly efficient Luftwaffe air cover[2]. Five MTBs[3] then left Dover to try to intercept the Germans. Once they encountered their opponents, the English quickly realized that they would not be able to cross the wall of fire created by the batteries of the destroyers and the S-Boote guns, and they could not expect to get any closer than 2 000 meters. Nevertheless the MTBs launched their torpedoes, but to no avail. Later a group of destroyers from the 16th and 21st fleets tried to approach, but the fire power of the large-caliber German battleship guns kept them at bay. By February 13, the three ships had reached the port of Wilhelmshaven[4].

A week after Operation *Cerberus*, the 2nd and 4th flotillas were again at work laying mines and attacking convoys. During the night of February 19, the 2nd S-Boote flotilla tried to intercept convoy FS 29, composed of 31 ships travelling south of tun 55B. As usual the gunboats were divided into two assault groups and headed toward their target in two parallel lines. The S70 and S105 were the first to open fire on the British freighters, but the English reacted immediately with two Hunt-class destroyers assisted by two MLs and two MGBs which blasted back with all

---

1 – At the beginning of operations, the units of the 4th flotilla were separated into 2 groups. The S64 was attacked by a Spitfire and slightly damanged, so turned back to Boulogne. During the morning of February 12, seven Swordfish from the 825th torpedo airplane squadron unsuccessfully attacked the second group of the flotilla. During the fighting the S69 shot down one of the planes.

2 – Twenty ME 109 and FW 190 fighter planes stayed constantly beside the battleships. 250 other planes were on alert at French, Belgian, Dutch and German airfields so that air cover could be maintained all the way back to a port within the Reich.

3 – MTBs 221, 219, 45, 44, and 48 were under the orders of Commander Pumphrey.

4 – At 15 :30 on February 12 near the mouth of the *Schelde*, the Sharnhorst hit a mine and had to stop about an hour for repairs. At nightfall the *Gneisenau* also hit a mine near Terschilling. Then at 22 :30 the *Scharnhorst* was again hit by an explosion. This time the ship took in 1 000 tons of water.

they had. The fire power of the English ships was too much for the two German groups: they turned away and scattered at full speed into the night. In the darkness, the S39 and S53 crashed into each other [1]. The S53 was seriously damaged and water had soon flooded the machine room. The S39 was able, in spite of her damage, to return to her base in Ijmuiden. As the *HMS Holderness* was arriving on the scene and trying to get a boarding crew onto the S53, Oberleutnant zur See Peter Block, who had stayed with his vessel, threw the lever to dynamite the boat and sacrificed himself, thus preventing the enemy from capturing the gunboat.

Poor weather was responsible for cancellation of several missions during the first ten days of March. It wasn't until March 10 that the S70 would sink the 951-ton British freighter *Horse Ferry*. Likewise the S105 fired two torpedoes and thought she had hit the destroyer *HMS Whitshead*, but the British ship had actually hit a mine that had been laid several days earlier near tun 55B by units of the German flotilla.

GUERILLA WARFARE IN THE ENGLISH CHANNEL.

During the night of March 14-15, the 2nd flotilla was in operation again, with two attack groups formed by the S105, S70, S111, S62, S104, S29 and S108. The Germans were heading for FN 55, a convoy of 41 freighters which had been reported by the radio-listening services of the Kriegsmarine near tun 37. The weather, as usual at this time of year, was bad: a force-3 to -4 wind, sheet rain pouring down so that it was impossible to see more than 150 meters, and a night black as ink.

At 2:50 AM the S104 and S62 sighted two freighters and a destroyer. The S104, commanded by Oberleutnant zur See Roeder, was right in line with the British wars-

---

1 – S39, commanded by Kapitänleutnant Félix Zymalkowski; S53, by Oberleutnant zur See Block.

B. PAUTIGNY

Schnellboote S62

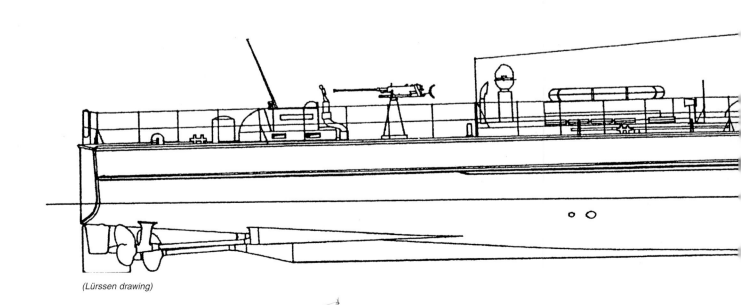

(Lürssen drawing)

The S62 seen here at the beginning of 1942 when the boat was fighting on the Western front as part of the 2nd flotilla and was commanded by Oberleutnant zur xSee Hermann Opdenhoff. She was a slightly modified series S38, entering service in the S-Bootwaffe in September of 1941. With a 115-ton displacement for a length of 34.94 meters, she was equipped with three 2000-hp Mercedes Benz MB 501 diesel engines and could reach a top speed approaching 40 knots for a radius of around 700 miles. The armament included, along with the two 533-mm torpedo tubes, two 20-mm pieces located fore and aft. In later production series the defensive weaponry was improved : the rear cannon was replaced by a 37-mm Flak L38 piece. This model was also equipped with a Metox Fumb passive radar. The crew was made up of 29 men. The S62 was surrendered to the Royal Navy in 1945 and sold in 1948.

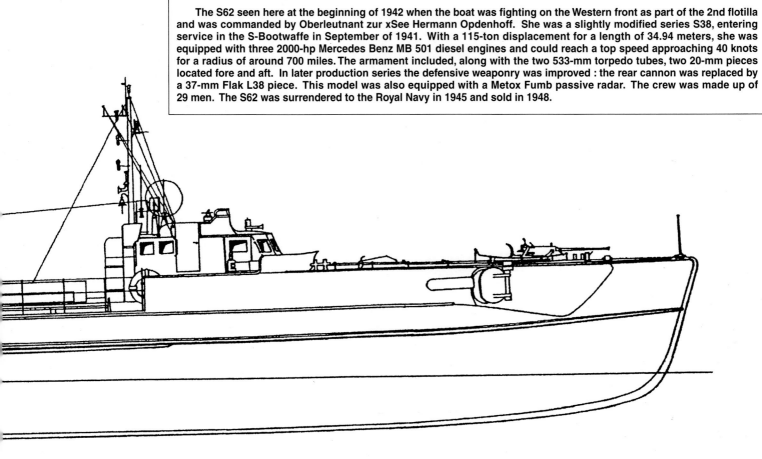

hip and in perfect firing position. Two torpedoes flew out of the S-Boote and struck the destroyer *HMS Vortigern* at the stern on the port side. She capsized in a matter of minutes. When the English learned of this attack they sent out MGBs 87, 88 and 91[1], belonging to the 7th MGB flotilla based in Lowestoft. The British sped straight for the coast of Holland, hoping thus to cut off the enemy boats heading back to base. They were lucky. Around 7: 30 AM, lost in thick fog, the S111 approached dangerously close to the Dutch coastline and ran into His Majesty's three boats, which immediately opened fire at close range. The fight was short, and the Germans, completely outgunned, surrendered to their attackers. The British immediately boarded the boat, herded the survivors onto their ships and left on the S-Boote a seizure crew composed of part of the crew of MGB 88; they immediately lowered the Kreigsmarine flag and raised the colors of the Home Fleet. On board they seized naval charts of German operational zones in the Channel, as well as weapons. Around 11: 00, after hitching the S111 up to be towed, the MGBs turned back to Lowestoft. After a few miles they were discovered by the S104, S62 and S29 which had been sent out a few hours earlier to look for the S111. After a short dogfight, the English broke off and abandoned their prize when MGB 91 was hit by several shots from one of the 20-mm cannons. The Germans in turn took the S111 in tow and headed back toward Ijmuiden. At 14: 00 the S-Boote were attacked by a dozen Spitfires and even

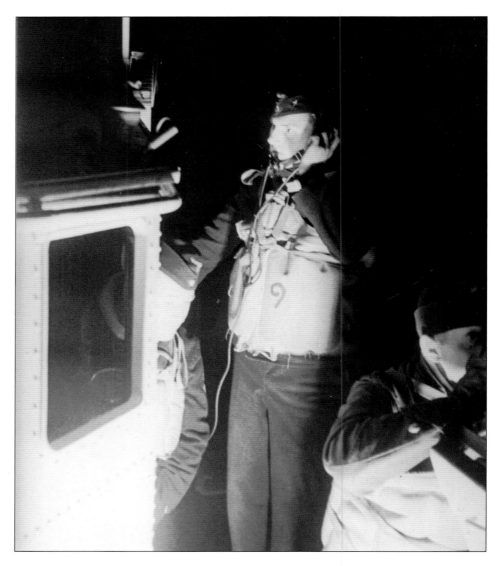

1 – MGB 87 : Lieutenant SB. Benett ; MGB. 88 : Lieutenant JBR. Horne ; MGB 91 : Lieutenant P. Thompson.

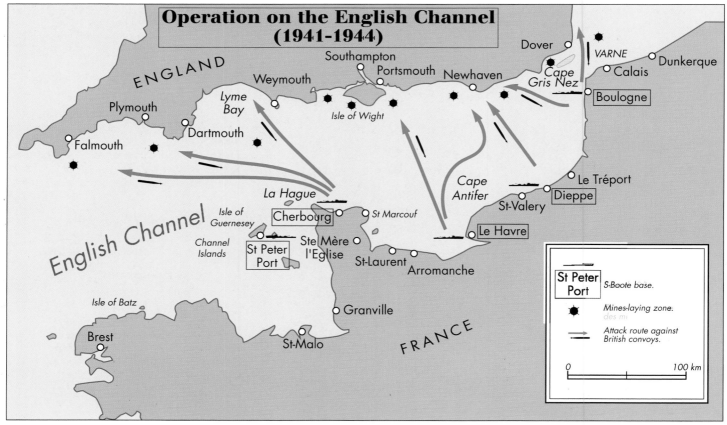

Operation on the English Channel (1941-1944)

ENGLAND

Dover — VARNE — Dunkerque
Southampton
Weymouth — Portsmouth — Newhaven — Cape Gris Nez — Calais
Plymouth — Lyme Bay — Isle of Wight — Boulogne
Dartmouth
Falmouth
Le Tréport
Cape Antifer — St-Valery — Dieppe
La Hague
English Channel
Isle of Guernesey — Cherbourg — St Marcouf — Le Havre
Channel Islands — St Peter Port — Ste Mère l'Eglise — St-Laurent — Arromanche
Isle of Batz — Granville
Brest — St-Malo — FRANCE

| St Peter Port | S-Boote base. |
| Mines-laying zone. |
| Attack route against British convoys. |

0 — 100 km

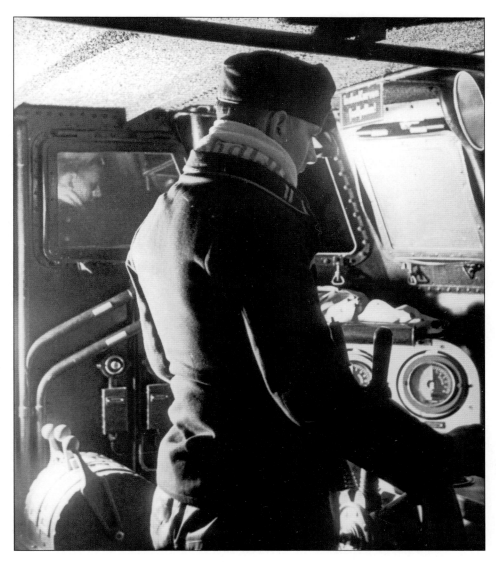

though they returned heavy fire, they were obliged to abandon the damaged gunboat which capsized after being hit by several bombs. Fourteen members of the crew perished during the English attack, including the commander, Oberleutnant zur See Paul Popp and his second-in-command Oberleutnant zur See Friedrich Wilhelm Jopping.

At the beginning of March, under orders from Admiral Bütow, mine-laying operations along the English coast were begun again, with some success. Over that month, the English lost 11 534 tons, representing 3 ships. On March 1, the 589-ton tanker *Audacity*, on March 4, the 6 675-ton tanker *Frumention*, and on March 16, the 4 270-ton steamship *Cressdone* were sent to the bottom. At the same time two destroyers were seriously damaged, the *HMS Whitshead* and *Cotswold*.

The raid on Saint-Nazaire launched on March 28, 1942 has been analyzed by numerous authors, as has the Anglo-Canadian invasion of Dieppe on August 19, 1942, better known under its code name Operation *Jubilee*. So there is no need to go into detail about these operations, which resulted in, for the first, the destruction of the locks and the pumping stations of part of the port of Saint-Nazaire, and, for the second, a tough defeat of the Anglo-Canadian forces who found themselves pinned down on the beaches of Dieppe. The British Coastal Forces played a major part in both of these operations, engaged in the front line along with other surface vessels providing escort and cover for ground troops. This proved that the English were now capable of sending large forces[1] against German land targets resulting in significant enemy losses. These first experiences would be the prelude and the testing-ground for the future major Allied invasions of North Africa in November of 1942 and Sicily and southern Italy starting in July, 1943.

REORGANIZATION OF THE S-BOOTE COMMAND STRUCTURE.

On April 16, 1942 an important change took place in the organization of the command structure of the S-Boote. Until that date, all eight flotillas had been placed under the authority of the *Führer der Torpedoboote*, with torpedo-boats and gunboats united under the orders of Admiral Hannes Bütow. Now a new structure specifically for the S-Boote was created. It was headed by Kapitän zur See Rudolf Petersen, who took the title of *Führer der Schnellboote*, a rank he would keep until 1945.

He established a new headquarters at Scheveningen in Holland. He had carte blanche to turn his units into a particularly dangerous Kriegsmarine combat tool. It was he who planned construction programs with the shipyards, developed improvements in the weapons and in the protection of the boats, and elaborated new combat tactics

1 – 1 MGB, 1 MTB, 15 MLs for the raid on Saint-Nazaire ; 12 MGBs, 20 MLs and 4 SGBs for Operation *Jubilee*.

Previous page : **An S-Boote on night operations somewhere in the Channel in 1942. The radio operator in the foreground is in permanent contact with the other flotilla units by VHF during the entire mission.**

Above : **An S-Boote pilot's bridge during a night mission. Notice on the left the transmitter box for orders concerning the three diesel engines.**

Below : **Four S30-type S-Boote waiting to leave on operations in an unidentified North Sea port.**

Petersen's headquarters in Scheveningen

Petersen's advisors were brilliant officers who had arrived in Scheveningen after exercising an operational command at the head of a flotilla. Among them, Kapitänleutnant Bernd Rebensburg was one of the indispensable operational links, helping plan the S-Bootwaffe missions. Rebensburg, as *operations officer*, worked directly with the unit commanders. He participated in the debriefings every time a boat came back from a mission, and systematically analyzed the circumstances of each combat with the British, seeking the little detail which would indicate that they were perhaps changing tactics. He also collaborated regularly with the B-Dienst services whose listening stations, installed at Dunkirk on the island of Jersey, had managed to identify the prefixes used by the British Admiralty in convoy movements. During the spring of 1944, the Germans were able to intercept and interpret the volume and direction of radio emissions between Portsmouth and Plymouth, which allowed them to deal a severe blow to the Americans in Lyme Bay in the night of April 27-28.

German mines

During the Second World War, more than 20% of Allied losses of commercial vessels resulted from mines. These can be classed in two categories, offensive and defensive. The barrier formed by the British in 1939 in the Straits of Dover and along the east coast of England was composed of mines of the first type. The English Admiralty wanted to reuse the concept of the Northern Barrage of 1918, which stretched from the Orkney Islands to Norway, thus preventing the German sea-going vessels from leaving their ports. Both the Allies and the Germans used different types of mines throughout the war. The traditional contact mines (called cable or submarine mines) were replaced early in the war by magnetic mines invented by the Germans. The next invention would be acoustical devices that were triggered by the vibrations of the boat engines. In 1944 appeared a new category, pressure or « oyster » mines, which reacted to the differences in water pressure created by the ship as she passed. These devices, used especially by the Kriegsmarine, gave considerable trouble to the Allied surface vessels, which had to send out explosives in areas they considered suspect, or reduce speed to a minimum.

MAGNETIC MINES

They go off when a metal hull goes by. It is the magnetic field created around the hull that triggers the explosion. These mines

Contact mines

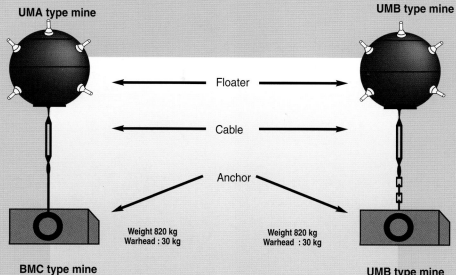

UMA type mine

UMB type mine

← Floater →

← Cable →

Anchor

Weight 820 kg
Warhead : 30 kg

Weight 820 kg
Warhead : 30 kg

BMC type mine

UMB type mine
with floating line

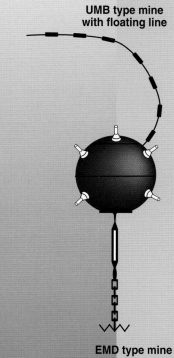

EMG type mine

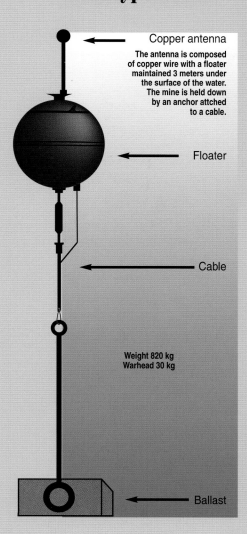

← Copper antenna

The antenna is composed of copper wire with a floater maintained 3 meters under the surface of the water. The mine is held down by an anchor attched to a cable.

← Floater

← Cable

Weight 820 kg
Warhead 30 kg

← Ballast

EMC type mine
with upper galvanic rod

Weight : between 1 808 and 1 170 kg
Warhead : 250 to 300 kg depending of the type.
Equippe with a clock movement triggering a scuttling chargee that could be set to go off at will within 80 to 200 days.

EMA et EMB type mine

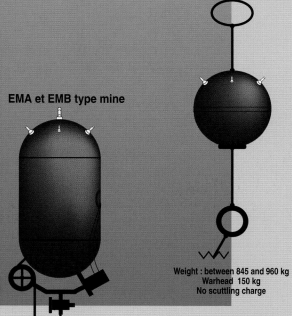

EMD type mine

Weight : between 845 and 960 kg
Warhead 150 kg
No scuttling charge

were dropped or laid in large numbers by the Germans in 1939, and in 1940 in the English Channel and the Thames River estuary. The mine contains a traditional clock movement, which will work up to a depth of 5.5 meters. If a ship passes over the mine lying on the sea bottom, the variation in the magnetic field created by the weight of the vessel moves a pointer which starts an electrical circuit which triggers the explosion. The only effective protection for ships was to surround them with an electric belt which demagnetized them, thus destroying any identifying signals.

Excerpt from a newspaper article appearing in a Portsmouth daily on November 25, 1939:

The British Admiralty has recently encountered a new menace, magnetic mines. These devices that the Germans lay in British waters are particularly dangerous weapons. On November 21, they sank the destroyer HMS Gipsy *and seriously dama-*

ged the new cruiser HMS Belfast. *Since the beginning of the month, they may have been responsible for the loss of 29 commercial vessels. Laid on the sea bottom by surface boats or dropped from planes, they are much more dangerous than the traditional floating mines which are easy to sweep. The Germans have scattered them close to the British coastline, at port entrances and also in the estuaries, especially that of the Thames. On November 20, the mine-sweeper* HMS Mastiff *was destroyed when the mine she was trying to pull up in a fish net exploded.*

The navy mines used by the Germans during the Second World War were of three distinct types.

CABLE MINES.

These are mines which can be triggered either by contact or by a magnetic field. They are either dropped from airplanes or laid by surface vessels or by submarines. The mechanism is relatively simple. The mine is composed of three parts: a floater, which is the explosive device, hitched to a cable which is in turn tied to an anchor that holds it down. Once the mine is in the water, the anchor pulls it down and the cable

Drift Mines

Weight: 34 kg
Mines either dropped by plane or laid by surface vessels.

← Stabilizing floater

Armoured drift mine.   Unarmoured drift mine.

On top:
A Kriegsmarine explosives expert taking apart the hydrostatic switch used for detonation security, transportation and laying of German DM-type contact mines with five electrochemical rods.

Centre, left:
A German EMD-type cable mine with electrochemical rods floating on the surface of the water, probably after having broken its cable. This type of device weighed around 150 kg and exploded when a boat touched one of the five rods on the floater.

Centre:
The destroyer *HMS Gipsy* going down in November, 1939, victim of a German magnetic mine. The same thing happened to the Dunler Castle off the southeast coast of England on January 9, 1940. 152 passengers perished.

Magnetic cable mines
(Immersion deph : between 15 and 30 meters)

EMF type mine
1939-1941 model

Weight: 1 220 kg.
Warhead: 320 kg.
Explosive use : aluminium TNT.

With scuttling trigeres
by a clock movement.

SMA type mine
1943 model

Weight: 1 570 kg.
Warhead: 350 kg.
Explosif : aluminium TNT.

With scuttling chage triggered
by a clock movement that
canbe programmed up
to 8 days in advance.

TMA type mine
Laid by submarine.

Charge: 230 kg.

LMF type mine
Dropped by plane.

Charge: 290 kg.

German sea-bed acoustic mines

BMA type mine
Laid by surface vessels.

Weight: 800 kg.
Warhead: 150 kg.

BM1000
Dropped by plane or by parachute.
Depth: between 15 and 35 meters.

Weight: 1 000 kg.
Warhead: 300 kg.

LMA type mine
Laid by surface vessels or
drop by plane or parachute

LMB type mine
Dropped by plane or parachute.
Depth: between 15 and 35 meters.

Weight: 350 kg.
Warhead: 80 kg.

stretches out taut, maintaining the floater about 3 meters under the surface of the water. When a boat goes by, the slightest touch on one of the rods sticking up on the floater sets off the explosion, resulting from an electrochemical reaction contained in the rod. The magnetic cable mine is composed, like the contact mine, of three parts: the floater, the cable and the anchor. The mine is triggered by the magnetic field created by the near-by passage of a surface vessel: the immersion depth is between 15 and 30 meters.

SEA-BED MINES.

These are the easiest to lay: they can simply be laid by surface vessels or submarines, or dropped by plane.

They are of three types: acoustic mines, magnetic mines (those most widely used during the war) and finally pressure mines that react to the variation in water pressure created by a displaced mass. This type of mine could be effective up to a depth of 60 meters. The change in pressure caused by the passage of a boat or the noise created by the propellers triggered the explosion of the device placed on the sea bed. There followed a shock wave whose size varied depending on the importance of the charge of explosives. The phenomenon was amplified as it approached the surface, spreading in the water five or six times faster than it would in the open air, creating a miniature underwater earthquake that would smash the hull of the ship sitting on top of the explosion. The force of the shock would generally break her in two.

DRIFTING MINES.

These are small contact mines (weighing 34 kg). They are set off by an antenna which sticks up above the surface of the

How the LMA type magnetic sea-bed mine works

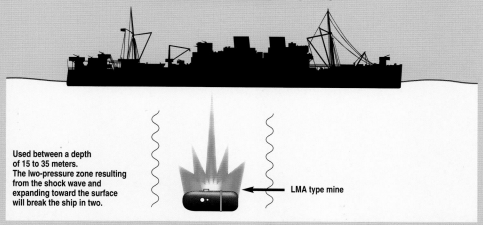

Used between a depth
of 15 to 35 meters.
The lwo-pressure zone resulting
from the shock wave and
expanding toward the surface
will break the ship in two.

LMA type mine

water. This type of mine (German type GL) was used mainly in rivers and estuaries, but not in the open seas, as it could not be pinpointed on a map and thus posed a threat to all navigators, friend or foe.

Top: Placing the triggering device in an EMC-type mine with an electro-chemical detonator. Each mine was anchored to the seabed by a cable and floated at a depth of between 0 and 55 meters. A vessel passing over it triggered the explosion of 300 kg of dynamite

Top: On patrol aboard the S105. The snapshot was probably taken in 1942 when the vessel was operating with the 2nd flotilla.

Centre: Loading a torpedo on board the S105. The view was probably shot in 1942, when the boat was operating with the 2nd flotilla based in Ostende.

Below: Several 2nd S-Boote flotilla heading back to the S-Boot-Bunker in Ostende in 1942. The vessel photographed in the middle ground has six anti-submarine DM 11-type grenades hitched to the back.

with his flotilla leaders. Facts and events proved the wisdom of the choice of Petersen as the man in charge. In the middle of 1942 the S-Boote were the only units capable of taking offensive action in the Channel or the North Sea against the Allied convoys. All of the other Kriegsmarine units except the U-Boote were reduced to undertaking mostly defensive operations along the coastlines. The S-Boote represented a serious threat to the commercial trade routes that had been organized from one end to the other of the British coastline, and their role as harassers can only be compared to that of Dönitz'submarines which were on the point of asphyxiating England's maritime traffic.

At the beginning of the spring of 1942, the eight operational flotillas were composed as follows:

1st S-Boote flotilla

under Kapitänleutnant Birnbacher: S26, S27, S28, S40, S72, S102, heading for the port of Constanza on the Black Sea.

2nd S-Boote flotilla

under Kapitänleutnant Feldt: S29, S39, S53, S70, S103, S104, S105, S108, S111, stationed in Ijmuiden.

3rd S-Boote flotilla

under Kapitänleutnant Kemnade: S30, S33, S35, S36, S54, S55, S56, S57, S58, S59, S60, S61, engaged in the Mediterranean since July, 1941.

4th S-Boote flotilla

under Kapitänleutnant Niels Bätge: S48, S49, S50, S51, S52, S64, S109, S110, S107, based in Ostende.

5th S-Boote flotilla

under Kapitänleutnant Bernd Klug: S27, S28, S29, S45, in the north of Norway.

6th S-Boote flotilla

under Kapitänleutnant Albrecht Obermaier: S18, S19, S20, S22, S24, S69, S71, S101, at Kristiansand, Norway.

7th S-Boote flotilla

under Kapitänleutnant Hans Trummer: S151, S152, S153, S154, S155, S156, S157, S158, crews in training at Swinemünde then sent into the Mediterranean in December, 1942.

8th S-Boote flotilla

under Kapitänleutnant Felix Zymalkowski: S44, S64, S66, S69, S108, S118, based at Bergen and then at Bödö.

On May 13, five boats from the 4th flotilla suddenly sped out of the port of Boulogne at 1:00 AM heading towards the Straits of Dover to meet the corsair Stier (n° 23) and her escort, composed of four torpedo-boats[1] belonging to the 5th Torpedo flotilla, and eight R-Boote. The English rapidly managed to pinpoint the German formation, and sent out 12 MTBs and MGBs to intercept it. Contact was made at 3:15 AM.

---

1 – Seeadler, Falke, Itlis and Kondor.

Soviet torpedeo boats

Top:
A Soviet G5-type torpedo launcher of the first generation, 1941-type. The boat has no auxiliary armament yet, and its mediocre performances make it an easy target for the Kriegsmarine S-Boote.

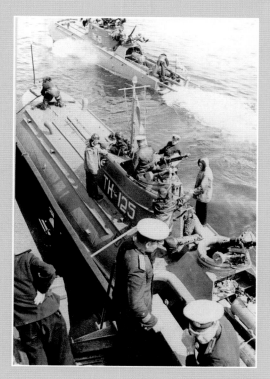

Right:
G5s docked at a base on the Black Sea in April, 1942. All the boats appear to be operational and ready to ship out, with their torpedo tubes loaded.

Left:
Two G5s getting ready to leave port. These are part of the 11th production series, operating in the Black Sea from April, 1944, on. Along with their two 533-mm torpedoes, these little boats can also carry eight R1-type anti-ship mines. Their auxiliary defense system is composed of two 7.62-mm pieces and a 12.7-mm heavy machine gun.

Below: A Soviet G5-type gunboat, 1944 model, part of the 11th production series. The Soviet G5s were 19.08 meters long for a weight of 16 tons, and propelled by two engines of 1150 hp each for the units of the last generation, allowing them to reach a speed of 38 knots. Their main armament was composed of two 533-mm torpedo-launching tubes located aft, and two 7.62-mm machine guns or a 12.7-mm heavy machine gun. They carried a six-man crew.

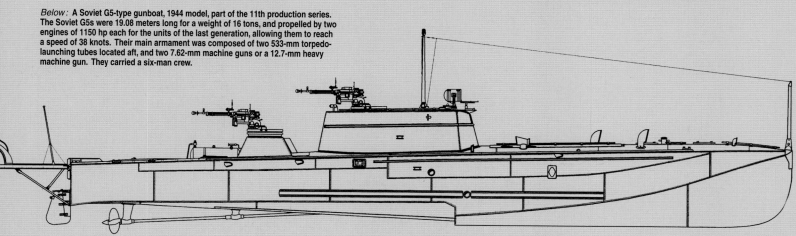

(Soviet Marine Collection)

Right and inset:
G5 torpedo-launching gunboats, 1944 model, travelling in formation in the Black Sea.

Bottom:
In the port of Libau, Latvia, Kriegsmarine personnel check out the Soviet G5-type rapid gunboat, model 41, captured intact during the initial phase of the invasion of the URSS.

The torpedo-boats *Itlis* and *Seeadler* were sunk, and the British lost MTBs 220 and 221. The *Stier* finally managed to take refuge in the port of Boulogne at 5: 45. The S107 stayed in the combat zone and was able to rescue 83 German sailors and three Royal Navy survivors. The last two weeks of May and the first days of June were used to lay mines in the zones around tuns 55A and 56 [1]. At the end of the afternoon on June 26, the S78 left Rotterdam for Boulogne. Halfway there, she was attacked by several British aircraft, probably Fairey Albacores. Two sailors were killed and nine others wounded, but the boat sustained only light damage and was able to continue on to Boulogne. On July 9 the 2nd flotilla[2] was once again out hunting. B-Dienst[3] reports reaching S-Boote headquarters in Wimereux in preceding days had mentioned several possible convoy movements in the zones around Weymouth and Darmouth.

Luftwaffe reconnaissance flights also confirmed important activity in several English ports along the coast. It was the S67, commanded by Kapitänleutnant Zymalkowski, which first spotted the British ships. Convoy WP 183 was progressing slowly, impervious to danger, apparently without escort, in spite of a rising sea and a force-4 wind. The S67 was in an ideal firing position at 800 meters from her target, and sent two torpedoes, one after the other, towards a 6 766-ton tanker, the *Pomella*, which immediately caught fire and capsized. Meanwhile, the S48, S109 and S70 were attacking the Norwegian freighters *Kongshang* (1,156 tons), *Rösten* (736 tons) and *Boku* (698 tons). At the same time the Dutch steamer *Reggestrom* (2 836 tons) was sent down by the S50. Finally the S63, which had just missed a 1 100-ton tanker, destroyed an armed trawler, the *Manor* (314 tons). In just a few minutes the S-Boote had sunk seven Allied vessels for a total of 22 000 tons, without any significant reaction from the British. Beginning in mid-July, the first Fumbs[4] started to be installed on the units of the 2nd S-Boote flotilla. This device was composed of an antenna capable of detecting radar emissions on a metric wave length corresponding to the search range of the centimetric radars installed on the planes of the Coastal Command. The antenna would start humming as it

intercepted waves from a distance of up to 60 kilometers.

On July 26, three vessels belonging to the 2nd flotilla received orders to proceed to Saint Peter Port on the island of Guernsey. They were met there on the 31st by five other S-Boote from the 5th flotilla that had left Rotterdam on the 30th. Then on August 1st, six more S-Boote from the 4th flotilla arrived in the Guernsey port. The decision to group these half-flotillas toge-

ther temporarily on the Channel island can be explained by the proximity of the British coastline and the natural characteristics of the port which had been reequipped especially for this type of small boat. Sorties would continue all during the month of August, following the same ritual: night attacks against convoys, dogfights with the British escort ships, victory bulletins, return to base and boat repairs, not to mention the continuing mine-laying e xpeditions sent out from Boulogne, Cherbourg or Saint Peter Port in the sectors around Lyme Bay, and periods of forced inactivity because of bad weather.

SUCCESSFUL GERMAN RAIDS AT THE END OF THE YEAR.

On October 1, the 5th flotilla took to sea again. As usual, the S-Boote were operating in Rotten: S77-S68, S81-S115, S112-S65. The S112 had just received new Lichtenstein-type radars designed to situate targets during torpedo attacks. She would be the first operational user of this new type of equipment and was able to sink the 444-ton armed trawler *Lord Stomhaven* in the Eddystone Rocks sector that night. On October 6 the 4th flotilla, with the S63, S69 and S117, proceeded to the Great Yarmouth sector to meet an important convoy.

1 – The 2nd and 4th flotillas were engaged in these operations and laid LMB- or UMB-type devices. .
2 –S48, S50, S63, S70, S104, and S109.
3 –B-Dienst (B = *Beobachtungs*) : the Kriegsmarine listening services in charge of decoding Allied radio messages.
4 –FUMB : acronym for *Funkmessbeobachtungsgerät* (radio location observation station).

Top : **Five S30-type S-Boote protected by camouflage tarpaulins in the port of Ivan Baba in Crimea in April, 1942.**

Centre : **An S26-type S-Boote from the 1st flotilla operating in the Baltic Sea in July 1941. The camouflage colors of grey, light brown and dark green are characteristic of the units operating in this battle zone at the time, and will later be used in the Mediterranean.**

Below: **S-Boote in a Black Sea port in June of 1943. These units are part of the 1st flotilla, operating in this sector since May, 1942, out of the Romanian port of Constanza.**

In less than 20 minutes the Germans were able to sink six commercial vessels, as well as an ML[1] with a second seriously damaged, without losing any of their own boats. In the evening of October 13, eight boats from the 5th S-Boote flotilla were sent out to wait for a convoy in the zone off Eddystone Rocks. They received an order on the morning of the 14th to abandon their mission and help rescue the crew of the corsair *Komet* (N° 45), which had been attacked several hours earlier by British gunboats beyond the cape of The Hague. It was MTB 236 that was responsible for the loss of the German cruiser. Two torpedoes literally pulverized the ship, and of the 251 crew members, the S-Boote could not find a single survivor. On October 14 Petersen's men carried out another successful raid. The 6th flotilla damaged two freighters, the 1 355-ton *Lysland* and the 1 570-ton *George Balfour*, right next to the English coastline, without any reaction from the Royal Navy.

In November missions continued with interruptions due to poor weather conditions, and the flotillas recorded several victories, especially along the south and east coasts of England. On November 9, two Allied vessels were destroyed, the 1 843-ton Norwegian freighter *Fidelio*, and the Wandler, a 1 850-ton English steamship, by units of the 6th flotilla. On November 19, the 5th flotilla left Cherbourg with two combat groups including the S82, S116, S77, and the S112, S65, S115 and S81. The two half-flotillas progressed in the dark

in conformity with the principles of *Lauertaktik*. The Rotten closed in on their targets, separated from each other by a respectable distance, so that the British escort boats would not be able to detect them until the last minute. Once again the S112 and her commander Oberleutnant zur See Müller would steal the show by sinking the 555-ton armed trawler *Ullswater*. Three other Allied boats[2], representing a total of 3 528 tons, were destroyed during the

night by the Rotte formed by the S77 and S116.

At the end of the year the S-Boote reported more successful missions. On December 3, the S115 sank the destroyer *HMS Penylan*,

1 –The ships destroyed were the freighter *Caroline Moller* (444 tons), the Danish ship *Jessie Maersk* (1972 tons), the steamships *Sheaf Water* (2 730 tons), *Ilse* (2 844 tons), *Shelldrake* (530 tons), and *Mimonia* (370 tons), and ML 399 (73 tons), for a total of 8 963 tons.
2 –The Norwegian steamship *Lab*, and the two British freighters *Yew Forest* and *Birgitte*.

Above:
Close-up view of the outside of an S-Boote bridge after a Coastal Command air raid on the port of Ostende in 1942. The structure visible here is typical of the first boats of the S38 series, not yet equiped with an armored cubicle.

Top:
Last-minute preparation aboard an S-Boote before leaving on operations from the Belgian port of Ostende in June, 1942.

Below:
The S79 in the port of Ostende in July, 1942, when the boat was part of the 4th S-Boote flotilla. This unit was part of the S38 series, but her armament has not yet been reinforced.

Above:
Inside view of a compartment in the Cherbourg S-Boote Bunker. 3 gunboats are visible, including the S24 on the right in the snapshot. That unit had undergone engine repair in Kiel and then joined the newly-created 4th flotilla. She was commanded by Leutnant-zur-See Hans Joachim Stöve. She was handed over to the Soviets in 1945.

Left:
The S-Boote Bunker in Le Havre under construction.

Below:
S-Boote type 30 in the S-Boote Bunker of Ostende.

The S-Boote Bunkers

Above:
Loading a G7a torpedo on board an S14-S25-type S-Boote in an unidentified S-Bunker. The triggering device is missing from the tip of the torpedo containing the explosives.

Right:
The Cherbourg S-Boote Bunker entrance in 1941. The building is finished and will shelter the units of the 4th and 5th flotillas.

Below:
The S-Boote Bunker in Le Havre under construction in February, 1941. The upper structure has just been started, and the docking spaces for the gunboats are visible.

Next page, on top:
Interior of the Cherbourg S-BooteBunker.

Next page, centre right:
Artist's view of a projected S-Boote Bunker in the port of The Helder executed in 1944.

Next page, centre right:
Close-up showing in detail the upper part of a compartment in the Cherbourg S-Boote Bunker sheltering the German gunboats.

A french base – Cherbourg

In August, 1940, Cherbourg would become the ideal base for the S-Boote involved in operations launched against British coastal traffic in that part of the English Channel. The 1st, 5th and 9th flotillas, commanded respectively by Heinz Birnbacher, Bernard Klug and Friedrich Götz von Mirbach, appreciated this port because of its installations that were particularly well adapted to the S-Boote missions. In the fall of 1940, the organization Todt started building a large S-Bunker, capable of containing two flotillas. Cherbourg, unlike Boulogne, had the advantage of being relatively distant from the British coastal defenses and their radar station. Moreover the port was protected by very effective Flak batteries. The imposing naval cannon installed near the cape of The Hague, and the Cape Levy batteries, dissuaded Royal Navy ships from trying to approach by sea. An English blockade of Cherbourg was just about impossible. The S-Boote could easily undertake attack and mine-laying operations in the Lyme Bay sector, only a few hours away by boat. On the other hand, Le Havre was much too far away from the British targets to offer an effective operational base for the S-Boote.

The crews stationed in Cherbourg were quartered in two outlying sections of the city. After the raids of 1942 and 1943, they were moved out into several villages in the Normandy countryside. The 5th flotilla installed its quarters in Urville, about 9 km from the port, while the 9th flotilla requisitioned a museum in Château-La-Tour-La-Ville.

B. PAUTIGNY

MTB 384 Type 1 VOSPER 73

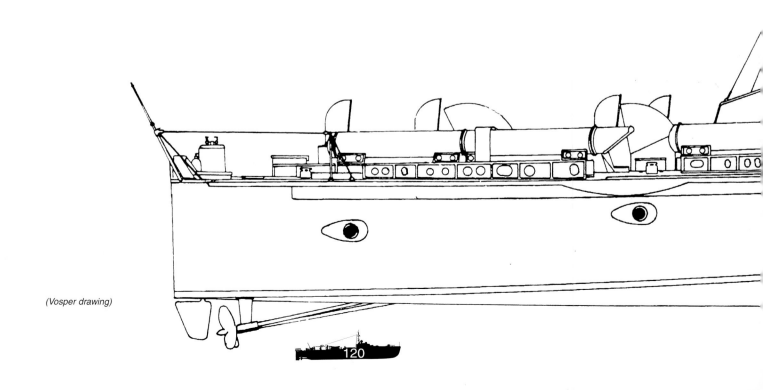

(Vosper drawing)

The ship shown here was operational in the English Channel and the North Sea starting at the end of 1943. She was 22.3 meters long and displaced 46.7 tons when fully loaded. She was driven by three 1400-hp Packard gasoline engines and a 210-hp auxiliary Ford V8. Top speed could reach 39.9 knots for an average cruising speed of 34 knots. 9500 liters of gasoline were stored in three tanks which had been separated to avoid risk of explosion. At top speed the gunboat had a 470-mile radius of action, which increased to 620 miles at 20 knots. The main weaponry included four 18-inch (457-mm) torpedo launching-tubes, plus a double 20-mm Oerlikon cannon in the front and four 7.7-mm Vickers machine guns positioned above each torpedo tube. Standard equipment on these units also included a Hydrophone permitting detection of submarine movements, even though the effectiveness of this instrument had only been proved when the ship was at a total standstill, and a 286-type radar permitting identification of friendly or unfriendly vessels. The crew was composed of two officers and 11 seamen.

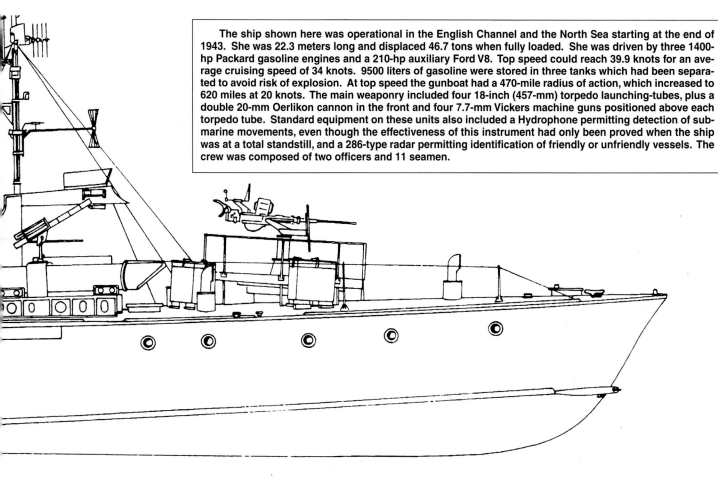

Below: **Bogen Bay on the west coast of Norway. The S10, S11, S13, S15 and S16 are hitched to a float. The photo was taken at the end of the year 1942. This series of S-Boote are no longer playing a front-line role, with the exception of the S11, which was integrated for a few months at the beginning of 1941 into the recently created 4th flotilla. The other boats were used for training in the S-Bootwaffe training flotillas. In December, 1942, they were sent to Norway to relieve units of the 8th flotilla, temporarily obliged to leave this operating zone.**

which capsized with part of her crew in less than 5 minutes. In the night of December 12-13, 17 gunboats from the 2nd and 4th flotillas left their Dutch bases to work off the east coast of England. The 2nd flotilla couldn't find the enemy, but its boats were attacked from a distance of 1 500 meters by a destroyer which opened fire with her 102-mm pieces. She couldn't hit the S-Boote as they darted away at top speed. The 4th flotilla was luckier. At 20: 15 its units sighted convoy FN 889 heading straight in their direction. The S-Boote immediately sped toward the freighters, which continued their route in the dark with no idea of the danger around them. The fighting would only last a few minutes and, as usual, end to the advantage of the Germans. The Rotten coordinated their attacks and then pulled back beyond range of the escort ships, which were not sufficiently versatile to intercept them. One after another, the British freighters would light up the night, torn apart by the torpedo explosions. During that night five transport ships disappeared, representing a total of 7 113 tons[1]. In spite of the presence of five destroyers, MLs 456 and 478, and MGB 75, the English were not capable of effectively protecting their ships; the escort was strung out over a distance which was much too long, and made up of boats whose speed was clearly inferior to that of their Kriegsmarine adversaries.

At the end of 1942, the S-Boote flotillas operating on the western front had sunk 43 000 tons of Allied ships, as follows: two destroyers, *HMS Vortigern*, *HMS Penylan*; One MGB (335), one ML (339); Four armed trawlers: the *Manor* (314 t.), the *Lord Stonehaven* (414 t.), the *Ullswater* (555 t.) and the *Jasper* (596 t.); nineteen freighters. To this total should be added 21 vessels damaged or sunk by mines, including two destroyers, the *HMS Whitshead* and the *HMS Cotswold*, making a total of 86 465 tons.

The English, on their side, had reinforced their defensive potential and had put together the following forces to protect their commercial traffic along the east coast: 45 MGBs, 24 MTBs, 35 MLs, including 20 MGBs, 7 MTBs and 17 MLs for the port of Dover, which also harbored 21 destroyers and 7 corvettes. In the south coast sector there were: 6 SGBs, 15 MGBs, 16 MTBs, 28 M.Ls, and 4 destroyers in Portsmouth, and 8 MTBs, 19 MLs, and 7 destroyers in Plymouth.

---

1 – The S48, commanded by Oberleutnant zur See von Mirbach, sank the *Avonwood* (1 056 tons) ; the S117, commanded by Oberleutnant zur See Bludau, sank the *Knitsley* (2 272 tons) ; the S63, commanded by Oberleutnant zur See Karcher, sank the *Lindisfarne* (999 tons) ; the S110, commanded by Oberleutnant zur See Graser, sank the *Glen Tilt* (871 tons) and the Norwegian freighter Marianne (1915 tons).

On top: **Patrolling in the English Channel in November, 1942.**

Left: **The S13 in Norway at the end of the year 1942. This unit was part of a group of five boats sent to Norway in December, 1942, to relieve the 8th flotilla. They ended the war there and were later turned over to the Allies.**

Next page: **A Daimler Benz MB 501-type diesel engine is being put back in place on board an unidentified S-Boote on a North Sea base.**

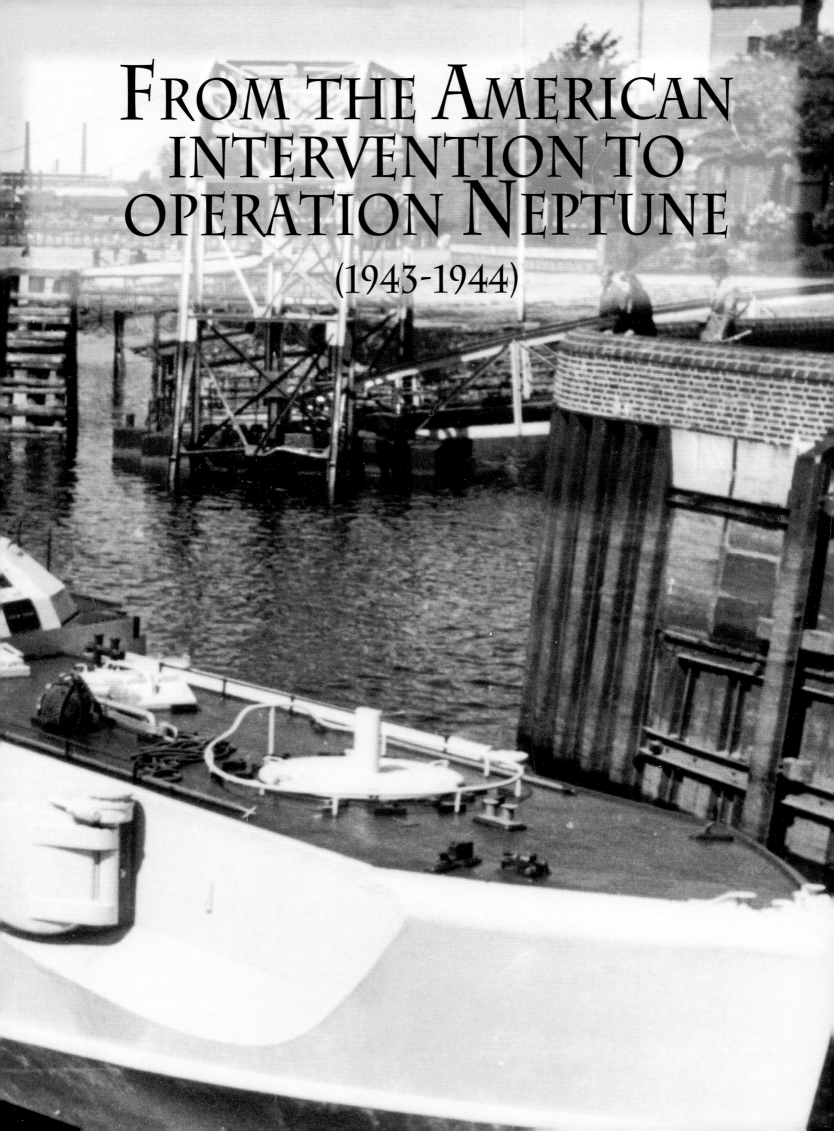

From the American intervention to operation Neptune

(1943-1944)

At the beginning of the year 1943, the Kriegsmarine could theoretically line up 90 S-Boote. Actually only 74 boats were being used for operational missions; the 16 others were assigned to training future crews. On January 1, these were the battle assignments of the flotillas: 1st flotilla engaged in the Black Sea, the 2nd, 4th, 5th, and 6th flotillas fighting on the western front, the 8th flotilla based in Norway, the 3rd and 7th flotillas operating in the Mediterranean.

If we consider the units that were under repair, the number of boats actually ready for battle did not exceed 54. For the British, the ratio was reversed! The Coastal Forces had at their disposal 9 000 men and 1 300 officers for a total of 263 operational vessels[1]. Because of the numerous victories of the Germans during the last months of 1942 on the south-east coast of England, the British Admiralty had realized the importance of the role the coastal forces were playing in the conflict with Germany and its allies. The English would give themselves the means, both quantitively and qualitively, to reinforce their strength. The differences between MGBs and MTBs would little by little disappear. The latter would receive torpedo launching tubes and their auxiliary weapons would be improved. Both types of boats would receive a 37- or 57-mm gun in the prow and two 20-mm cannon in the stern, so as to be able to effectively return fire during S-Boote attacks.

SEA BATTLES CONTINUE.

Operations began again at the beginning of January. Early in the afternoon on January 5, a large convoy was reported by the Luftwaffe planes in the sector around Cromer. A half-hour later, the 2nd, 4th and 6th flotillas sent out 16 S-Boote to intercept it. They were met later on by five other boats from the 5th flotilla which had left Cherbourg to participate in the attack. But bad weather spoiled the German plans and all the vessels had to return to their bases. Other sorties were to take place during the month without significant results. In the night of January 8-9, the S104[2] hit a mine. Damage was so important that the crew scuttled the ship. On January 18, the same thing happened to the S109, during a sortie where the 4th, 2nd and 6th flotillas had engaged almost all of their units northwest of Cromer. In spite of the damage, the S109 was able to make it back to Ijmuiden. On the 24th, the Germans made another try, but were turned back by several MLs assisted by the destroyers

Windsor (D42) and *Mendip* (L60), which kept the S-Boote from getting close to the target convoy.

The Germans undertook new operations around the middle of February. On the 18th, the three flotillas with 15 boats participated in minelaying in the channels of access to Great Yarmouth and Sheringham. But the English were waiting for them. First the Germans were attacked by Fairey Albacores who dropped 5 bombs on the boats of the 2nd flotilla, but without any direct hits. A little later, the S71[3] was attacked by the destroyers *Garth* (L20) and *Montrose* (D01), as well as the sloop *Kittiwake* and a group of MGBs who had been waiting in ambush in the Hatwick-Yarmouth zone, thinking that the S-Boote were going to attack in this sector. The S-Boote was hit several times and her engine failed. Finally *HMS Garth* rammed into her and broke her in two. Seventeen crew members perished in the fighting. On February 20, the units of the 5th flotilla stationed in Le Havre moved to Cherbourg[4]. In the afternoon of the 26th, Luftwaffe reconnaissance planes sighted a convoy of twenty vessels, escorted by five destroyers in the sector of Start Point going towards Leere. The S77, S65, S85, S81 and S68 started out immediately to intercept the English. Several freighters were unsuccessfully attacked. The first hit was made by the S85 commanded by Oberleutnant zur See Erich Kolbe, which seriously damaged LCT 381. The Germans were even able to board the vessel

Above:
June, 1943. Admiral Dönitz is visiting the crews of the 4th flotilla, commanded by Korvettenkapitän Werner Lützow. At that time the vessels of this flotilla were participating in operations against British convoys, and based in the ports of Boulogne and Saint Peter Port on the island of Guernesey. Behind Dönitz is standing the Kriegsmarine Chief of Operations, Rear Admiral Martin Baltzer; in the center Korvetten Kapitän Rudolf Petersen, leader of the S-Bootwaffe, and on the right with his face partially hidden, Korvettenkapitän Werner Lützow.

Below:
An S38-type S-Boote probably photographed during operations in the English Channel during the winter of 1942. On the bridge notice the round antenna characteristic if the Metox Fumb radar, just beginning to be used on S-Bootwaffe units. It is a passive radar, giving off a hum if the boat has been detected by an enemy ship within a radius of 6000 meters. An MG 34 machine gun is also visible on the starboard side near the pilot's bridge.

Next page:
German propaganda poster dating from 1943 and representing an S-Boote beside an 18th century Dutch ship heading out to attack England. German war propaganda in the occupied countries continued right up until 1945. Goebbels was quick to capitalize on historic ties between Germany and the powers conquered in 1940 to try to isolate England and make her appear as the archenemy which had to be defeated by any and all means.

1 – 85 MGBs, 61 MTBs, 111 MLs, 6 SGBs
2 – The S104 was commanded by Oberleutnant zur See Ullrich Roeder
3 – The S71 was commanded by Oberleutnant zur See Rudiger
4 – S81, S77, and S65.

Radars

The *Metox Fumb*[1] radar was designed by a team of technicians led by Admiral Sturmel, Kriegsmarine transmissions director. The Germans were able to recover a Leigh projector and its radar from an English plane shot down by the Flak. These devices were being used after 1942 by the planes of the Coastal Command tracking U-Boote in the Atlantic. The system was triggered automatically as soon as a submarine was spotted on the surface at a distance of less than 2000 meters. Sturmel's team used this model to create the Metox, operational at the end of 1942 on the most vulnerable Kriegsmarine ships, notably the U-Boote and the S-Boote. During the winter of 1943 the S-Boote started to receive the *Hohentwiel*. It was an improved version of the Metox radar. The principle was the same.

(1) – Fumb: *Funkmessbeobachtungsgerät*

It was a passive radar designed to determine if a boat had been detected by the enemy, but with no way of exactly pinpointing the danger. The last version, developed in 1944, was the Naxos, with identical characteristics. The German engineers, in spite of their inventiveness, were unable to create a ship radar capable of indicating the exact position and direction of the Allied planes and ships.

and take the crew prisoners. The S65 gave it the final blow that sent it to the bottom. A second Rotte formed by the S68 and S8[1] destroyed the British steamship *Moldavia* (4 858 tons) east of Berry Head, and two armed trawlers: the Norwegian *Harstad* (258 tons) and the British *Lord Hailsham* (445 tons).

In March, the month named for the war god Mars, the tables started to turn and the Germans ran into difficulties. On March 4, the 123rd Luftwaffe reconnaissance group reported to the S-Boote headquarters a group of 15 boats located 15° north 4° west. Six gunboats of the 5th flotilla took to sea immediately but were unable to find the convoy. On the way back, the S68 and S65 smashed into each other at full speed and had to limp back to Cherbourg as rapidly as possible. On March 5, the 2nd flotilla was operating in the same sector with the S70, S29, S80 and S89. Suddenly the S70 struck a mine. The explosion touched off the reserve torpedo which exploded in turn, sinking the boat. At the same time, ten gunboats from the 4th and 6th flotillas were patrolling in the sectors around Lowestoft and Great Yarmouth, looking for the same target. But the Germans were held at bay by two destroyers and a sloop, so they gave up trying to attack the convoy. The 6th flotilla decided to go back to Ijmuiden. The S74 and S75 held back in the rear in case the units of the British escort decided to try something, They suddenly found themselves under fire from four Spitfires and two Typhoons. The S75 was sunk during the first pass of the British planes, and eleven sailors lost their lives. The S74 was luckier. Her crew managed to pick up the survivors of the S75 and get back to her base on one engine and with three dead and eight wounded.

Then on March 7 came the final German setback. The S119 and S114, part of the 6th flotilla, were attacked as they were operating around the Great Yarmouth sector by the destroyer *HMS MacKey* (D70). At the same instant appeared MTBs 20 and 21, coming to help the British vessel. The S-Boote were surrounded, and had to push their engines as far as they could go. They broke out of the trap but, travelling at more than 42 knots, they couldn't avoid each other and collided violently. The S119 was partially destroyed and abandoned on the spot after her crew had been picked up by the S114. By the middle of March, the four flotillas on the western front had only fifteen boats left in battle shape[2]. The German operational capacity had never been so low, and the month of April would bring numerous battles with the Coastal Forces all along the English Channel.

Starting on March 12, Petersen decided to contentrate his flotillas around the English Channel. In October of 1940 the B-Dienst had installed listening stations on the Channel Islands, and they now reported important movements of Allied ships in the British ports on the south coast. The Germans were afraid of a major operation planned for the month of April, inspired, but on a larger scale, by the attempted invasion of Dieppe in August, 1942. The 5th and 6th flotillas left Ijmuiden for Cherbourg. The 4th flotilla took up quarters in Boulogne, while the six operational S-Boote of the 2nd flotilla moved to Ostende.

As had happened in previous years, when the weather improved, operations could

start again at the end of March. On March 28, the 4th and 2nd flotillas left respectively Hoek-van-Holland and Ijmuiden to try to intercept convoy FS 1 074. The British destroyers *Windsor* (L94) and *Blencathra* (L24) kept the Germans from penetrating the protective barrier created by the Royal Navy. As the S-Boote were turning back, a group of MGBs[3] appeared out of nowhere and gave chase. The S29[4] was overtaken by the British boats which fired at her from close range. She couldn't get away and was literally cut in two by MGB 333. Persistent mechanical problems, the Coastal Command planes, and bad weather kept the flotillas from intercepting several convoys during the first ten days of April[5]. But on April 13, convoy PW 323 was identified by two planes from Luftwaffe reconnaissance group N° 123[6] flying out of Saint-Brieuc. As soon as it received the report, the 5th flotilla took to sea with six gunboats[7]. There were 22 British ships, including two large tankers, travelling at a speed of about 12 knots, under the protection of two destroyers[8] and three armed trawlers. The S-Boote hunkered down in the sector around Lizard Head and waited. The S121[9] went into action first at 1: 03 by torpedoing the British freighter *Stanlake* (1 742

tons). The S-Boote missed many vessels during the attack, but at 2: 10 the S90, S65 and S112 ganged up on the Norwegian destroyer *Eskdale*, which was hit by three torpedoes and capsized wihin a few minutes. During the second half of April weather was so bad that all operational sorties had to be cancelled. Mine-laying in the Berny Head and Start Point zones followed convoy attacks during the month of May[10].

On May 21, the S-Boote headquarters left Wimereux and settled in Boulogne. New flotilla assignments came starting in June. The 2nd and

1 – The S68, commanded by Oberleutnant zur See Jurgen Goetschke; the S81, commanded by Oberleutnant zur See Hugo Windler.
2 – 2nd S-Boote flotilla: four operational boats, 4th S-Boote flotilla: six operational boats, 6th S-Boote flotilla: five operational boats, 5th S-Boote flotilla: none (20 S-Boote were under repair).
3 – MGBs 321 and 333.
4 – Commanded by Oberleutnant zur See Hans Lemm.
5 – On April 5, the 5th flotilla left Cherbourg to intercept convoy WP 318 reported west of Needles Point. The S65 had mechanical problems and the other boats were unable to find their target.
6 – *Fernaufklärungsgruppe* 123 (Long-distance reconnaissance group N° 123).
7 – S81, S82, S90, S121, S112, S65
8 – *HMS Glaisdale* and the Norwegian destroyer *Eskdale*.
9 – Oberleutnant zur See Johan Konrad Klocke.
10 – Between May 23 and June 12, the flotillas laid 321 mines: 135 LMFs, 166 UM.s, 20 LMBs.

Elco PT Boat Type 80

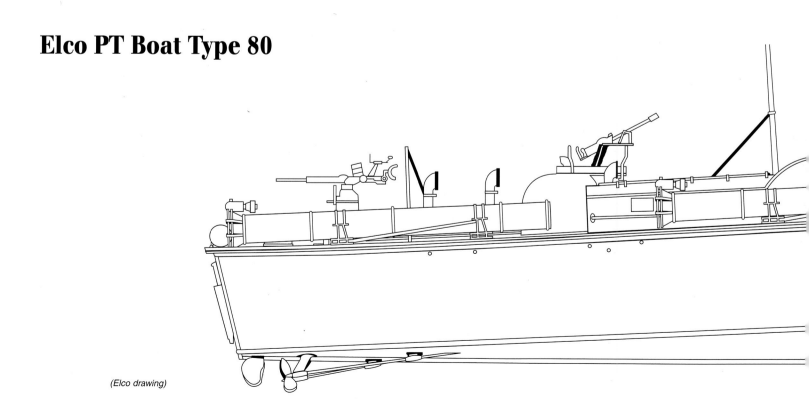

(Elco drawing)

An Elco 80-type PT Boat shown in 1943 in the Mediterranean with a zebra-striped camouflage designed to hide the shape of the boat and prevent enemy ships from determining her speed and direction.

The Elco 80 was 24.4 meters long for a fully loaded displacement of 51 tons. The gunboat was propelled by three Packard 4 M 2500 gasoline engines for a total of 3600 hp, and could reach a top speed of 41 knots. Her weapons included four 533-mm torpedoes, a 37-mm Bofors cannon, a 20-mm Oerlikon cannon, four twin 12.7-mm machine-guns mounted on two turrets. Two 127-mm rocket launchers were installed on the last models. The radius of action at 25 knots was 550 miles. The crew was composed of 18 men. 322 units were built for the US Navy during the war.

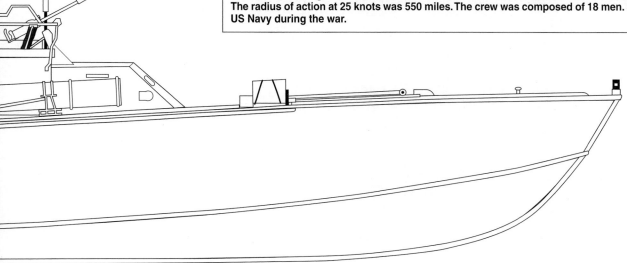

6th flotillas left Ostende for Ijmuiden and the 4th flotilla was sent to Saint Peter Port. On June 17, as they were leaving the port of Ostende heading for Ijmuiden, the S80 and S86 were attacked by British planes. They were nevertheless able to zigzag among the falling bombs without sustaining any major damage[1]. On June 20, it was the S122 and S90 which were attacked by the Coastal Command as they were returning to Hoek-van-Holland. The S90 received a hit and started taking in water. The two boats were nevertheless able to get back to their base in Holland.

These repeated attacks by the Royal Air Force along the coast of Holland were the proof that the British no longer hesitated to chase the S-Boote beyond the French ports on the Channel, in spite of the presence of the Luftwaffe, whose planes occupied many airfields in Belgium and the Netherlands. The offensive tactics of the English were beginning to prove their worth. On every German sortie, increasing pressure would be exerted above Petersen's flotillas, up until the Allied invasion and the great raids on the ports of Le Havre and Boulogne in mid-June, 1944, at which time the Luftwaffe planes would no longer be able to counter English and American air operations.

S-Boote activity slowed down over the summer. Many boats went into dry dock to have their anti-aircraft armament modified. Because of the persistent threat represented by the Coastal Command planes to all of the flotillas, Petersen and his boat commanders decided to reinforce the auxiliary weapons on their units. 40- and 37-mm cannon were installed, along with 20-mm 4-gun turrets, the famous rapid-fire *Flakvierling*, terribly effective against low-flying aircraft. Firing would now take place from low dugouts situated in the bow and reinforced by armored shields. MG 34- or MG 42-type double machine guns would complete the defensive weapons of the ships. Likewise the S-Boote pilot's bridge was systematically replaced by an armored structure, the *Kalottenbrücke*, which would provide better protection for the crew during the increasing violence of the fights with the British ships.

THE ARRIVAL OF THE AMERICANS.

In April of 1943, three PT boats[2], belonging to the US Navy 2nd fleet[3], arrived in Darmouth, England. They were ships of the Higgins 78 type, 23 meters long for a 43-ton displacement. The boats were first used for landing operations involving American agents of the OSS (Office of Strategic Services) on the French coast, with the mission of contacting elements of the French resistance. About twenty sorties were carried out by the units of the 2nd flotilla between mid-May and the end of the year 1943. At the same time, new US Navy flotillas were arriving in England[4]: the 34th, in May of 1944, followed by the 35th and 30th at the beginning of June. These boats participated in Operation *Neptune*. Together they were placed under the command of Frigate Captain John Bulkeley, who had made a name for himself in the Philippines in January of 1942 by attacking Japanese troop transport ships with his PT 34 near Bataan.

During the Second World War, the US Navy would build several types of rapid torpedo-launchers. The best of these were the *ELCO 80* and the *Higgins 78*, of which there were built respectively 320 and 205 models. As compared to the S-Boote, the American boats were much smaller and their maximum speed was slightly inferior. Their auxiliary weapons, as was the case for all the other powers, would be considerably reinforced starting in 1943-1944.

At the end of July, the Allies took over operational initiatives. As German units were moving

---

1 – The S80's Fumb disappeared overboard during the attack.
2 – Patrol Torpedo Boat. These first boats were PT 71, PT 72, and PT 199.
3 – This unit had participated in fighting in the Pacific the year before, including the battle of Guadalcanal.
4 – Starting in April 1943, the Americans also engaged 18 P.T. boats in the Mediterranean. PTs 201 to 218 were transported from the port of Norfolk, Virginia to Gibraltar by U.S. Navy transport ships. They were operational at the end of the month and undertook their first patrols at the beginning of May along the Tunisian coast, with the mission of preventing the Kriegsmarine from evacuating the remaining elements of the Afrika Korps.

Below:
Two S38-type S-Boote covered with tarpaulins decorated with geometric designs used to camouflage their shape. These two photos come from an issue of the German magazine Signal published in October, 1943.

between Boulogne and Ostende on July 24, the S68 and S77 were attacked by an MGB and MTB patrol north of Dunkerque. The S77 was hit several times by MGBs 40 and 42, destroying her two 20-mm pieces and provoking the explosion of her spare torpedo, which ended in the loss of the boat. Only four survivors were picked up by the English, and her commander, Oberleutnant zur See Joseph Ludwig, was killed during the fighting. The S68, which was on the scene, sped away from the fighting, without so much as a thought about helping the survivors. Oberleutnant zur See Jürgen Moritzen, the commander of the boat, was court-martialed for cowardice in the face of the enemy, and was relieved of his command.

In the afternoon of July 25, 118 B17s from the US Air Force 8th bombing group dropped 522 tons of bombs on the port of Kiel. The Americans

sank two U-Boote, the U 395 and U 474, as well as the S44 and S66[1] belonging to the 8th flotilla. On the morning of July 29, a new American raid took place, with 139 B17s this time, appearing suddenly over the German port and dropping 315 tons of bombs. The brand new S135 and S137, which had just been delivered to the 6th flotilla, were seriously damaged. In the afternoon on August 11, the port of Brest was also targetted by the British. Twenty-five B26 Martin Marauder bombers dived over the Kriegsmarine installations and the moored boats. At the same time 7 German gunboats from the 4th and 5th flotillas which had left Saint Peter Port several hours earlier heading toward Brest, arrived in view of the Aber-Wrac'h. They found themselves right under the Royal Air Force planes. The S121 took two hits, immediately killing the commander, Oberleutnant zur See Johan Konrad Klocke, and eleven crew

members. A bit later a second attack by four fighter-bombers damaged the S117. This series of raids showed that the Allies had changed tactics[2]. Instead of fighting the S-Boote at sea, they preferred to hit the enemy bases, trying to prevent offensive actions against convoys. The increased pressure would reach a climax with the intense bombing of Le Havre in June of 1944.

BRITISH VICTORIES AND REINFORCED GERMAN DEFENSES.

In September and October two violent combats opposed the British escort forces and the Schnellbootwaffe flotillas. The first took place in the night of September 24-25. A major mine-laying operation[3] was scheduled by the Germans under the code name *Probestück*, between Long Sand and the Sunk lighthouse boat. All the flotillas operating on the western front were involved and 29 S-Boote[4] in all took to sea that night. The S87 of the 4th flotilla soon had to turn back because of engine problems. Three hours later, the S38, S74 and S90[5], travelling at more than 38 knots not far from each other, collided. Damage was quite important and their commanders decided to return to Hoek-van-Holland. Around 1:00 AM, the S88, S96 and S99 came nose to nose with four armed trawlers[6], part of a convoy escort. The S96 launched a torpedo that ripped through the hull of the Franc Tireur (327 tons), sinking her immediately. The English soon reacted by sending MLs 145 and 150, who were patrolling in the area near the attack, to intercept the Germans before their gunboats had time to escape as they usually did. ML 145 was more than happy to inter-

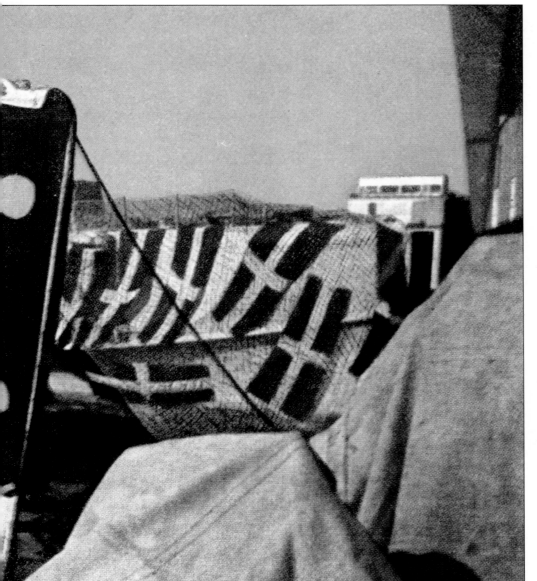

1 – S44, under the orders of Leutnant-zur-See Joachim Quistorp S66, under the orders of Oberleutnant zur See Horst Schuur
2 – The British had been the first to launch air raids over the ports occupied by the Kriegsmarine; from 1943 on, U.S. Air Force planes would also participate in these raids in increasing numbers.
3 – New mines, type Zundmittell MA II, would be used in addition to L.M.B.s.
4 – 2nd and 6th flotillas: 11 S-Boote; 4th flotilla: 7 S-Boote; 5th and 8th flotillas: 11 S-Boote.
5 – 4th S-Boote flotilla.
6 – *Stella Leonis* (FY 706), *Stella Rigel* (FY 657), *Donna Nook* (FY 1559), *Franc Tireur* (FY 1560).

Top left:
he S40 and S52 caught in the ice
in the port of Breila in January, 1943.
These two units were part of the 1st S-Boote
flotilla, engaged on the eastern front almost
continuously from June,1941, on. The S40 was
attacked and sunk by Soviet aircraft
in the Black Sea on August 19, 1944.
The same thing happened to the S52
the next day off the Romanian port of Konstanza.

Top right:
An S38-type S-Boote from the 4th flotilla,
identified by its insignia painted
on the hull: a black panther.

vene and rammed into the S96 so violently that she ended up imbedded in the S-Boote. The shock resulted in considerable damage, but by pulling the throttle wide open, the three diesels of the S96 managed to free the boat from the embarrassing embrace of her opponent. It was not long, however, before ML 150 reached the German boat and prevented her from escaping. The two crews shot at each other from just an arm's length away, using the deck guns, while the German boat was going up in smoke. The show was worthy of the best scenes from old pirate movies. In spite of the confused fighting, the Germans managed to scuttle their flaming S-Boote, which was abandoned at the last minute. Thirteen crew members were picked up by the British, including the commander, Oberleutnant zur See Herman Sander and the second-in-command, Oberleutnant zur See Wilhelm Ritter von Georg.

After a three-week period of mine-laying operations, there was new fighting with the units of the Royal Navy. In the evening of October 23, the S-Boote headquarters sent out an alert to all its flotilla commanders. An important convoy (FN1160), composed of 31 ships, escorted by destroyers[1] and armed trawlers, was travelling towards the estuary of the Humber River[2]. Twenty-eight S-Boote from the 2nd, 4th, 5th, 6th and 8th flotillas were ready for action, but the bad weather in the Channel prevented them from leaving port. On October 24, they made another try against the same target; weather conditions were better and thirty-one vessels[3] awaited the order to attack. It was the 6th flotilla which first established contact with the back end of the British convoy. Its nine gunboats sped forward in groups of three with their diesels wide open, but were unable to approach the freighters. The 40-mm guns of the MGBs kept them at bay. The S73 and S74 were hit several times but could not get themselves into firing position. Kapitänleutnant Witt's S74 was luckier and managed to sink the 235-ton

armed trawler *William Stephen*.

Then around midnight the 4th flotilla was able to position itself in the lane of the approaching convoy. The first attack group was composed of four boats[4] under the orders of the fleet leader, Korvettenkapitän Lützow, in person, who decided to come upon the English from the south. The second group, with four gunboats, commanded by Kapitänleutnant Causemann, approached from the west. The British had been warned about the presence of S-Boote by Lancasters from the Bomber Command on their way back from a bombing mission over the Ruhr. The destroyers, alerted at the last minute, hastily positioned themselves to meet the enemy attack. The Pytchley's radar[5] was the first to detect a German presence and she opened fire at a distance of 2 000 meters, thus preventing the Germans from approaching

closer. The *HMS Eglinton* received orders to stay beside the convoy to protect it, while *the Worcester*, the *MacKay* and the *Campbell* headed toward the *Pytchley* to try to intercept the S-Boote. They were assisted by the MGBs which had been providing cover for the British operation. The cat-and-mouse game between the English and the Germans was to last for four hours. Each time the S-Boote were attacked they were able, thanks to their speed, to escape from the enemy trap. Around midnight Causemann's S120 was seriously assailed by the Worcester. The S88, S63, S110 and S117 came rapidly to her assistance. But MGBs 603 and 607 also arrived to support the destroyer and tried various maneuvers to approach the S-Boote. There was strong fire around the boats of the 4th flotilla, which had to reduce their speed so as to avoid the risk of collision. During the fighting, the S63[6] received a shell in the machine room which caused a lot of damage and seriously wounded four crew members. The gunboat had to reduce her speed to 20 knots. Lützow on the S88 tried to come to the assistance of his comrades, but the intense gunfire from the MGBs[7] prevented him from getting close.

The S-Boote were caught under a storm of steel. The power of destruction of the 57- and 20-mm cannon, along with the heavy machine guns, was devastating so close up. The deck and the top sections of the gunboat were riddled with holes, and the fire that had started on the bridge soon spread to the rest of the vessel. Korvetten-kapitän Werner Lützow was killed, as was

---

1 – *HMS Campbell* (D 60), *HMS MacKay*, *HMS Worcester*, *HMS Eglinton* (L 87), *HMS Pytchley* (L 92).
2 – Eight MGBs and two M.L.s were positioned further from the convoy, forming a screen: MGBs 609, 607, 610, 603, 315, 327, 329, 332; M.L.s 250 and 517.
3 – 6th flotilla: 9 S-Boote; 8th flotilla: 6 S-Boote; 2nd flotilla: 8 S-Boote; 4th flotilla: 8 S-Boote
4 – S88, S63, S110, and S117.
5 – Starting in 1941, the Royal-Navy escort ships were equiped with the Asdic 144, capable of detecting by hydrophone the presence of a surface vessel within a radius of 6 000 meters. This system of detection was completed by several types of radars, the Mark IV 271, which was capable of spotting a boat the size of an S-Boote at a distance of 8 000 meters, the Mark V 291, which could follow an airplane up to a distance of 20 nautical miles, the Mark VI which allowed night firing with no visibility or anti-aircraft barrage fire using the Auto-Barrage-Unit system.
6 – S63, commanded by Leutnant-zur-See Dietrich Howaldt. Accosted by MGB 603, she sank shortly later.
7 – Fairmile D-type MGBs 603 and 607

the commander of the S88, Oberleutnant Heinz Räbiger, and three crew members. The fire spread, and caused the explosion of the S88 a few minutes later; the English picked up 19 survivors.

The failure of the attack on convoy FN 1 160 would lead Petersen and his advisors to undertake an analysis of the tactics to use in the face of an enemy who was becoming more and more agressive, and who had managed to create an impenetrable screen of destroyers and gunboats around the Allied ships, preventing the Germans from getting close. The Germans decided to try to deal with this new situation by reinforcing once again the protection and the auxiliary weapons on their vessels. Starting in October of 1943, a new torpedo, the T5 Zaunkönig[1] replaced the old G7As of the first generation.

On November 2, nine gunboats from the 5th flotilla left the port of Boulogne on a mission to intercept convoy CW 221 which had been spotted south of Dungeness by the reconnaissance planes of the Luftwaffe. The S-Boote were rapidly on the scene, and the first *Rotte*, formed by the S112 and the S141, just missed a tanker and a large freighter. The S100 and the S138[2] managed to get close to three other Allied ships but could not get into firing position. The two boats repeated their maneuver a little later, and this time the torpedoes hit their targets and simultaneously sank the steamships *Foam Queen* (811 tons), and *Storia* (1967 tons). A third group, formed by the S136, S142 and S143, went after three freighters moving along slowly at the tail end of the convoy, without any apparent protection. Once again the S-Boote were in a position of force. The 1 179-ton Dona Isabel lit up the sky after she was hit by a torpedo launched from the S136[3].

In spite of the presence of several destroyers and five MLs, the English were unable to react to

the German lightning attack. This was a reversal of what had happened on October 24. The freedom of movement which was characteristic of the small formations involving 8 to 10 units working in Rotten was appreciated by the Schnellbootwaffe headquarters, and it was decided henceforth to use these small groups for interception of convoys, rather than a bigger group of several flotillas involving a large number of vessels.

The end of November was mostly used for mine-laying operations. Over a relatively short period the British would successively lose the freighter *Cormount* (2 841 tons) which sank on November 11 after hitting a UMB near Harwich. On November 26 the steamer *Morar* (1 507 tons) was also destroyed. In December, the destroyers *Worchester* and *Holderness*, belonging to the *Nore Command*, were seriously damaged by magnetic mines. At the beginning of December, the S142, commanded by Oberleutnant zur See Hinrich Ahrens, sank the armed trawler *Avanturine*, participating in the escort of a large convoy. Other boats were attacked by units of the 5th flotilla, without much success. The year ended with a slow-down in activity for all the flotillas because of the poor weather which kept them from intervening against the British convoys. The year 1943, with the reinforcement of theBritish escorts, left bitter memories for Petersen's men. Only 16 ships had been sunk for a total of 26 000 tons.

NEW RAIDS LAUNCHED FROM THE FRENCH AND DUTCH PORTS.

On January 1, 1944, the general situation of the S-Bootwaffe was as follows. The 1st S-Boote flotilla was operating in Crimea out of the port of Ivan-Baba on the Black Sea. It had seven operational boats. Four more gunboats were being repaired in the shipyards of the port of Constanza in Romania, and three others were expected from Germany. The 2nd, 4th, 5th, 6th, 8th and 9th flotillas were based in either Ijmuiden, Rotterdam or Cherbourg with missions of mine-laying and attacks on convoys along the east and south coasts of England. They had a total of 46 operational S-Boote. In the Mediterranean, the 3rd and 7th flotillas were fighting the Royal Navy, and in the last six months had also had to deal with the American units operating out of Gibraltar since May of 1943. The two flotillas included 16 boats, but only half of these were capable of navigation. The eight others were under repair in the Genoa naval shipyards. Finally two training flotillas were operational in the Baltic Sea with fifteen gunboats.

As usual the weather was terrible at the beginning of January, and all the flotillas operating

1 – The T5 was equiped with a seaker which was attracted by the noise of the propellers of the Allied ships and ended up exploding against the stern. During the spring of 1944 the T5 was improved by the German engineers so that it was capable of following a crooked path.
2 – S100, commanded by Kapitänleutnant zur See Ulrich Kolbe; S138, commanded by Oberleutnant zur See Jurgen Stohwasser
3 – S136, commanded by Oberleutnant zur See Hans Gunter Jürgensmeyer

Top: **S-Boote protected by a camouflage net at dock in the Dutch port of Ijmuiden at the beginning of the year 1944. These units are part of the 8th flotilla. The boat in the center of the snapshot is probably the S93, whose number appears above the pilot's bridge. She was under the orders of Oberleutnant zur See Hans Joachim Quistorp. The S93 was sunk on March 26, 1944 with the S129 after an American air raid on the port of Ijmuiden**

Insert: **Kriegsmarine insignia.**

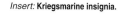

on the western front stayed at dock or under shelter at their bases. From the second week on, better weather would allow them to start work again. On January 5, the boats of the 5th flotilla, grouped in three Rotten[1], attacked convoy WP 457, following reconnaissance reports from the Lufwaffe Junker 88s, which had taken off at the end of the afternoon from the Caen-Carpiquet airport. Five freighters were sunk by the S-Boote, for a total of 12 500 tons, plus the armed trawler Wallasea (545 tons)[2]. During the attack the Germans had used new T5 and T4 Falke[3] acoustic-guidance torpedoes. On January 30, the 5th flotilla was out on operations again. A large convoy had been identified by the B-Dienst listening stations and seven S-Boote[4] immediately took to sea in the late evening. Suddenly the S112's Fumb started buzzing. This meant there were enemy ships within 6 miles of the boat. The three Rotten immediately positioned themselves for the attack. Convoy CW 243 was located southeast of Beachy Head, with not much of an escort. At 2 : 00 the second Rotte, composed of the S138 and S142, attacked the end of the line of English ships. For the English, it was a total surprise. The Germans had been able to approach the Allied ships in the darkness. From a distance of 800 meters, the S142[5] launched a torpedo toward the trawler Pine (542 tons). She disappeared a few minutes later, cut in two by the blast. The next victim was the British freighter Emerald (806 tons). The first shot missed, but the second sank her. The S138[6] sent down the 1 813-ton steamer Caleb Sprague. During this action, the two other S-Boote pairs had been held at bay by two destroyers and several MGBs which had effectively prevented them from approaching the convoy.

At the beginning of February, the 2nd, 5th, 8th and 9th flotillas were engaged in mine-laying operations around the estuary of the Humber. These sorties lasted two weeks and during one of them the S85 and S99[7] together sunk the 207-ton British trawler Cap d'Antifer. Nothing else spectacular happened in February: the month

1 – 1st group: S141, S142, S143; 2nd pair: S100, S138; 3rd pair: S136, S84.
2 – Sunk by the S138 and Oberleutnant zur See Hans Jürgen Stohwasser.
3 – During this operation 23 torpedoes were fired, including thirteen T4s.
4 – S112, S143, S142, S138, S141, S100, S136.
5 – S142, commanded by Oberleutnant zur See Hinrich Ahrens.
6 – S138, commanded by Oberleutnant zur See Paul Stohwasser
7 – Units belonging to the 8th S-Boote flotilla: Kapitänleutnant Walter Knapp (S99), Oberleutnant zur See Horst Schuur (S85).

Top: **LST 283 entering the English Channel at the mouth of a river to participate in landing exercises in the spring of 1944. The Allies decided to organize their exercises in zones frequently raided by the S-Boote, and they paid a heavy price for this overconfidence during the night of April 27-28 at Slapton Sands.**

Centre: **The LCI 125 off The Solent on June 5, 1944, preparing to cross the Channel with Canadian troops on board. 245 boats of this type were used by the Allies during Operation Neptune. The S-Boote sank two of them.**

Centre: **LST 507 photographed crossing the Atlantic in April, 1944, heading for England. In the night of April 27-28, this was the first boat to be attacked by the S-Boote of the 5th and 9th flotillas in Lyme Bay.**

Left: **LST 289 in the port of Dartmouth after being seriously damaged by the attacks of the 5th and 9th flotillas on April 27-28, 1944. 13 American sailors who were manning the 40-mm cannon on the wrecked superstructure visible in the photo were killed.**

Next page: **An S-Boote commander before leaving on mission.**

Tallboy against S-Boote

Engineer Barnes Wallis and his team master-minded the « Tallboy » penetration bombs used during the Le Havre bombing on June 14, 1944. The bomb was designed to destroy industrial sites, coastal batteries, the underground V1 launching sites, as well as the U-Bunkers and S-Bunkers spread out along the Atlantic coast as far as the North Sea. The British were able to develop an explosive device that would only be surpassed during WWII by the American atomic bombs dropped on Hiroshima and Nagasaki in 1945. Three types of bombs were built: model S (small), 2 tons, model M (medium), 5.5 tons, and finally the 10-ton type L (large), which was not operational until the spring of 1945.

The Tallboy was a traditional bomb with great penetrating power. It could also be fired from a surface vessel, in which case its destructive effect was increased by the shock wave resulting from the explosion. Dropped from a height of 2000 feet[1], model S could rapidly attain a speed of Mach 1. At the moment of impact, the bomb penetrated inside the target to a depth of several meters without exploding. When it finished its path against the first of its target structures, the shock wave, associated with the quantity and power of the explosives used for the deflagration, created a truly devastating effect. The explosive used was Torpex, a combination of 40% T.N.T.,

Top:
An Avro Lancaster coming back from a mission. This type of plane, slightly modified, was used by Squadron 617 of the Bomber Command, notably for the great Le Havre air raid of June 14, 1944.

Above:
A 5443-kg model-M Tallboy, used by the planes of Squadron 617 for bombing the S-Boot-Bunker in Le Havre on June 14, 1944. A 9979-kg device called the *Grand Slam* was also developed to equip the Bomber Command planes at the end of 1944.

Left:
On the afternoon of June 14, 1944, Royal Air Force ground crews are starting to load the Squadron 617 Lancaster bomb compartments with the medium model 5.5-ton Tallboys that will be dropped on Le Havre a few hours later.

Above:
Aerial photograph taken of Le Havre en June 15, 1944, after the raid of the 14th. A giant crater beside the S-Bunkers shows the impact created by the explosion of the Tallboys.

Top right:
Overall view of Le Havre in June, 1945. Allied bombings, along with German destruction and probable Resistance sabotage, have annihilated the city.

Bottom Right:
An Avro Lancaster getting ready to take off from a British airfield for a nighttime bombing raid over the Ruhr. This is the type of plane, modified to carry Tallboys, which was used by Squadron 617.

Bottom left:
After the Allied bombing of the Ijmuiden S-Bunker on March 26, 1944. That afternoon 344 Martin Maurauder B26s from the US Air Force 9th fleet dropped several thousand 435-kg bombs to try to destroy the S-Boot-Bunker located in the outer harbor of Amsterdam. The raid was only partially successful. Barely 30 cm of the concrete structures was destroyed. The S93 and S129, docked outside, were sunk by the American bombs.

42% cyclonite[2], to which had been added 18% aluminum powder. This last ingredient, associated with the two others, considerably raised the temperature at the moment of explosion.

In May, 1944, Squadron 617[3] of the Royal Air Force received their first Tallboys. On June 8 and 9, 25 Lancasters for the first time dropped their model M Tallboys on a railway junction near Saumur where large numbers of enemy troops and quantities of material had been identified during previous reconnaissance flights. During the attack one bomb hit a tunnel underneath a mountain. Within a fraction of a second, 30 meters of rock and earth were easily penetrated and the device exploded against the tunnel vault, creating a hole 10 meters in diameter, through which 10 tons of rubble immediately caved in.

1 – 660 meters
2 – Cyclo-trimethylene-trinitramine
3 – In July of 1943 a special bombing squadron was created with a first group of twelve crews placed under the orders of squadron leader George Holden. The men received special training on modified planes. New equipment was installed on the Lancasters of the Bomber Command which were to participate in future raids.

Above and left:
The result of the explosion of two Tallboys on the upper structures of the S-Bunkers in Le Havre. Part of the concrete roof has caved in on the boats docked underneath.

Centre:
The Ijmuiden S-Bunker after the air raid launched by the Bomber Command Squadron 617 aircraft on December 15, 1944. Two 5,5-ton Tallboys penetrated inside the building, destroying the S198 and damaging the S193, S195 and S701. In less than ten minutes the entire 8th flotilla was out of action.

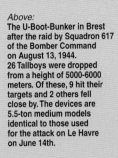

Above:
The U-Boot-Bunker in Brest
after the raid by Squadron 617
of the Bomber Command
on August 13, 1944.
26 Tallboys were dropped
from a height of 5000-6000
meters. Of these, 9 hit their
targets and 2 others fell
close by. The devices are
5.5-ton medium models
identical to those used
for the attack on Le Havre
on June 14th.

Left:
The lower part of the
Boulogne S-Boot-Bunker
after the Bomber Command
raid on June 15, 1944.
The building was unable
to resist the impact of the
Squadron 617 Tallboys.

Above:
The Brest U-Boot-Bunker after
the Squadron 617 raid on August 13, 1944.
Five of the nine Tallboys pierced the roof
of the building, creating a hole 5 meters in diameter.
There was not much damage inside the building
because the penetrating power of the bombs
was absorbed by the perforation
of the 3-meter thick concrete slab.

Below:
Aerial view of the Le Havre port
taken by a Bomber Command
plane during a raid in October, 1944.
In spite of the June 14th bombing,
some installations of the Normandy
port are still intact. On the left notice
the smoke from the explosions
in fuel tanks hit by British bombs.

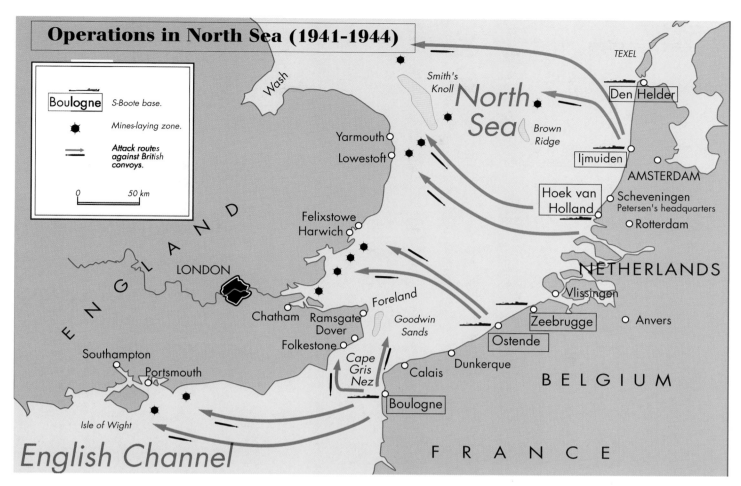

Boulogne S-Boote base.

Mines-laying zone.

Attack routes against British convoys.

0   50 km

TEXEL

Smith's Knoll

North Sea

Brown Ridge

Den Helder

Ijmuiden

AMSTERDAM

Scheveningen Petersen's headquarters

Rotterdam

Hoek van Holland

NETHERLANDS

Vlissingen

Anvers

Zeebrugge

Ostende

BELGIUM

Wash

Yarmouth

Lowestoft

Felixstowe

Harwich

LONDON

E N G L A N D

Chatham   Ramsgate Dover

Folkestone

Foreland

Goodwin Sands

Cape Gris Nez

Calais

Dunkerque

Boulogne

Southampton

Portsmouth

Isle of Wight

English Channel

F R A N C E

was basically devoted to major mine-laying actions accompanied by attempted convoy interceptions where the S-Boote[1] didn't have much luck. In spite of the new type T3 and T5 torpedoes, Petersen's crews missed their targets every time. With five boats in operation, an average of twenty torpedoes was launched during each attack, for only one which hit its mark.

In March the escorts of the British convoys were considerably reinforced. The English were now using several groups of MTBs along with destroyers and cruisers[2]. The Allies now had the ball in their camp, and they had the necessary means to launch the largest naval operation of all times: the Channel and the North Sea would soon be British again. On the afternoon of March 26, 344 B26 Martin-Marauders from the US Air Force 9th bomber fleet arrived over the port of Ijmuiden at an altitude of 4 000 meters. In just a few seconds 1 120 453-kg anti-bunker bombs rained down onto the huge S-Bunkers sheltering the ships of the 6th and 8th flotillas. Even though they were powerful, they barely scratched the surface of the concrete, penetrating to a depth of 30 cm but leaving untouched the remaining 3,70 meters of concrete surrounding the inner core of the buildings. Only the S93 and S129[3], which were moored at the pier at the time of the raid, were sunk by the American bombs.

On April 26, six boats from the 5th and 9th flotillas[4] left Boulogne in the evening, heading west. Their mission: intercept the Allied invasion landing barges and pick up as much information as possible about their movements, their weapons, their speed and their tactical formations. Along the way the Germans were detected by the coastal radars in Portsmouth, which immediately

alerted the frigate *HMS Rowley* and the FNFL ship *La Combattante*[5] which were patrolling south-east of the Isle of Wight. The two ships also soon picked up the signal of the S-Boote, rapidly approaching from a distance of 3 000 meters, on their radar screens. The two groups of gunboats were zigzagging at 35 knots and using their smoke pots to try to get as close as possible to the destroyers to get into good firing positions. *La Combattante* opened fire first. She took on the Germans from a distance of 2 000 meters with her 102-mm double cannon. The S167 took a hit, but with only minor damage her commander was able to direct her away from the combat zone. The S147[6] wasn't as lucky. A shell exploded in the bow, igniting a fire which had soon spread over the rest of the boat. Part of the crew were able to evacuate the flaming ship, which sank a few minutes later. On April 27, 30 miles off Barfleur, two MTBs picked up ten survivors drifting in two lifeboats.

ALLIED DEFEATS: THE LYME BAY DISASTER.

In the afternoon of April 27, a Luftwaffe reconnaissance flight warned the S-Boote headquarters about a group of seven ships proceeding slowly west of Start Point 50° north 4° west. The 5th and 9th S-Boote flotillas[7] were immediately put on alert and left Cherbourg at 22: 00. At first the Germans were unable to find the convoy, but came practically nose-to-nose with eight American LSTs[8], travelling in Lyme Bay at a speed of 3 knots, with a single escort ship, the frigate *Azalea*. The Allied ships had actually left the port of Brixham, Devon, during the afternoon to participate in a beach-landing exercise[9] on the south

coast of England, in a spot closely resembling the Normandy beaches around the Cotentin peninsula where they would be invading for good two months later. The exercise, baptized *Tiger*, was to take place with heavy material, and so the LSTs had taken aboard armored tanks, Jeeps and brand new Dukws, strange amphibious vehicles half-boat half-truck which were able to go right up out of the water and drive along on the sand.

The Americans encountered several problems during this attack. The LSTs were relatively slow ships; their two diesel engines propelled them at a maximum speed of 12 knots, and their displacement, around 4 000 tons when fully loaded, made them difficult to maneuver. Moreover, they carried few weapons and counted on destroyers to insure their protection. For Exercise *Tiger* only one of the two British vessels[10] originally desi-

---

1 – Because of the foul weather, the Luftwaffe reconnaissance planes were unable to fly; the information about convoy movements transmitted by the B-Dienst listening stations to the S-Boote headquarters was insufficient to allow them to pinpoint the exact positions and needed to be confirmed by aerial reconnaissance.
2 – On March 15 convoy WP 492 was protected by no less than eight MTBs, the cruiser *HMS Bellona*, two corvettes, *HMS Pimrose* and *Azalea*, and four destroyers, *HMS Tartar, Ashanti, Brissenden,* and *Mealbreak.*
3 – S93, commanded by Oberleutnant zur See Hans Joachim Quistorp S129, commanded by Oberleutnant zur See Ulrich Toermer
4 – 9th flotilla: S147, S167, S146; 5th flotilla: S136, S138, S140.
5 – FNFL = *Forces Navales Françaises Libres* (Free French Naval Forces). The Combattante would participate in Operation Neptune on June 6, 1944.
6 – S147, commanded by Leutnant zur See Benhard Theenhauser.
7 – 5th S-Boote flotilla: S136, S138, S140, S142, S100, S143 9th S-Boote flotilla: S130, S145, S150
8 – LS.s 507, 515, 531, 511, 496, 289, 512, 497
9 – On Slapton Sands.
10 – The second ship originally scheduled to protect the convoy was the *HMS Scimitar*, a former US destroyer built during WWI and loaned to the Royal Navy under the lend-lease act. Her 36 years of good and loyal services had led her into dry dock for extensive repair work.

S-Boote Flotillas Insignas

1st S-Boote Flotilla

1st S-Boote Flotilla

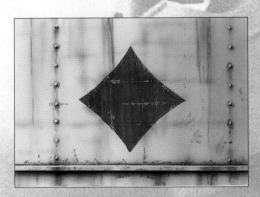

2nd S-Boote Flotilla

2nd S-Boote Flotilla

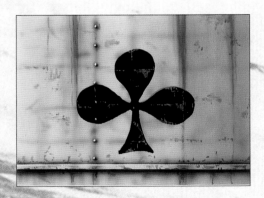

2nd S-Boote Flotilla

2nd S-Boote Flotilla

gnated to escort the LSTs was available. *HMS Azalea* was an anti-submarine corvette and her commander and crew had never before had to deal with an S-Boote attack. The inexperience of the sailors and troops on board the ships would also play against the Americans. The US Navy units had arrived in British waters barely a month before and the personnel had been assigned to their ships just two weeks before.

At midnight the *Azalea* received a radio message from the Naval Commander in Chief (NCC) in Plymouth alerting her to the presence of several S-Boote in her navigating zone. In spite of the danger, the British commander decided to go ahead and not cancel the exercise. At 1: 30 a.m. LST 507 detected echos on her radar indicating that several small boats were rapidly approaching to the north of the convoy.

Here is the account of the S-Boote attack from L.S.T. 507's health service officer, John Eckstam, who was on board at the time:

The explosion surprised everyone. The torpedo impact and the shock wave following it shoved me forward and I found myself on my knees on the steel bridge of the ship. I was lucky, I was unhurt. The situation appeared to be dramatic. The boat was quiet, as if dead in the middle of the ocean. A fire had broken out in the spare engine room and flames were starting to lick the upper deck where our landing vehicules were strapped down. Before leaving Brixham, all the gas tanks had been filled, and to make the exercise even more realistic, the Jeeps and the Shermans were loaded with ammunition. I had the feeling at that moment that I was looking through the gate to hell. Everything around me was burning: the Jeeps were afire and the ammunition was exploding and I heard the cries of the men who were caught in that trap of world-ending fury.

The burning LST 507 (1 490 tons) was abandoned by part of her crew. A few minutes later, two torpedoes hit LST 531 (1 650 tons), sinking her in less than 10 minutes. At 2: 28, it was LST 289's (1 490 tons) turn to be targetted by the S-Boote. She managed to avoid destruction and was able to get back to Brixham on only one engine. The attack took the lives of 197 US Navy sailors and 441 GIs The S-Boote didn't pick up any American survivors and turned back to Cherbourg.

The Allied invasion plans were not yet evident to the Germans, but Eisenhower learned a lot from Lyme Bay. During the meeting he had the next day with General Marshall, a series of questions was raised which it had become urgent to answer. How was it that such a reduced force had been able to attack American ships so easily in a zone supposedly under Allied control and only a few miles away from battleships that could have intervened? How could a handful of wooden boats inflict such damage on units of the US Navy without sustaining any losses themselves? The English and Americans, only two months away from Operation *Overlord*, had to find a quick solution if they wanted to prevent a tragedy of considerably larger proportions[1].

The Allied response was worked out little by little starting in May with the preparation of major air raids on the ports of Le Havre for June 14 and Boulogne for the 15th. On the German front, the beginning of May was devoted to mine-laying around the Isle of Wight and Needles Point by vessels of the 4th flotilla. During the night of May 12-13, the *Combattante* was once again operating south-east of the Isle of Wight, along with the Greek corvette *Tombazis*, the British frigates *Stayner*, *Trollop* and *Stevenstone*, and further west the corvette *Gentian*. This large number of boats around Spithead and The Solent was due to the presence in the sector of 600 ships preparing to participate in less than three weeks in Operation *Neptune*[2]. The British Admiralty had decided to use its force for two purposes: defense and mine-laying. Defense against the S-Boote which had been particularly active in April and during the first week of May in the zone around The Solent. Mine-laying to protect the edges of the portion of the Bay of the Seine where 10 channels would have to canalize the 5 *Overlord* fleets, taking each one to its landing zone on the Cotentin beaches.

At 0: 34, the *Combattante* recorded a contact 4 000 meters away; four echos appeared on the radar screen, representing boats travelling very fast. The corvette, flying the flag of Free France, immediately opened fire with her two 102-mm pieces, and hit an S-Boote. On board the S141[3],

1 – 236 LSTs were used during Operation *Neptune*.
2 – The naval phase of Overlord.
3 – S141, commanded by Oberleutnant zur See Walter Sobottka.

Top: LST 289 in the port of Dartmouth after the Lyme Bay attack. LSTs 507 and 531 were sunk during the operation. 197 sailors and 441 US Army soldiers died that day.

Below: An American liberty ship, priority target for the S-Boote before D-Day in Normandy.

Armement of S-Boote

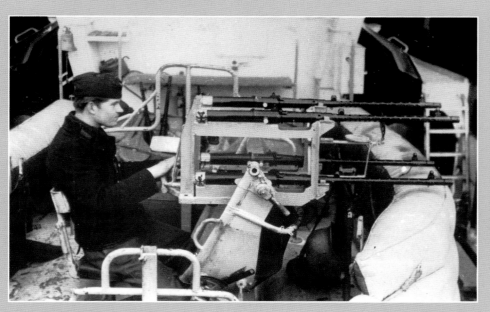

Previous page:
Two S-Boote patrolling in the Atlantic probably before Operation Overlord. The boats are travelling at high speed and the gunners are wearing their helmets. Because of the Allied air superiority this type of sortie in broad daylight required the crew to be particularly vigilant, as they could be attacked at any minute by Allied planes.

Above:
Firing exercise on an S10-type S-Boote with a 20-mm Flak cannon. Many of the warring powers used Swiss-designed Oerlikon cannon of identical caliber manufactured under licence, but the German engineers with the Mauser Company developped an original weapon which was produced in several different versions depending on the type of utilization.

Top right:
A 7.92-mm 4-gun turret, mounted from four MG 34 machine guns and installed in back of the cabin on the S105.

Right:
Firing practice with an early-generation 20-mm piece located at the rear of an S-Boote. This type of weapon will disappear starting in 1942, replaced by the more powerful rapid-fire Bofors 40-mm cannon or 37-mm Flaks, on the new S-Boote series.

Below:
Firing exercise with a 20-mm cannon on a 2nd-flotilla S-Boote off the port of Ostende in September, 1940.

B.PAUTIGNY

Schnellboote S150

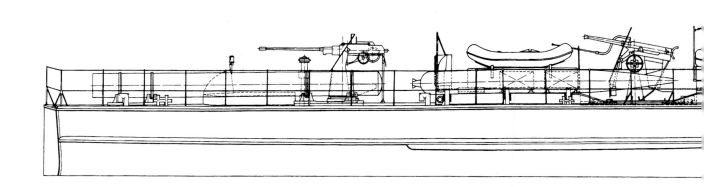

(Lürssen drawing)

The S150 during the first days of June, 1944. The gunboat, commanded by Kapitänleutnant Götz Friedrich von Mirbach, was operating with the 9th flotilla based in Cherbourg. The S150 had been delivered to the S-Bootwaffe en December of 1943 and was part of the S139-S150 series, a derivative of the S100. With a fully loaded 117-ton displacement and a length of 34,94 meters, she was propelled by three 2500-hp Daimler Benz MB 501 A engines which allowed her to easily top 42 knots with a 700-mile radius of action. The main armament had not changed : two 533-mm torpedo launching-tubes with four LUT-type torpedoes. Her auxiliary weapons had been improved over those of the S38 series. A 37-mm Flak M42 cannon was installed at the rear and three 20-mm pieces protected the center and front of the boat. The pilot's bridge had been completely transformed ; it was now entirely armored, with a lower, more streamlined profile. This series was equipped with the new FUMB 24 radar, permitting identification of enemy ships or planes within a radius of 10 miles. The crew was made up of 29 men. The S150 was destroyed on June 14, 1944 during the bombing of Le Havre by the Squadron 617 Lancasters of the Bomber Command.

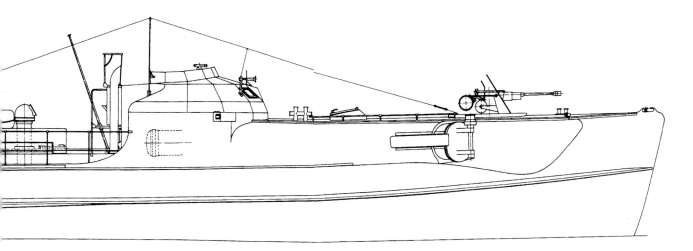

the crew had a hard time managing the fire which had just broken out at the rear. Two shells had struck the boat, and the fire was spreading rapidly. A group of S-Boote[1] tried to approach the French ship close enough to torpedo her, but her commander[2] executed an unexpected maneuver to starboard allowing her to again open fire on the Germans while at the same time remaining out of reach of their torpedoes. After that maneuver the *Combattante* attacked the S141 again from the port side and was practically on top of her when she finished her off with her 40-mm Pom-Pom and her light weapons. Seventeen crew members were killed during the fighting, including the son of Admiral Dönitz[3], Leutnant zur See Klaus Dönitz, whose body washed up on the French coast several days later.

FIGHTING DURING THE SUMMER OF 1944.

On June 3rd at 23:00 Petersen's headquarters in Scheveningen received information from the *Marinegruppewest* indicating that the Allied invasion would take place during the night of June 4th between Cherbourg and Le Havre. That same day 534 English and American bombers[4] escorted by 447 fighters[5] attacked the coastal batteries along 60 km of the French coast across the Straits of Dover. They also targetted the Boulogne S-Bunker[6], but were unable to make a dent in the solid concrete structure.

On June 5, from his Paris headquarters situated at the corner of Boulevard Suchet and the Place de Colombie, Admiral Theodore Krancke, commander-in-chief of the Kriegsmarine on the western front, launched code *Körbchen*[7]. All units stationed between the southern end of the Channel and Zeebruge received orders to pass from Alert level 2 to level 3. In spite of the events of that day, tension among the Kriegsmarine crews soon dropped. The sunny weeks of May had made the Germans fear that a European landing on the continent was imminent. But particularly bad weather at the beginning of June, with heavy rain and force-4 winds, misled them into relaxing and lowering their guard, especially since the weather forecast for June 6, 7 and 8 made it theoretically impossible for any large-scale combined air, sea and land operations in the Straits of Dover.

Petersen and his leaders had nevertheless taken the necessary measures, and since the end of May movements of units among the flotillas had been taking place from the North Sea ports toward Cherbourg and Boulogne. New boats had also been sent into the Channel zone, so that on June 5, battle order of the S-Bootwaffe on the western front was as follows:

• **2nd S-Boote flotilla based in Ostende:**
Korvettenkapitän Opdenhoff,
S177, S178, S179, S181, S189.
(Under repair: S176, S180, S182, S190.)

• **4th S-Boote flotilla based in Boulogne:**
Korvettenkapitän Fimmen,
S169, S171, S172, S173, S174, S175, S187, S188.

• **5th S-Boote flotilla based in Cherbourg:**
Korvettenkapitän Klug,
S84, S100, S136, S138, S139, S140, S142.
(Under repair: S112, S143.)

• **8th S-Boote flotilla based in Ijmuiden:**
Korvettenkapitän Zymalkowski,
S83, S117, S127, S133.

• **9th S-Boote flotilla based in Cherbourg:**
Korvettenkapitän von Mirbach,
S130, S144, S145, S146, S150, S167, S168.

There were thus 31 operational vessels which could be reinforced by eight units belonging to the 6th flotilla, operating in the Baltic Sea and ready to leave at a moment's notice for the western front. Opposing them, just before the Normandy invasion, the English and Americans were able to line up 28 MTB. MGB flotillas, 20 ML flotillas, 11 HDML flotillas and 4 flotillas of PT Boats, in addition to the naval forces of *Overlord*[8].

---

1 – S140, S142, S136.
2 – Under Commander Patou's instructions, the *Combattante* changed directions several times, allowing her to avoid a torpedo which ended its path on a line parallel to and less than 10 meters from the side of the ship.
3 – A year earlier his second son, Peter Dönitz, had disappeared on board the U 954
4 – 300 B-17s, 234 B-24s
5 – 201 P-38s, 163 P-47s, 83 P-51s
6 – 1 580 tons of bombs were dropped that day.
7 – *Little Basket*
8 – 7 battleships, 2 monitors, 23 cruisers, 105 destroyers, 25 Hunt-class destroyers, 71 corvettes, 63 frigates, 287 mine-sweepers, 60 armed trawlers, 14 sloops and 495 reserve coastal vessels, 236 LSTs, 245 LCIs, 911 LCTs, 481 LCMs, 1 484 LCV.s

On June 6 at 2:34 Petersen received information at his headquarters in Scheveningen indicating that parachute-jumpers had landed at several points on the west side of the Cotentin peninsula. Ten minutes later, the 4th, 5th and 9th flotillas received orders to support the Kriegsmarine ships operating on the western front. In the morning of June 6, four S-Boote belonging to the 4th flotilla left the port of Boulogne to reconnoiter the zone between Le Tréport and Dieppe. The Germans were hardly out of the port before being detected by Allied radars, and were immediately attacked by a group of MTBs and *HMS Obedient*. In the face of the numerical superiority of the enemy, the S-Boote had no solution but to turn back, and as usual the extraordinary performances of their diesels, reaching 42 knots, were able to save them.

During the night of June 7, the 2nd flotilla, under the orders of Korvettenkapitän Opdenhoff, left Ostende with the S177, S178, S179, S181 and S189, immediately followed by the 8th flotilla from Ijmuiden with the S83, S117, S127 and S133. The two units had received orders to proceed to the Allied landing zone and to torpedo the ships they might find there[1]. At the same time, the 4th flotilla left Boulogne travelling south with the S169, S171, S172, S173, S174, S175, S187 and S188. The S172 launched a torpedo against a British destroyer without managing to hit her. The 5th flotilla, coming from Cherbourg with seven boats[2], also attacked two Royal Navy destroyers, but the German gunboats were unsuccessful in their attempts to find the right firing angle. A few minutes later the S139[3] hit a mine which had probably been laid the day before by British MTBs from the 64th flotilla. A little later, the 9th flotilla[4] joined up with the elements of the 5th flotilla in the same operating zone. During a combined action involving several pairs of gunboats belonging to these two units, the British LST 875 (611 tons) and LCI 105 (380 tons) were sunk off Saint-Vaast la Hougue. The Germans lost the S140 which struck an English mine east of Barfleur. The attacks against the Allied ships continued during the following days.

In the night of June 8, the Americans were the S-Boote victims. In the evening, the 4th flotilla was operating in the estuary of the Seine. The S174, S175, S187 and S172 launched several torpedoes, and in spite of barrage fire coming from the British escort ships, were able to sink LSTs 376 (1 490 tons) and 314 (1 490 tons), and to damage the destroyer *USS Meredith* (2 200 tons)[5]. On June 11, the 5th and 9th flotillas again took to sea. MTB 448 was sunk during a dogfight with the S84 and S100, but the S136[6] was surprised east of Barfleur by the Canadian destroyer *Sioux*, the British frigate *Duff*, and the Polish escort ship *Krakowiak*. The three of them sent her to the bottom. A little later, north of Barfleur, the frigate *HMS Halstead* was attacked by a Rotte from the 9th flotilla. Her prow was ripped off by a torpedo, but she did not sink and was able to make it to Juno Beach under her own power.

Around midnight it was also the S-Boote from the 9th flotilla that attacked several towboats pulling *Mulberry* artificial pontoon sections 10 miles from Omaha Beach. After several tries to move in close, they were able to direct a torpedo against the 730-ton *USS Partridge*

1 – During the first days of the invasion, the German S-Boote principally attacked the escort ships, without much success. Finally, after June 9, Petersen intervened personally to encourage his unit commanders to give top priority to targetting the large transport ships landing the troops, which were much more vulnerable.
2 – S136, S138, S140, S142, S100, S139, S84
3 – S139, commanded by Kapitänleutnant Hans Jürgen Dietrich: 22 killed and 4 prisoners.
4 – The 9th flotilla was composed of the S130, S144, S145, S150, S167, S168.
5 – At the moment of the explosion, 1:52, her commander thought the ship had hit a mine. 2 officers and 33 men died during the attack.
6 – The S136 was part of the 5th S-Boote flotilla: Oberleutnant zur See Hans Günter Jürgensmeyer.

Top: An S-Boote photographed just before D-Day in an unidentified French port. This is an S30 type, with streamlined tubes, quite different from the rest of the gunboats used by the five flotillas engaged by the Kriegsmarine on the western front at that time. Note the MG 34 machine guns mounted in the prow.

Previous page: On board an S-Boote in the North Sea. Two members of the crew are busy unloading a 20-mm Flak 38 cannon located at the rear of the boat. On the lefthand side notice the metal net basket, the *Hütsenfankorb*, used for ejected cartridges.

Below: S-Boote from the 8th flotilla in may 1944 in front of the entrance of the S-bunker of Ijmuiden.

which capsized, carrying with her 32 American sailors. The British towboat *Sesame* (700 tons) was likewise sunk a few minutes later. After this series of attacks the S-Boote turned their attention to a convoy of LSTs travelling towards the coast in the same sector. LST 538 (1 490 tons) received a torpedo under her water-line. However the flat bottom of the boat kept her from sinking, and even though she was badly damaged she was able, under escort, to reach Omaha Beach.

On June 12, the whole day was devoted to actions directed against the Allied ships by the 2nd, 4th and 9th flotillas. The S177 and S178[1], off Juno Beach, were able to sink the ammunition transport ship *Dungrange* (621 tons) and the British steamers *Ashanti* (534 t.) and *Brackenfield* (657 t.), which were together in the process of delivering 660 tons of ammunition and fuel to the Anglo-Canadian troops. In the evening on the same day, six boats[2] from the 5th and 9th flotillas left Cherbourg. Their goal: attack the U force off Utah Beach and thus repeat the operation that had been so successful on June 7th against LSTs 376 and 314. The Allied defensive perimeter was rapidly pierced and the S150, S167, S138 and S142 found themselves face-to-face with several American destroyers[3]. The S138 then moved as close as possible to the USS *Nelson*, and her commander, Oberleutnant zur See Stohwasser, found himself in good firing position 800 meters from the righthand side of the American ship. It was too good to pass up. In a fraction of a second the torpedo had left its

tube and exploded in the stern of the destroyer. Twenty-four men were killed on the spot, but the boat did not sink and was able to be towed to Portsmouth.

On June 13, the S178, S179 and S189[4] were attacked by Bristol *Beaufighters* from Royal Air Force squadrons 143 and 236, as they were patrolling off Boulogne with R-Boote from the 8th flotilla. The British executed several passes, sinking the three S-Boote as well as the R97 and R99, without sustaining any losses themselves. In spite of their meager success during the first days of Operation Neptune, the S-Boote managed nevertheless to considerably hinder the landing operations of the Allied ships, creating a permanent threat for the English and American leaders out of proportion to their numbers.

Starting on June 12, OIC[5] reports indicated an abnormally large group of S-Boote concentrated in the port of Le Havre[6] ready to intervene rapidly in the Allied landing zones. This situation, and the shock caused by the Lyme Bay attack in May, would lead the Allies to launch several air raids against the French Channel ports, of which the most devastating would be the June 14th attack on the port installations of Le Havre. The mission was assigned to the Bomber Command under the orders of Air Field Marshal Arthur Harris[7]. The Bomber Command attack on the port began on June 14 at nightfall. A fleet of 337 planes, including 223 Lancasters[8], 100 Halifaxes and 14 Mosquitos, attacked the entire port structure. The first bombs exploded at 22: 32 dropped from a height of 18 000 feet[9]. At the same

moment, the 22 Lancasters of Squadron 617 dropped their *Tallboys* on the docks and the huge S-Bunker sheltering several units from the 4th, 5th and 9th flotillas. The S142, S143, S144 and S146 were moored outside, along the floating pier situated east of the Theophile basin. All of the crew members had left the boats, with the exception of the S144, where Oberleutnant zur See Hans Shirren and his men were at their stations. His original boat, the S145, had been seriously damaged a few days before in a fight with US Navy PT boats. The Germans were

1 – Leutnant zur See Karl Bosenink: S177 (2nd S-Boote flotilla)
Oberleutnant zur See Georg Braune: S178 (2nd S-Boote flotilla)
2 – S84, S100, S150, S167, S138, S142
3 – *USS Sowers, USS Laffly, USS Nelson*
4 – S178, commanded by Oberleutnant zur See Georg Braune
S179, commanded by Oberleutnant zur See Kurt Neugebauer
S189, commanded by Oberleutnant zur See Alois Sczesny.
5 – Operational Intelligence Center of the British Admiralty.
The OIC had managed to decipher the Kriegsmarine Ultra code, and the English were thus able to anticipate movements of S-Boote flotillas between their base ports and their operational zones in the Channel or the North Sea. The Allies could at any time intercept the radio messages sent between Petersen's FDS. and his units. Thus they knew every movement of the enemy during the week following D-Day. Nevertheless the Germans came out ahead during the actual fighting and were able to escape from the British ships because of the high speed of their boats.
6 – 6 boats in Ostende, 5 in Boulogne, 4 in Cherbourg, and 15 in Le Havre.
7 – Arthur Harris was named to head the Bomber Command in February, 1942.
8 – Including 22 Lancasters from Squadron 617.
9 – 18 000 feet, that is 5 486 meters.

Below:
An S-Boote equiped with an experimental *Panzerkalotte* photographed in 1944.

Above: **A Bofors 40-mm cannon used on an S38-type S-Boote at the end of the year 1942.**

intending to make a sortie at nightfall and were checking the engines and the weapons on board. At 22: 30 the first shots of the Flak[1] batteries were heard over the basins. *Shirren* had just enough time to yell to his men to man their battle stations when a cluster of bombs started exploding around the vessels. Within a few seconds all hell had broken loose around the four S-Boote.

At the same moment, a reception was taking place in the officers' mess-hall on the 900-ton torpedo ship *Möwe*. The commander of the 5th torpedo flotilla, Kapitän zur See Heinrich Hoffman, had invited on board his colleague Kurt Johansen, who had just taken over leadership of the 5th S-Boote flotilla. And they were especially celebrating the Knight's Cross of Korvettenkapitän Götz Friedrich von Mirbach who had just been decorated that very morning for his heroic actions in combat. The leader of the 4th flotilla, Kurt Fimmen, had also joined his comrades a bit later. At 22: 32 the English bombs started raining down on the German ships at mooring. In the general panic that followed, the men tried either to reach shelter in the S-Bunker or to reach their boats in an attempt to respond to the enemy attack. Götz von Mirbach was wounded by shrapnel in the legs and neck, Kurt Fimmen was miraculously spared with just a slight concussion. Kurt Johansen was not as lucky. He was thrown into the port by the blast of an exploding bomb and died instantly. Herman Opdenhoff, commander of the 9th flotilla, had not participated in the party and was at home in his requisitioned villa near the Tourneville fort on the heights of Le Havre.

From there he helplessly witnessed the deluge of fire raining down on his comrades.

At the same time, three *Tallboys* struck the north-west side of the S-Bunker. They pierced through to the inside of the upper part of the concrete structure, even though it was 3,5 meters thick and reinforced by metal bars. They did considerable damage to the north and west walls, respectively 2,5 and 2,7 meters thick, and created a crater of more than 6 meters in diameter in the vault. Another bomb exploded between the two middle levels of the S-Bunker, leading to the total destruction of the floors above and below, which caved in on the gunboats moored in the basins. During the 22 minutes that the raid lasted, 1 230 tons of bombs hit the installations of the Le Havre port. The Kriegsmarine lost three torpedo ships: the *Falke*, the *Jaguar* and the *Möwe*, 14 S-Boote[2], 2 R-Boote and 20 other boats. 700 homes were destroyed and 76 Le Havre civilians were killed that night[3].

On the day following the Le Havre air raid, Admiral Krancke, commander of the German western naval group, noted in his war journal:

Losses are extremely heavy and our situation is catastrophic. The naval situation in the bay of the Seine has completely changed and it will now be difficult to try to accomplish the planned operations with the forces remaining.

In the evening of June 15, a new air raid took place over Boulogne. 155 Lancasters, 130 Handley Page Halifaxes and 12 Mosquitos from the Bomber Command flattened the port under 1 300 tons of bombs. Seven R-Boote were sunk, along with fifteen other smaller boats.

During this period, from June 7 to 30, the Allies landed 850 229 men, 148 803 vehicles and 570 505 tons of material on the Normandy beaches. These numbers represent 13 armored divisions and 30 motorized infantry divisions.

On June 16, 1944, the Schnellbootwaffe could muster the following boats:	
Ostende:	8th flotilla S83, S127, S133.
Boulogne:	2nd flotilla S176, S180, S181, S182. 4th flotilla S174, S175.
Le Havre:	9th flotilla S167.
Cherbourg:	9th flotilla S130, S145, S168.

Operational activity of the flotillas was to continue on the western front in spite of the terrible losses incurred during the bombing of Le Havre. Sorties took place between June 16-19, involving all units participating in mine-laying operations or in attempted convoy attacks which would all be effectively repulsed by the British escort ships. During the night of June 22, the 2nd flotilla[4] left Le Havre with units S167, S174, S175, S177, S180, S181 and S190 to undertake mine-laying operations in the bay of the Seine. At 1: 00 a.m. the S190 was attacked by the 102-mm cannon of two British destroyers. After several direct strikes her commander, Kapitänleutnant Hugo Wendler, was obliged to abandon his boat which soon capsized.

In the night of June 23-24, the Germans evacuated Cherbourg. The Kriegsmarine had lost a valuable operational base that would be reoccupied by the Americans on June 26.

Above: **The S128 on patrol in the North Sea in November 1943. This boat is part of the S101-S133 series. On February 23, 1944, while participating in operations with other units of the 2nd flotilla, the S128 was attacked by the destroyer *HMS Garth* as she tried to approach a convoy. She capsized after hitting the S94 which also went down trying to escape fire from the British ship.**

1 – Flak is the acronym of *Flugabwehrkanone* (anti-aircraft cannon).
2 – S84, S100, S138, S142, S143, S144, S146, S150, S169, S171, S172, S173, S187, S188
3 – The Kriegsmarine lost eighteen men from the S-Boote crews.
4 – During the night of June 18-19, the six boats of the 2nd flotilla were transferred from Boulogne-sur-Mer to Le Havre.

Flotilla movements would continue until the end of the month. During the night of June 25-26, the 6th flotilla[1] was transferred from Cuxhaven to Ijmuiden, leaving the Baltic for the North Sea in an attempt to reinforce the Kriegsmarine western forces and compensate for the losses sustained during the previous two weeks of fighting. One month day for day after D-Day, the S-Boote flotillas still occupied three French ports.

The condition of the flotillas (July 1944)	
Saint-Malo:	5th flotilla: S112.
	9th flotilla: S145 damaged.
Le Havre:	2nd flotilla: S174, S177, S180, S181 damaged.
	8th flotilla: S83, S127, S133 damaged.
	9th flotilla: S167 and S175 damaged
Dieppe:	9th flotilla: S130, S168 damaged.
Vlissingen:	2nd flotilla: S176, S182 damaged.
Amsterdam:	6th flotilla: S39, S114 damaged.
Rotterdam:	6th flotilla: S76, S90, S97, S132, S135 damaged.
Ijmuiden:	6th flotilla: S91 damaged.

Of 23 boats only 13 were shipshape and ready for operation.

During the night of July 4-5, elements of the 8th flotilla[2] were heading toward Le Havre. At half past twelve, near Cap d'Antifer, several MTBs[3] accompanied by the frigate HMS Trollope suddenly appeared. The fighting was particularly violent and the S83 was hit by several shells that destroyed her 37- and 20-mm pieces. The Germans were nevertheless able to get to Le Havre without losing the boat. On July 5 the Kriegsmarine had another stroke of ill luck. The Le Havre torpedo repair depot was destroyed by an explosion, undoubtedly a sabotage action organized by the French resistance. 41 torpedoes were destroyed, and this would have a direct impact on the operational capacities of the S-Boote in the following days. On the night of July 8,

all units of the 2nd flotilla had left Le Havre for the bay of the Seine River. They were organized into two attack groups: the S176, S177 and S182 on the one hand, and the S174, S180 and S181 on the other. The first group made contact with two destroyers which were immediately attacked. 6 torpedoes flew almost simultaneously out of the 3 S-Boote's tubes. 1 400 meters away, the frigate HMS Trollope (1 300 tons) was hit in the stern. 54 sailors and 7 officers were killed. The British ship was seriously damaged but was nevertheless towed to Portsmouth.

Poor weather conditions accounted for a lull in activity during the following days, but the fighting began again with the same intensity starting in the middle of July. In the night of July 26-27, the 6th flotilla left Boulogne with eight boats under the orders of Kapitänleutnant Matzen heading out to meet a convoy which had been spotted by the B-Dienst services off Dungeness. In spite of the presence of several MTBs and 3 destroyers[4], the S97 and S114[5] were able to launch two Fat-type[6] torpedoes from a distance of 1,800 meters. The freighters Fort Perrot (7 171 tons) and Empire Beatrice (7 046 tons) were hit but did not sink, even though they were seriously damaged. The other S-Boote attacked the British escort ships, but without much luck. At the same time, the 2nd

flotilla was operating out of Le Havre with the S176, S182, S174, S181 and S180. Near Cap d'Antifer the Germans met a group of 12 MTBs assisted by the frigate HMS Retalick. The S-Boote immediately went into action against the British boats, with the S182[7] smashing MTB 430. The latter was so hard hit that she was abandoned by her crew. As the sinking ship was drifting away, she was hit by MTB 412 which had no way of avoiding her. The operation cost the Royal Navy Coastal Forces two MTBs, and the Germans were obliged to scuttle the S182 as she was unable to get back to Le Havre under her own power.

On July 30, the S97, S114 and S91 [8], belonging to the 6th flotilla, left Dieppe to try to cut off a convoy located to the east of Eastbourne. The three S-Boote found themselves in good firing position, and launched their six Fat torpedoes,

1 – (25)S39, S76, S90, S91, S97, S114, S132, S135
2 – S83, S127, S133
3 – MTB 459, MTB 462, MTB 464 belonging to the 29th MTB flotilla of the Canadian Navy
5 – MTB 436, MTB 432, MTB 418, destoyers HMS Obedient, Opportune and Savage.
5 – S97, commanded by Oberleutnant zur See Wilhelm Waldhausen S114, commanded by Kapitänleutnant Hans Karl Hemmer.
6 – Fat: Flächen Absuchender Torpedo (circular-seak torpedo)
7 – S182, commanded by Kapitänleutnant Kurt Pinger
8 – The 6th flotilla was made up of the S97, S114, S90, S132, S29, S135, S79, S91.

striking several British freighters. The *Samwake* (7 219 tons) was sunk, and four other ships, the *Fort Dearborn* (7 160 tons), *Fort Kaskaskia* (7 187 tons), *Ocean Volga* (7 174 tons) and *Ocean Courier* (7 178 tons) were seriously damaged. Even though the frigate *HMS Thornbrough* intervened, firing 150 40-mm and almost 700 20-mm shells during the combat, none of the S-Boote were hit, which shows once again how successful these rapid boats were in harassing the enemy in spite of their small number.

On August 2, at the end of the day, another air raid, launched by 54 Lancasters from the 1st and 8th Bomber Command groups, showered the port of Le Havre with bombs. The S39 and S114[1] were sunk and the S91 and S97 badly damaged. On August 7, the brand new 10th flotilla, under the orders of Kapitänleutnant Karl Müller, with the S183, S184, S185, S186, S191 and S192, left Cuxhaven for Ijmuiden. On the 9th, the S198, S199 and S701 also arrived in the Dutch port, to be assigned to the 8th flotilla. Between August 4 and 15, the 2nd and 6th flotillas launched several operations from Le Havre, during which new long-distance T3a torpedoes[2] were used against

Allied ships. On August 9, the light cruiser *HMS Frobisher* (9 860 tons) was hit, as well as the minesweeper *HMS Vestal* (960 tons), near Juno Beach. On August 10, it was the freighter *Iddesleigh* (5 205 tons) which was torpedoed off Sword Beach, along with the repair ship *HMS Albatross* (4 800 tons). By mid-August the five flotillas present on the western front had 33 gunboats available and operational.

On August 18, the 8th flotilla operated off Dover intercepting a large convoy. The steamer *Fort Gloucester* (7 127 tons) was unable to avoid the path of a T5 which hit her back side and resulted in important flooding on board. Once again the escort ships of the Royal Navy were unable to keep the S-Boote away from the convoy, in spite of the presence of 5 MTBs and 2 destroyers[3]. On August 23, the Germans would start evacuating Le Havre. The pocket was completely isolated and at the end of its tether when the Kriegsmarine decided to attempt a sortie under the protection of the gunboats of the 6th flotilla. Over 6 days, one hundred boats managed to make it through the blockade of English and American ships surrounding the port[4]. The last move took place at night on

August 29-30, when 19 ships left the largest port in Normandy under the protection of the units of the 8th flotilla. The convoy was attacked by the escort destroyer *HMS Cattistock* and the frigate *HMS Retalick*. But the English didn't sink a single boat that day. Korvettenkapitän Zymalkowski's S-Boote (S196) kept them at bay.

Bottom, previous page:
The S210 photographed on September 27, 1944, after entering service in the 2nd flotilla whose distinctive insignia appears on the boat: an ace of spades. She was commanded by Oberleutnant zur See Günter Weisheit, and participated in operations in the North Sea in 1944 and 1945. At the end of the war she was turned over to the US Navy, which ceded her to the Norwegians.

Top and bottom:
The S176 with an unidentified S-Boote on her left. The snapshot appears to have been taken at the end of 1944 in the port of Ostende. The boat was operational since March of 1944 in the 2nd flotilla, and was commanded by Oberleutnant zur See Friedrich Wilhelm Stockfleth. The S176 went down on April 7, 1945 during a dogfight with MTBs 494, 493 and 497 from the 22nd flotilla. 26 crew members and the commander were rescued by MTBs 497 and 775.

1 – S39, commanded by Leutnant zur See Enno Brandi
S114, commanded by Kapitänleutnant Hans Karl Hemmer.
2 – The T3a is a G7e torpedo equipped with a Fat or Lut system
3 – *HMS Walpole, HMS Opportune* Only ten ships were sunk, by MTBs and PT Boats operating with destroyers.

THE FINAL COMBATS
ON THE WESTERN FRONT
(1945)

RETREAT TO HOLLAND AND NORWAY.

On September 3rd and 4th, the last S-Boote units stationed in the English Channel retreated to Rotterdam and Ijmuiden.

At the beginning of September, the six flotillas operating on the western front included 34 boats of which 27 were operational. Operations started again on September 5[1], mostly night mine-laying in the zone around Cromer, since every attempted attack of an English or American convoy was foiled by the superior Allied air power[2]. Petersen finally intervened personally at the Luftwaffe headquarters to try to get night fighter

New units put into service between July and December 1944 :

July 1944	: eight units in service.
August 1944	: five units in service.
September 1944	: six units in service.
Octobrer 1944	: ten units in service.
Novembrer 1944	: two units in service.
Decembrer 1944	: four units in service.

planes that would maintain security in the skies over the zones of S-Boote operation, but all available aircraft were assigned to the defense of the Reich. At this time the British Coastal Forces started operating out of Dover, patrolling the coast along Dunkerque. The Germans in that pocket were surrounded on land and the only possible liaisons were by using the small boats of the Kriegsmarine. On several different occasions the S-Boote had unsuccessfully tried to force the British blockade. In the night of September 18-19, the Kriegsmarine organized a new operation. Two groups from the 10th flotilla[3], commanded by Korvettenkapitän Müller, transporting eight tons of ammunition, tried to get through to the blockaded port. This time the operation was a success, and the four S-Boote made it back to Hoek-van-Holland and Vlissingen, with on board the commander of the 226th Infantry Division, Generalleutnant Wolfgang von Kluge, and several of his officers, who they had ben able to evacuate.

Encouraged by the result of this operation, three more boats[4] left Hoek-van-Holland to test the British defense forces. Half way there, the German craft were identified by a Coastal Com-

mand reconnaissance plane and intecepted by the frigate *HMS Stayner* and MTBs 724 and 728 from the 64th flotilla. The fighting was extremely violent and left no hope for the S-Boote crews. The S183[5] came under direct fire from the Stayner's main guns and sank immediately. The S200 and the S702 were hopelessly confused and ran into each other after having been hit by several 40-mm shells. Sixty survivors were picked up by the British.

At the beginning of October, new mine-laying operations were planned, and Petersen now had at his disposal 21 S-Boote based in the ports of Ijmuiden, Hoek-van-Holland and Rotterdam[6]. On October 10, fourteen boats participated in a major mine-laying operation in the estuary of the Schelde in an attempt to prevent the Allies from reopening the port of Antwerp. The Germans were

1 – The S184 was sunk by the Dover coastal batteries as she was laying mines with units of the 10th flotilla during the night of September 4-5.
2 – In August, 1944, the Luftwaffe had 680 operational aircraft on the western front (France, Belgium, Netherlands). Opposing them, the Allies totaled 3,467 four-engine aircraft, 1 800 twin-engine planes, 5,500 fighter bombers. The ratio was 26 to 1.
3 – S186, S185, S198, S199
4 – S183, S200, S702
5 – S183, commanded by Oberleutnant zur See Klaus Ulrich ; S200, commanded by Leutnant zur See Alfred Kellinghusen ; S702, commanded by Oberleutnant zur See Hilmar Blum.
6 – Ijmuiden : S201, S202, S203, S204, S205, S219, S220, S703 (4th flotilla), and S186, S185, S199 (10th flotilla) ; Rotterdam : S130, S167, S168, S175, S206, S207 (9th flotilla) ; Hoek-van-Holland : S194, S195, S197, S198 (10th flotilla).

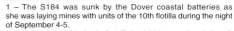

Top : **Close-up view of the *Kalottenbrücke* on an S170-type gunboat belonging to the 4th flotilla. The snapshot appears to have been taken in the fall of 1944 when the boats were operating out of Rotterdam. The letters painted on the righthand side of the *Kalottenbrücke* probably correspond to the commander's initials. Small bullet holes are visible on the fairing of the torpedo tubes, the proof that fights with Allied ships still took place regularly in spite of a power ratio in their favor.**

Left : **April 1944. Three S38-type S-Boote from the 1st training flotilla taking part in grenade exercises in the Baltic Sea. The S-Bootwaffe operated three training flotillas right up until 1945.**

Previous pages : **S38-type S-Boote on maneuvers in the Baltic Sea.**

Above :
The S199 photographed in autumn, 1944. The boat joined
the 8th flotilla units in Ijmuiden at the beginning of August.
On September 17, with the S198 she took part in the operation
designed to get supplies through to Dunkerque and helped
to deliver nine tons of ammunition to the besieged garrison.
She sank on January 23, 1945 after crashing into the S701
during an attempted attack of a British convoy. At the time
she was commanded by Oberleutnant zur See Achim Quistorp.

Bottom:
The S195 at the end of December, 1944,
after being hit during an air raid launched
by Royal Air Force Squadron 617 Lancasters over
the port of Ijmuiden. On December 15, all of the 8th
flotilla units were hit by British bombs, and it
would be several months before the S-Boote
which were not completely destroyed
could be operational again.

soon rewarded for their tenacity, for at the beginning of November, the mines hidden along the coasts of Belgium would give the Allies plenty of problems.

On November 1st, twelve S-Boote left Hoek-van-Holland during the night heading for the zone situated north of Dunkerque. 21 UMBs and 14 LMBs were dropped in this zone which was now being used by Allied maritime traffic. Four days later, LCT 457 (600 tons) hit a mine and capsized off Ostende. Then on November 7, LCT 976 (200 tons) became the second victim. The boat broke in two and had to be abandoned near the Escaut River. On the same day, LST 420 (2 750 tons) exploded and sank almost immediately off Ostende.

<table>
<tr><td colspan="1">Allied losses due to mine-laying
operations during November
and December, 1944 :</td></tr>
</table>

• November 8, 1944 : ML 916 (75 tons)
sunk off Walsoorden

• November 10, 1944 : Squadron mine-sweeper
Hydra hit by a mine off Ostende and irretrievable.

• December 3, 1944 : American freighter *Francis
Asbury* (7 176 tons) sunk off Ostende

• December 7, 1944 : American freighter *Samsip*
(7 219 tons) irretrievable in the estuary
of the Escaut.

• December 15, 1944 : British freighter *Fort Maison
Neuve* (7 128 tons) finished off by cannon in the
estuary of the Escaut.

• December 16, 1944 : British tanker *War Diwan*
(5 551 tons) sunk off Ostende.

• December 24, 1944 : American freighter *Empire
Path* (6 140 tons) sunk off Ostende.

• December 29, 1944 : MTB 782 sunk in the *mouth
of the Escaut.*

The British invasion of the island of Walcheren[1], located in the mouth of the Schelde, on November 1st, triggered an immediate Ger-

man reaction. Twelve boats from the three flotillas based in Holland moved out to try to attack the British forces. But the Royal Navy escort ships, with the help of the 29th MTB flotilla, were able to repulse the Germans' repeated attacks. Nevertheless a 1 141-ton tanker, the Rio Bravo, and an armed trawler, the Colsay (384 tons) were sunk[2]. Once the Allies had taken Walcheren, the balance of force was modified in their favor. Henceforth the maritime route between the Thames River and Antwerp was under their control. On November 4, the Royal Navy mine-sweepers cleared a channel into this important Belgian port, which was to become rapidly operational and give the Anglo-Saxons a foothold[3] from which they would be able, in the coming months, to launch their major assault against the Reich.

During the month of November, mine-laying missions still proceeded, but with greater and greater difficulty. On November 15, six boats from the 9th flotilla left Hoek-van-Holland for the estuary of the Escaut River. They had hardly arrived in the zone when they were assaulted by the British frigates HMS Retalick and HMS Thornbrough, along with several MTBs. The fighting was brief, but they were forced to abandon their mission after the S168 was hit several times by the MTBs. As winter arrived, weather conditions in the North Sea became worse, with force-8 winds that prevented any sorties until mid-December.

When better weather returned, the operations continued, but it was now the Allies who had the initiative. In the afternoon of December 15, 17 Lancasters from the 617th Squadron of the Bomber Command, performed a remake of the mid-June attack over Le Havre. This time the target was the port of Ijmuiden. 69.8 tons of bombs were dropped during a period of seven minutes, and two 5.4-ton Tallboys penetrated inside the S-Bunker, destroying the S198[4] and damaging the S193, S195 and S701, as well as four other ships. In less than ten minutes the entire 8th flotilla was K.O. After the attack, Petersen's headquarters published the following bulletin:

*This raid leaves the entire S-Bootwaffe bitter.
It is clear that the concrete shelters no longer
offer sufficient protection from the enemy.*

1 – Operation *Infatuate.*
2 – The S-Boote also took on the venerable battleship Warspite several times, without succeeding in touching her ; also the monitors Erebus and Roberts.
3 – At the beginning of December 18,000 tons of material transited through the port of Antwerp.
4 – S198, commanded by Kapitänleutnant Walter Knapp.

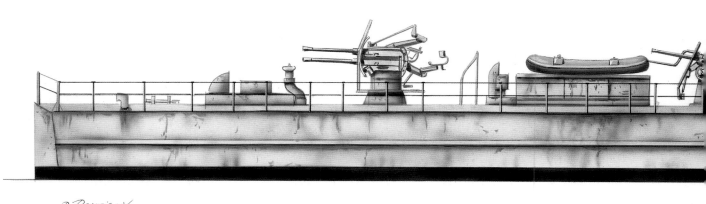

B PAUTIGNY

Schnellboote S174

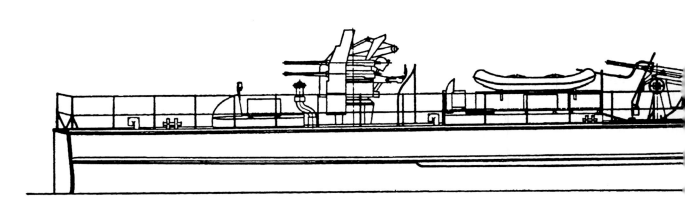

(Lürssen drawing)

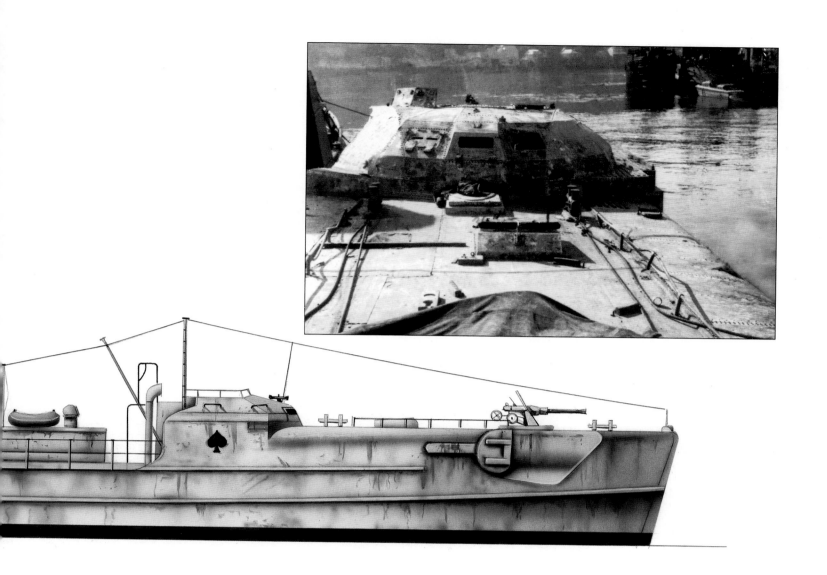

The S174 in July, 1944, while fighting with the units of the 2nd flotilla based in Le Havre. The gunboat was commanded by Kapitänleutnant Hugo Wendler. The S174 entered service in March, 1944, and was part of the S171-S186 series, slightly modified versions of the S170. She measured 34,94 meters long for a 122-ton displacement when fully loaded. Her three 2500-hp Daimler Benz MB 511 engines gave her a top speed of 42 knots and a radius of 700 miles. Her weaponry had not changed from that of previous models. It was made up of two 533-mm torpedo tubes with four G7a-tpye traditional or acoustic torpedoes. The pilot's bridge has an armored structure, the Kalottenbrucke. The boat is equipped with two passive radars, a FuMO 62 Hohentwiel and a FUMB 10 Borkum. Secondary weapons include the 20-mm Flakvierling L 38/43 main cannon mounted on a four-gun rapid-fire turret, terribly effective against low-flying enemy aircraft, and three 20-mm Flak 38 L41 cannon located in the center and prow of the ship. 31 men, including two officers, make up the crew. The S174 was surrendered to the U.S. Navy in 1945, then sold in 1947 to the Norwegian armed forces.

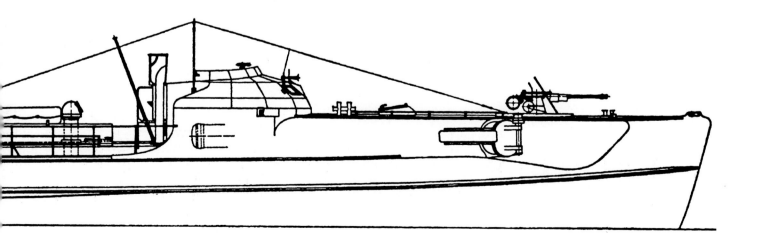

S-Boote Flotillas Insignas

4th S-Boote Flotilla

6th S-Boote Flotilla

7th S-Boote Flotilla

8th S-Boote Flotilla

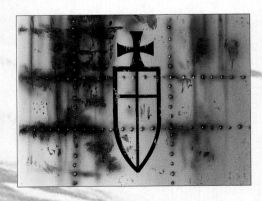

8th S-Boote Flotilla

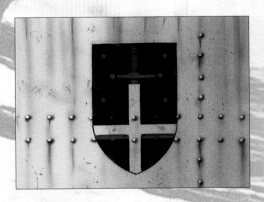

9th S-Boote Flotilla

Left:
A 700-type S-Boote from the 9th flotilla photographed at the end of 1944 in the North Sea. The flotilla insignia is visible on the prow : a sword with a Baltic cross.

Centre:
The support ship *Carl Peters* in 1944 with five boats belonging to the 3rd training flotilla in the Baltic Sea during an exercise.

For the time being, the units will be dispersed among our ports and camouflaged to escape the Allied bombs.

On December 29, 16 RAF Lancasters again bombed the port of Amsterdam. But all of the gunboats had left the S-Bunker and been carefully camouflaged, saving them from the English bombers. There were no losses [1].

The end of the year marked a new defeat for the Germans. The S185 and S192[2], belonging to the 9th flotilla, were sunk by the frigates HMS *Torrington*, *Curzon* and the sloop *Kittiwake* while participating in a major combined operation of mine-laying off Ostende. Several Rotten tried to get through to pick up survivors, but the British escort ships prevented them from nearing the spot. The English were able to save 22 crew members from the S185, but none of the men from the S192 were ever found. On December 29, the 4th flotilla, with the S202, S204, S205, S219 and S201, left Norwegian waters to be transferred to Rotterdam.

1 – Only the S167 and S207 were slightly grazed.
2 – S185, commanded by Oberleutnant zur See Klaus Degenhard ; S192, commanded by Leutnant-zur-See Reinhard Heinrich Holz.

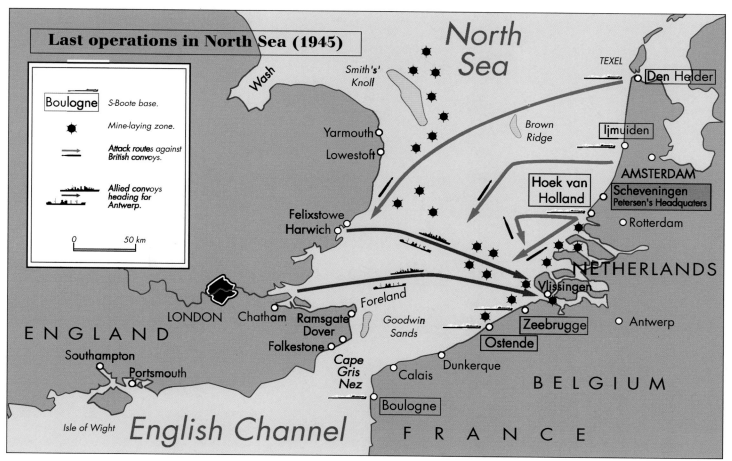

Last operations in North Sea (1945)

Boulogne — S-Boote base.

Mine-laying zone.

Attack routes against British convoys.

Allied convoys heading for Antwerp.

0   50 km

North Sea

Wash
Smith 's' Knoll
TEXEL
Den Helder
Brown Ridge
Ijmuiden
Yarmouth
Lowestoft
AMSTERDAM
Hoek van Holland
Scheveningen
Petersen's Headquaters
Rotterdam
Felixstowe
Harwich
NETHERLANDS
Vlissingen
LONDON
Chatham
Ramsgate
Dover
Foreland
Goodwin Sands
Zeebrugge
Antwerp
ENGLAND
Folkestone
Ostende
Southampton
Portsmouth
Cape Gris Nez
Calais
Dunkerque
BELGIUM
Boulogne
Isle of Wight
English Channel
FRANCE

Günther Rabe, « the crow »

Günther Rabe was certainly the most brilliant S-Boote commander of his generation. He was named Kapitänleutnant in April 1943 and took command of the S130 during the month of October of that same year. He was among those Kriegsmarine officers who were the most familiar with their British opponents and their tactics. Throughout the war, Rabe would continue adapting the offensive S-Boote techniques to the new challenges to which they were confronted. He was notably the person who suggested replacing the Lauertaktik (hide-and-seek, or ambush, tactic) by the Stichtaktik (sting tactic). From then on, the S-Boote would attack convoys by forming a more compact navigational group. After creating a gap in the enemy defense, the Germans used the *sting* technique, moving in several *Rotten* at top speed while at the same time coordinating the launching of their two torpedoes against the Allied ships. Then, still in formation, the S-Boote sped away. This maneuver required tight collaboration and extreme vigilance on the part of the different crews, to avoid any risk of collision at a speed of 40 knots. The Stichtaktik was also tough on the S-Boote diesels. The average speed for the

whole length of the mission was 38 knots, with several minutes at 42 knots [1] as the boats left the scene after launching their torpedoes.

Rabe also had some original ideas about equipment. He had his men wear, under their reglementary uniforms, leather underwear that would protect them from the cold and the spray, as the boat was racing along at more than 38 knots. The ends of the underwear, on wrists and ankles, were tight and almost waterproof, so that if a crew member fell into the water, his chances of survival were doubled. (The English Channel in autumn can kill a man in less than 20 minutes if he is not sufficiently protected from the cold.) A model-35 steel helmet would be required equipment on the S130 when on operation against Allied ships.

Rabe had realized by studying the Kreigsmarine statistics that a large number of German sailors on S-Boote had been mortally wounded in the head or at the nape of the neck during fighting against British crews, either by direct gunfire or by shrapnel, because they were not wearing their helmets.

(1)The Daimler-Benz diesel engineers calculated that after a half hour at more than 42 knots, the engines could develop serious problems.

The Stichtaktik
Attack technique of the S-Boote

Right:
A school flotilla on Baltic Sea in 1944.

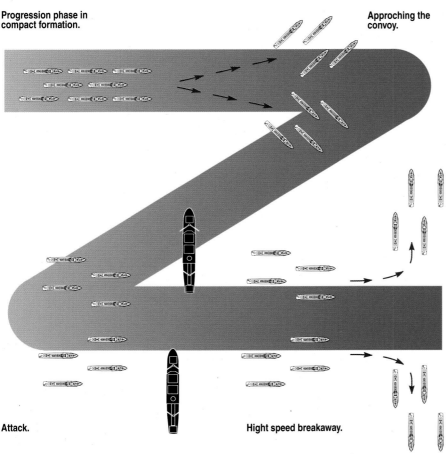

Progression phase in compact formation.

Approching the convoy.

Attack.

Hight speed breakaway.

Total Allied losses in 1944 :

Ships sunk by the S-Boote:

- 12 British merchant ships.   25 856 tons
- 21 warships, including :
- 4 armed trawlers,
- 3 fleet towboats (2 GB, 1 US),
- 5 American L.S.T.s
- 4 British L.C.T.s   14 619 tons
- 1 British L.C.I.
- 2 British frigates
- 2 British MTBs

Total:
33 ships representing 40 475 tons

Total Allied losses due to mines between June and December 1945 on the western front:

- 4 squadron mine-sweepers :
  1 US, 3 GB   4 678 tons
- 8 coastal mine-sweepers :
  5 US, 3 GB   1 720 tons
- 8 destroyers : 4 US, 4 GB   13 351 tons
- 1 corvette GB
- 1 submarine chaser US   370 tons
- 1 troop transport ship US   8 101 tons
- 1 troop transport ship GB   7 177 tons
- 1 hospital ship GB   4 220 tons
  tank transport ship GB   2 678 tons
- 1 mine-layer US   3 056 tons
- 1 light cruiser GB   5 600 tons
- 1 MGB   142 tons
- 1 MTB

TOTAL :
30 warships, for   51 093 tons
28 merchant ships for   95 855 tons

Grand total of ships sunk: 146 948 tons.

the S-Bootwaffe deployment on the Western Front :
(At the beginning of January 1945,)

2nd S-Boote flotilla stationed at Den Helder :
S174, S177, S180, S181, S209, S210, S221. (The S176 was under repair in the Wilhelmshaven naval shipyards).
Flotilla leader : Kapitänleutnant Hermann Opdenhoff

4th S-Boote flotilla based in Rotterdam :
S202, S204, S205, S703 [1].
Flotilla leader : Korvettenkapitän Kurt Fimmen.

5th S-Boote flotilla : had left the eastern Baltic Sea in August 1944, and also moved to Den Helder in mid-January: S48, S67, S85, S92, S98, S110, S127.
Flotilla leader : Kapitänleutnant Hermann Holzapfel.

6th S-Boote flotilla, also stationed in Rotterdam :
S211, S212, S222, S223, S704. (The badly damaged S705 and S706 were in dry dock at Wilhelmshaven).
Flotilla leader : Kapitänleutnant Jens Matzen.

8th S-Boote flotilla, based in Ijmuiden :
S194, S196, S197, S199, S701. (The S193, badly damaged after an air raid, was no longer capable of participating in operations. The S195, partially destroyed, was in dry dock at Emden.)
Flotilla leader : Korvettenkapitän Felix Zymalkowski.

9th S-Boote flotilla, with only 4 out of 6 boats operational : S130, S168, S175 and S206. (The S167 and S207 were under repair in Rotterdam with hull and propeller damage [2].
Flotilla leader : Korvettenkapitän Götz Friedrich von Mirbach.

---

1 – The S201 was in drydock in Bergen under repair and the S220 in Wilhelmshaven for rudder trouble.
2 – The S112 was also under repair in Saint Peter Port with two damaged propellors.

Top:
An S171-type S-Boote from the 8th flotilla based in Ijmuiden photographed off the coast of Holland at the end of 1944. The design of the boat has changed drastically since the first models came off the drawing boards at the beginning of the war. The bridge has been modified to create the *Kalottenbrücke*, an armor-plated cubicle, and the auxiliary weapons have been improved with a low-lying rapid-fire 20-mm piece in the prow, a Bofors 40-mm cannon in the stern, and two MG 34s mounted on a turret on each side behind the pilot's bridge. Notice the flotilla insignia, an antelope in a circle. The letter « A » was a means of rapidly identifying the unit within the flotilla.

Above:
The S99 zooming along in the Baltic Sea in 1945 as part of the 2nd training flotilla. She was commanded by Leutnant zur See Nienstedt.

Below:
The S212 photographed at the end of 1944 or the beginning of 1945. At the time she was assigned to the 6th S-Boote flotilla commanded by Kapitänleutnant Jens Matzen. The « S » painted on the hull beside the *Kalottenbrücke* is the first letter of the name of the gunboat commander, Leutnant zur See Alfred Schannow. The S212 was turned over to the Royal Navy in 1945 and rebaptized MTB 5212. She remained in service until 1957.

Above : S-Boote maneuvering in the Baltic Sea in 1945. The number « 6 » on either side of the hull of the first boat could mean that these are units belonging to a training flotilla with novice crews.

Below : An S170-type S-Boote at top speed launching a torpedo. In spite of the mediocre quality of the snapshot, we can see the members of the crew on the bridge wearing their leather clothing which protected them from the cold and the spray.

Above:
Exercises in the Baltic Sea in 1944 involving S38-type vessels from the 3rd training flotilla. The old battleship *Schleswig-Holstein,* launched in 1906, can be seen in the background. She was used during WWII as a training ship.

Including the 5th flotilla brought in for reinforcement, that made a total of 32 craft ready for battle. Petersen's staff had established a previsionary estimate at the beginning of the year for 50 operational units with stores of 950 mines (450 LMBs, 400 UMBs), 1 600 m³ of fuel and 140 model T1 G7A torpedoes. Supply problems prevented the different flotillas from receiving the planned quantities.

Until January 9, all operations were suspended because of bad weather. When it wasn't rain and fog so thick you could cut it with a knife, it was snow and a force-4 to – 5 wind which made any kind of sorties impossible. A first major mine-laying operation took place during the night of January 14-15, between Dunkerque and the mouth of the Humber, with the participation of the 2nd and 5th flotillas and a total of fourteen gunboats [1]. 39 mines were scattered during that night by the S-Boote. On January 19, convoy FN6 became the next victim of the German mines [2]. During this sortie, the S180 [3] hit a UMB and sank south of Hoek-van-Holland.

In the night of January 15-16, the 2nd and 5th flotillas [4] again left their base in Den Helder with the mission of intercepting a convoy spotted north of Cromer. The Germans were attacked several times without sustaining any losses, but they were unable to locate the British ships and so the gunboats had to turn back to their base in the early morning. During the same night the 8th flotilla sent out the S194, S196, S197, S199 and S701. This time, and in spite of several attacks

by the Coastal Command planes, the S-Boote were able to find the Allied ships and seriously damaged a British tank transport ship, LST 415 (1 625 tons). Sorties and mine-laying were to continue in spite of difficult weather conditions.

In the night of January 22-23, three convoys were once again detected in the zone around the Schelde. The 8th, 9th, 4th and 6th flotillas, with a total of 16 boats, left Hoek-van-Holland and Ijmuiden to cut off the British and American ships. On the enemy side, the Royal Navy had lined up 44 MGBs, the frigate Torrington and the sloop Guillemot to insure protection of their ships. The 8th and 6th flotillas were the first to establish contact with one of the convoys, but the Germans were unable to get in close enough. At 22 :54, S-Boote from the 9th flotilla were finally able to break through the Royal Navy defenses. From 1 500 meters away, the S168 and S175 launched their four torpedoes toward a large freighter. The British steamship *Halo* (2 365 tons) was hit twice and capsized within ten minutes, taking with her her crew members. The English reacted immediately with the frigate Stayner and four MTBs [5] opening fire simultaneously on the two gunboats, which had not had time to retreat. The S168 received a 76-mm shell that destroyed one of her torpedo launching-tubes. In spite of the damage, the two boats, with their diesel engines wide open, were able to escape from their enemies.

All night long the flotillas would try to get into the convoys, but they were unable to prevail against the Royal Navy fighting ships [6]. Around

3 :00 AM, several units of the 8th flotilla [7] reached the mouth of the Thames near the Fort Tongue Sand [8] batteries. Suddenly the Metox Fumb on the S701 started to crackle, meaning there were boats at a distance of 6 000 meters. The 5 S-Boote immediately spun around and sped off in the direction of what appeared to be a convoy, in an attempt to intercept it. The English ships suddenly loomed up less than 1 500 meters away, and within a few seconds ten torpedoes [9] had almost simultaneously ripped out of their tubes.

1 – 5th flotilla, with the S98, S67, S127, S48, S92, S85 ; 2nd flotilla, with the S221, S176, S210, S180, S174, S209, S181, S177. British convoy FS 97 was in that zone on the morning of the 15th and lost the Dalemoor (5 835 tons).
2 – Ships sunk : the English steamship *Grainton* (6 341 tons) and the Norwegian freighter *Carrier* (3 036 tons).Ships damaged : the tanker *San Nicolas* (2 391 tons) and the freighters *Empire Milner* (8 135 tons) and *Leaside Park* (7 160 tons).
3 – S180, commanded by Oberleutnant zur See Albrecht Pillet. The gunboat hit a German mine probably laid during night operations on January 14-15.
4 – 2nd flotilla : S221, S174, S209, S181 ; 5th flotilla : S98, S67, S92, S48.
5 – MTBs 495, 496, 497 and 446.
6 – The 4th and 6th flotillas were intercepted north and northeast of Ostende by several groups of MTBs which repelled every attempted attack.
7 – S194, S196, S197, S199 and S701
8 – The *Tongue Sand Fort* was part of a group of seven concrete towers built to reinforce the air defense system around greater London. The Admiralty had furnished Navy guns which had been installed in four towers. Their range permitted them to fire on small Kreigsmarine boats.
9 – Eight T1 G7As and two T5 G7 es Zaunkönigs.

S186: Oberleutnant zur See Ludwig Ritter
S191: Leutnant zur See Günther Benja
S215: Oberleutnant zur See Heinz-Dieter Mohs
S224: Leutnant zur See Bruno Klockow

11th flotilla
Leader: Kapitänleutnant Nikolai Baron von Stempel
S170: Obstrm. Odermann
S208: Obstrm. Mauroschat
Support ship: Tanga
Commander: Oberleutnant zur See Johann Wortmann

1st S-Boote division

Division leader: Fregattenkapitän Herbert Schultz
3rd S-Boote flotilla
Leader: Kapitänleutnant Günther Schulz

Group 1
Group leader: Oberleutnant zur See Günther Milbradt
S30: Oberleutnant zur See Gunnar Kelm
S36: Leutnant zur See Rudolf Svoboda
S61: Oberleutnant zur See Jürgen Hardtke

Group 2 (former 7th flotilla)
Group leader: Oberleutnant zur See Hans-Georg Buschmann
S151: Leutnant zur See Hellmuth Greiner
S152: Obstrm. Erich Mensch
S153: Oberleutnant zur See Hans Wulf Heckel
S154: Obstrm. Erwin Schipke
S156: Reserve Oberleutnant zur See Marxen
S157: Oberleutnant zur See Hans-Ulrich Liebhold

Group 3 (former 24th flotilla)
Group leader: Oberleutnant zur See Hermann Bollenhagen
S621: Oberleutnant zur See Wernicke
S623: Oberleutnant zur See Elksneit
S626: Leutnant zur See Klaus Burba
S627: Leutnant zur See Paul Overwaul
S628: Under repair
S629: Leutnant zur See Ernst-Günter Müller
S630: Oberleutnant zur See Cartagna (Italian crew)

S-Boote Training Division

Division leader: Korvettenkapitän Klaus Feldt
Support ship: Buea
Commander: Oberleutnant zur See Ludwig Stölzer
Support ship: Hermann-von-Wissmann
Commander: Oberleutnant zur See Gert Vassel

1st training flotilla
Leader: Kapitänleutnant Friedrich-Wilhelm Wilcke
S62: Oberleutnant zur See Hermann Rost
S79: Oberleutnant zur See Hermann Zeiler
S89: Oberleutnant zur See Jasper Osterloh
S90: Reserve Leutnant zur See Gärbers
S109: Reserve Leutnant zur See Kopperneck
S133: Leutnant zur See Günter Schiersmann
Support ship: Adolf-Lüderitz
Commander: Oberleutnant zur See August Gauland

2nd training flotilla
Leader: Kapitäntleutnant Hans-Helmut Klose
S64: Oberleutnant zur See Karl Deckert
S69: Leutnant zur See Eberhard Runge
S76: Oberleutnant zur See Wildner
S81: Oberleutnant zur See Bernhard Wülfing
S83: Leutnant zur See Carl Hoffmann
S99: Leutnant zur See Nienstedt
S117: Oberleutnant zur See Hans-Viltor Howaldt
S135: Oberleutnant zur See Hans-Jürgen Schwepcke
Support ship: Tsingtau
Commander: Oberleutnant zur See Kurt Kmetsch

3rd training flotilla
Leader: Kapitänleutnant Hans Detlefsen
S21, S22, S24, S25, S65, S65, S68, S82, S95, S97, S101, S103, S105, S107, S108, S113, S115, S116, S118, S120, S122, S123
Support ship: Carl-Peters
Commander: Oberleutnant zur See Walter Reuthal

The three training flotillas wer stationed in the Baltic Sea.

Organisation of the S-Bootewaffe in febuary 1945

Leader of the S-Bootwaffe: Kommodore Rudolf Petersen
Chief of staff: Korvettenkapitän Heinrich Erdmann

1st flotilla
Leader: Korvettenkapitän Hermann Büchting
S216: Kapitänleutnant Ernst-August Seevers
S225: Oberleutnant zur See Gërhard Behrens
S707: Oberleutnant zur See Peter Neumeier

2nd flotilla
Leader: Korvettenkapitän Hermann Opdenhoff
S174: Kapitänleutnant Hugo Wendler
S176: Oberleutnant zur See Friedrich Stockfleth
S177: Oberleutnant zur See Karl Boseniuk
S181: Oberleutnant zur See Martin Schlenck
S209: Oberleutnant zur See Kurt Neugebauer
S210: Oberleutnant zur See Günter Weisheit
S221: Oberleutnant zur See Schneider

4th flotilla
Leader: Korvettenkapitän Kurt Fimmen
S201: Obstrm. Wilhelm Kohrt
S202: Kapitänleutnant Joachim Wiencke
S204: Reserve Leutnant zur See Claus Hinrichs
S205: Oberleutnant zur See Hans Neuburger
S219: Oberleutnant zur See Dietrich Howaldt
S220: Kapitänleutnant Helmut Dross
S703: Reserve Oberleutnant zur See Dieter Steinhauer

5th flotilla
Leader: Kapitänleutnant Hermann Holzapfel
S67: Leutnant zur See Heiko Buddecke
S85: Leutnant zur See Hans-L. Reimers

S92: Oberleutnant zur See Fritz Schay
S98: Leutnant zur See Heinrich Horkisch
S110: Oberleutnant zur See Johann Schmölzer
S127: Oberleutnant zur See Hinrich Ahrens
S132: Obstrm. Heinz Deppe

6th flotilla
Leader: Kapitänleutnant Hens Matzen
S211: Oberleutnant zur See d August Licht
S212: Obstrm. Alfred Schannow
S213: Leutnant zur See Reinhard Bucher
S222: Leutnant zur See Breithaupt
S223: Oberleutnant zur See Enno Brandi
S704: Oberleutnant zur See Georg Korn
S705: Kapitänleutnant Hans Karl Hemmer
S706: Oberleutnant zur See Wilhelm Waldhausen

8th flotilla
Leader: Korvettenkapitän Felix Zymalkowski
S193: Under repair
S194: Kapitänleutnant Siegfried Wörmcke
S195: KapitänleutnanWalter Knapp
S196: Oberleutnant zur See Günter Rathenow
S197: Oberleutnant zur See Wulff Fanger
S199: Oberleutnant zur See Horst Schuur
S701: Oberleutnant zur See Ulrich Toermer

9th flotilla
Leader: Korvettenkapitän Götz Friedrich von Mirbach
S130: Kapitänleutnant Günter Rabe
S167: Leutnant zur See Seifert
S168: Oberleutnant zur See Dau
S175: Oberleutnant zur See Franz Behr
S206: Kapitänleutnant Ulrich Roeder
S207: Oberleutnant zur See Hans Schirren
S214: Oberleutnant zur See Rudolph Beck
S112: Leutnant zur See Nikelowski

10th flotilla
Leader: Kapitänleutnant Dietrich Bludau

They missed all their targets, but two destroyers and several groups of MTBs[1] rushed in to counter the Germans. As always happened during direct fighting, everything went very quickly in a deluge of fire and spray. The S701[2] and S199 rammed into each other. The former was nevertheless able to move away, thanks to her powerful engines, but the S199[3] was so badly damaged that her crew decided to abandon her. The Fort Tongue Sand coastal batteries dealt the final blow and sank her several hours later. MTB 495 was seriously damaged by German fire during the action.

The daily activity of the S-Boote and the losses incurred because of the German mine-laying operations[4], resulted in a decision by the Bomber Command headquarters to bomb the port of Ijmuiden again. On February 3, between 16:07 and 16:11, 17 Lancasters from the 9th squadron dropped 17 5.4-ton Tallboys on the S-Boote bunker. A second raid took place on the 8th, with this time 15 Lancasters from Squadron 617 using the same types of bombs against the same target. The Germans had learned their lesson in Le Havre, and had scattered their units around and carefully camouflaged them during the two attacks. There were no German losses. In spite of their numerical inferiority, the Schnellbootwaffe crews still represented a serious threat to the Royal Navy. Even though the number of British escort ships was constantly increased, and the English and Americans overwhelmingly controlled the skies, the presence of these little gunboats in the paths of the convoys, where they continued to undertake daily offensive action, would create a real problem for the Allied High Command right up to the end of the war.

Mine-laying operations continued throughout the month of February. During the night of the

1 – HMS Seymour, HMS Guillemot, MTB.s 451, 452, 450, 495, 446, 454, 447
2 – The S701 was immobilized until the end of the war when she was ceded to the American Navy.
3 – S199, commanded by Oberleutnant zur See Achim Quistorp
4 – Two freighters torpedoed, five freighters sunk by mines, two others seriously damaged and a 165-ton British coastal minesweeper sunk during the month of January.
5 – MTBs 763 and 770.

18th, the 2nd flotilla operated in the sector around the Humber, where 20 mines were laid. Five days later, the Combattante was patrolling north of the Norfolk coast with 2 MTBs[5]. Around 23:45, near the East Dudgeon buoy, the French ship was hurtled into the air by a violent explosion which cut her in two at the level of her smokestack. The magnetic mine, which had been triggered twenty meters below at the moment the ship passed

Top :
The S204 arriving in the port of Felixstowe on May 13, 1945. The boat, part of the 4th flotilla, had left her base in The Helder that morning with the S205. On board Rear Admiral Erich Alfred Breuning, Commander in Chief of the German naval forces stationed in Holland, coming to surrender to the British. He is accompanied by Korvettenkapitän Kurt Fimmen, leader of the 4th flotilla, and Kapitänleutnant Bernd Rebensburg, Chief of naval operations at Petersen's headquarters.

Right:
The S98 photographed in mid-May, 1945, in an unidentified port. This boat was part of the S92-S99 series launched in 1943 and built by the Lürssen shipyards. She has a low armored pilot's bridge and more powerful guns used only on this series. The S98 was turned over to the American Navy in 1945, then transferred in 1950 to the Norwegian Navy and renamed *Kvikk*. She remained in service until July, 1957.

Below :
The S95 photographed beside the suppport ship *Carl Peters*. This unit entered service in February, 1943, then became part of the 3rd training flotilla. She was turned over to the Royal Navy in 1945.

directly over it, had worked perfectly. 64 men died during the wreck, many having been blocked inside the vessel, and 120 were picked up by the Royal Navy ships sent out immediately to the site. These included the commander, Corvette Captain Pépin Lehalleur. Less than a year after she had sunk the S147 and S141[1], fate turned against the Free French ship.

On February 25, the armed trawler *Aquarius*

Left:
Five S-Boote of the S701-709 type, photographed after the German surrender on May 8, 1945. The boats are intact. Among them notice the S219, launched in 1944, and which ended the war in the 4th S-Boote flotilla under the orders of Korvettenkapitän Kurt Fimmen. The gunboat had been commanded by Oberleutnant zur See Dietrich Howaldt and was surrendered to the Russians on November 5, 1945.

(187 tons), was the next victim. And on February 28, the freighters *City of Lincoln* (8 039 tons) and Cydonia (3 517 tons), were also badly damaged by German mines. Six flotillas[2] with a total of 22 boats left their Dutch bases on the night of February 22, heading for the east coast of England with a mission of intercepting convoy FS 1734, travelling north-east of Great Yarmouth. The 2nd and 5th flotillas were the first to attack,

with nine gunboats racing forward in the dark at a speed in excess of 38 knots. Two British freighters, the *Goodwood* (2 780 tons) and the *Blacktoft* (1 109 tons), were sunk, and a Norwegian steamship, the *Skjold* (1 345 tons) badly damaged by the S-Boote artillery. In the meantime, the 8th flotilla had targetted a small convoy of landing vessels in the Thames estuary and sunk LCP 707. However they lost the S193[3], destroyed by the British escort ships. And the 4th, 6th and 9th flotillas[4], laid a barrage of mines along the convoy route between the Thames and the Escaut. In spite of several passes by the Coastal Command planes over their heads, the S-Boote were able to complete their mission and get back to their bases in Holland[5]. Mine-laying operations would continue without interruption to the end of the month.

On the night of February 28, four gunboats from the 4th flotilla set out for the estuary of the Schelde. In less than 20 minutes, 20 UMBs disappeared into the icy waters of the North Sea. At 23 :00, with their mission accomplished,

1 – S147 sunk on April 26, 1944 ; S141 sunk on May 13, 1944.
2 – 2nd, 4th, 6th, 5th, 8th and 9th flotillas
3 – S193, commanded by Oberleutnant zur See Horst Schuur
4 – The S167, commanded by Oberleutnant zur See Seifert, ran into another boat on the way back and was scuttled on the spot by her crew.
5 – The outcome of this operation was the loss of four Allied ships:
On February 26: the British freighter *Auretta* (4 751 tons)
On February 26: the American freighter *Nashaba* (6 054 tons)
On February 27: the British freighter *Sampa* (7 219 tons)
On March 10: the Liberty Ship *Robert L. Vann* (7 176 tons).

Top: **Three S-Boote from the 9th flotilla have just surrendered to the British with their crews in May 1945. These S700-type gunboats were put into service in July, 1944. The first unit has already docked ; her deck armament is complete with the exception of the 20-mm cannon located in the prow which has been dismantled.**

Left: **The surrender of the S76 in May, 1945.**
An S38-type vessel, entering service in May, 1942, s he was among the first to receive an armored bridge. She was engaged with the 6th flotilla in Norway and then transferred to the western front until February, 1944, when she left for the Baltic to participate in operations against the Soviets. In June, 1944, the S76 was back on the western front as part of the 6th flotilla based in Ijmuiden. Then at the end of 1944 she was assigned to the 2nd training flotilla, and participated on May 8 and 9, 1945, in the evacuation, through the port of Libau, Latvia, of part of the troops of the German 16th and 18th Armies surrounded by the Russians in Courland.

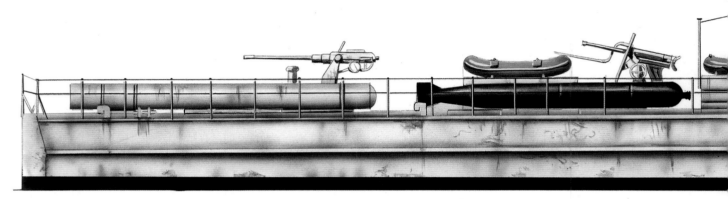

B.PAUTIGNY

Schnellboote S701

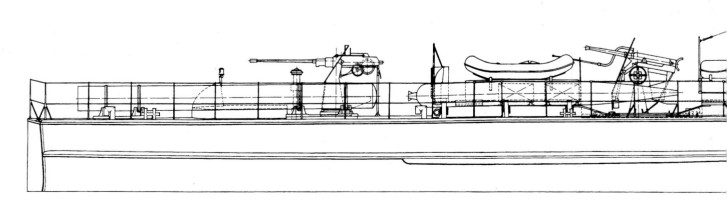

(Lürssen drawing)

The S701 in April, 1945. This gunboat was part of the 8th flotilla based in Ijmuiden, and was commanded by Oberleutnant zur See Ulrich Toemer. The S701 had been delivered to the S-Bootwaffe in July, 1944, by the firm Danziger WaggonFabrik which built the S701-S709 series. She was 34,94 meters long with a 124-ton displacement, and propelled by three 2500-hp Mercedes Benz MB 511 engines allowing her to reach a top speed of 44 knots using the Lürssen Effekt. Her radius of action at 35 knots was 700 nautical miles. As were the preceding series, the vessel was armed with two 533-mm torpedo tubes, capable of launching four G7es T5 Zaunkönig torpedoes with acoustic heads, as well as traditional torpedoes. Secondary weapons included a 40-mm Bofors Flak 28 cannon in the rear, the double 20-mm Flak 38 turret in the center and a 20-mm Flak 38 piece in the low firing dugout up front. The following models of the S702-S709 series had two 20-mm model 41 Flak 38 cannon mounted on a three-gun turret located in the center of the boat. Radar equipment : a FUMB antenna, a FUMB 10 Borkum radar, a FUMO 62 Hohentwiel radar. The crew was made up of two officers and 28 men. The S701 was surrendered to the U.S. Navy in 1945 and then sold to the Dutch Navy.

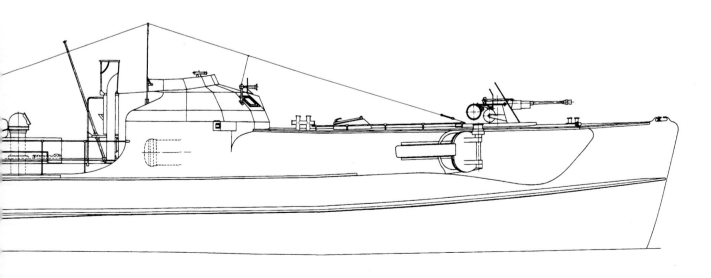

the Germans headed back toward Rotterdam, travelling at a speed of 25 knots. But the English were waiting for them. The destroyer *Cotswold* and the frigate *Seymour* opened fire with their main guns. The S220 took a hit in the machine room, setting off a fire which rapidly spread to the rest of the boat. The commander, Kapitänleutnant Dross, sent out the order to abandon ship, and she soon capsized. The crew was saved by the British escort ships. The score for February was thus 2 freighters torpedoed by the S-Boote for a total of 3 889 tons, and 10 other Allied ships (19 551 tons) lost to the lethal mines planted near the Belgian and Dutch coasts[1]. It was just two months before the German capitulation, but S-Bootwaffe activity on the western front had not let up. Witness this excerpt from a note from the Home Fleet dated May 1, 1945 :

Attacks by German motor torpedo boats against our convoys have increased during the last three months, notably by the use of new and more daring approach techniques. Our enemies use two or three boats operating in small independent groups, which makes the possibility of interception by our escort ships increasingly difficult. The action of the Coastal Command planes, in spite of regular sorties and a total absence of enemy aircraft, is unable to stem the offensives of the Kriegsmarine units. In spite of a power ratio unfavorable to them, they represent a constant threat to our maritime traffic.

131 sorties took place during March and several convoys were attacked. During the night of March 18-19, the S705 and S706 were patrolling off Lowestoft with other units of the 6th flotilla[2]. After having laid their mines, the S-Boote intercepted convoy FS 1759, which lost two freighters, the *Rogate* (2 871 tons) and the *Chrichtoun* (1 097 tons). The next day four flotillas [3] repeated the previous day's operation between the Thames and the Escaut. The mines laid by the S-Boote were responsible for the sinking of the British transport ships *Samselbu* (7 523 tons) and *Empire Blessing* (7 062 tons) on March 19. Then on the 20th, the British tank transport LST 80, displacing 2 750 tons, and the American Liberty Ship, the *Hadley F. Brown* (7 176 tons). The series continued until March 22 with three other ships, the Greek freighter *Eleftheria* (7 247 tons), the Liberty Ship *Charles D. MacIver* (7 176 tons) and the British ML 466 (75 tons)[4].

On March 26, the 4th flotilla was again operating on the Thames-Schelde line. In spite of several attempts by a destroyer and a group of MTBs to intercept them, the four S-Boote, two hours after leaving their ports, were able to lay sixteen UMBs which would be responsible for sinking three ships[5] two days later. The English reacted during the night of March 21st, when three Bristol Beaufighters from Squadron 236 launched a rocket attack against elements of the 2nd flotilla north of Texel Island. The S181 [6] took several hits on the pilot's bridge and on section VII of the gunboat structure where the fuel tanks were located. Kapitänleutnant Hermann Opdenhoff, leader of the 2nd flotilla, who had come on board to participate in

1 – Between January 1 and May 8, 1945, the S-Boote torpedoed six ships for a total of 12 972 tons. 25 other Allied ships, for 75 999 tons, were lost to mines. And seven more boats representing 26 408 tons were damaged and immobilized for several months.
2 – S211, S212, S213, S222, S704, S705, S706.
3 – 2nd, 4th, 5th and 9th flotillas.
4 – The March 22 losses were probably the result of mines laid by the 9th flotilla ; those of March 26 from mines laid by the 4th flotilla.
5 – British LCP 840 (11 tons), the Belgian trawler *Saint Jan* (11 tons) and the English tanker *Belinda* (8 325 tons).
6 – The S210 was also hit by the British fighter-bombers and 14 sailors were killed.

the operation, was killed instantly, as was the commander, Oberleutnant zur See Martin Schlenck and four crew members[1].

On April 6, in spite of the losses of two weeks before, the 2nd flotilla was once again back in operation with a new leader, Kapitänleutnant Hugo Wendler. Six gunboats[2] would try to intercept a convoy that had been sighted near the Humber River estuary. Two British escorters, the frigate *Cubitt* and the destroyer *Haydon*, were able to prevent the Germans from approaching. Facing an opponent with superior numbers and fire power, the S-Boote preferred to retreat, but not before laying 36 LMBs, nevertheless. But luck would be against Petersen's men that night. The gunboats were sighted by a Coastal Command Wellington, which immediately radioed the news to three MTBs belonging to the 22nd flotilla based in Lowestoft. It took the British boats only 20 minutes to suddenly erupt in the center of the German formation. The fighting lasted for an hour and a half. MTBs 494 and 493 were blasting away so close to the S176 and S177[3] that they all ran into each other. The result was heavy losses on both sides. The S176 sank along with MTB 494; the two boats had crashed into each other and the ensuing fire was impossible for either boat to extinguish. The situation of the S177 was no better. Her commander, Oberleutnant zur See Karl Boseniuk, was seriously wounded by fire from MTB 497, and her crew had to abandon ship. The English managed to tow MTB 493 back to Lowestoft, but she was declared irretrievable[4].

The following night, and in spite of the losses incurred the previous day, the Germans were back in operation[5]. The 4th and 6th flotillas with thirteen vessels[6] were able to lay 52 mines in the lanes used almost daily by the convoys travelling between the mouths of the Thames and the Schelde. During this mission the MTBs would once again try to intercept the enemy boats. The S202 and S703, travelling at full speed to try to escape their assaillants, were unable to avoid each other and crashed[7].

The last sortie of the Ijmuiden-based units took place during the night of April 12, 1945. Twelve S-Boote, including parts of the 4th, 6th and 9th flotillas, laid 48 mines around the Flessingen north channel. The Royal Navy units were immediately alerted and reacted hastily, with several MTBs accompanied by the destroyer Hambleton and the frigate Ekins, responding to the German intrusion. The S205 was hit by a 76-mm shell which exploded in compartment VI, damaging the radio cabin. In spite of the damage, her commander, Kapitänleutnant Hans Jürgen Seeger,

---

1 – Three S-Boote were sunk in March. On March 30, 1945, 358 B-24 Liberators from the American 8th Air Force launched a raid over Wilhelmshaven and destroyed the S186, S194, and S224.
2 –S174, S176, S177, S209, S210, and S221.
3 –S176, commanded by Oberleutnant zur See Wilhelm Stockfleth; S177, commanded by Oberleutnant zur See Karl Boseniuk.
4 –M.T.B. 5 001 was also sunk by simultaneous fire from the canons of the S209 and S210.
5 –On April 7, between 19 :24 and 19 :40, Bomber Command Squadron 617 attacked the Ijmuiden base with 15 Lancasters, 2 Mosquitos and 24 Spitfires, targetting the S-Bunker and the port installations. 80 tons of bombs were dropped onto the port.
6 –4th S-Boote flotilla: S205, S204, S219, S202, S703, S304; 6th S-Boote flotilla: S222, S705, S211, S223, S704, S212, S706.
7 –S703, under Oberleutnant zur See Dieter Steinhauer; S202, under Kapitänleutnant Joachim Wiencke, who was killed in the crash. Both boats capsized shortly later. The S223, commanded by Oberleutnant Erno Brandi, hit a mine on the same night and sank off Ostende.

Left: **Three S-Boote from the 9th flotilla have just surrendered to the British with their crews in May 1945. These S700-type gunboats were put into service in July, 1944. The first unit has already docked ; her deck armament is complete with the exception of the 20-mm cannon located in the prow which has been dismantled.**

was able to leave the combat zone, once again thanks to the exceptional power of the three M.B. 511 engines, reaching a speed of more than 41 knots[1].

On the German home front, the situation started deteriorating rapidly from April on. On the 3rd, Münster fell, then Essen and Hanover on the 10th. By mid-April the Ruhr was invaded and the 320,000 men of Army Group B capitulated. Holland was ready to fall, under pressure from the British and American armies. The situation of the Schnellbootwaffe, compared to that of the rest of the German military machine, was not so bad. 21 boats[2] were still operational at their Dutch bases, but they were severely lacking in fuel, torpedoes and spare parts[3]. Likewise the port of Egersund in Norway harbored nine gunboats right up to the German capitulation: the S195, S302, S303 and S709 belonging to the 8th flotilla, and the S62, S79, S86, S89 and S133, being used for training by the 1st training flotilla. Between January and the end of April, the S-Boote destroyed 31 transport ships, sunk mostly thanks to the mines laid along the Allied convoy shipping lanes, for a total of 88,971 tons [4].

S.W. Roskill, the British naval historian, expressed the general feeling of the British as regards their adversaries:

The S-Boote were remarkably designed and their crews fought valiantly up until the end of the war. If they had been used with efficient support vessels and in tight collaboration with the Luftwaffe planes, they could have caused much greater losses to our shipping. The tenacity and the crusading spirit of their crews made them respectable adversaries.

On May 13, 1945, two S-Boote from the 4th flotilla, the S204 and S205, undertook for the last time the crossing of the North Sea toward England. They left their base at Den Helder at 9 :00 AM with on board Rear Admiral Erich Alfred Breuning[5], coming to sign the surrender of the German naval forces based in Holland. He was accompanied by Korvettenkapitän Kurt Fimmen, leader of the 4th flotilla, and Kapitänleutnant Bernd Rebensburg, Petersen's chief of naval operations. The English left Felixstowe at the same time, with ten MTBs, to meet the Ger-

THE EVACUATION OF THE KURZEME PENINSULA

The order to evacuate the Kurzeme beachhead in Latvia came on May 3, 1945: once again the Kriegsmarine units stationed in the Baltic Sea were confronted with an impossible situation. 250 000 soldiers had pulled back into the ports of Windau and Libau, completely surrounded by several Soviet armies. The only alternative to the Soviet steam roller was a massive operation involving all available German sea-going vessels.
On May 7, all the S-Boote working with the 2nd training flotilla arrived at the docks of the port in Libau with orders to begin evacuating the troops. At the beginning of December the battle front had been stabilized twelve kilometers outside the city, and the Soviet advanced guard had not yet appeared. In the afternoon the German gunboats started taking the men on board, one hundred for each S-Boote, with the support ship Tsingtau providing cover. The latter alone could transport two thousand wounded. By the end of the afternoon the 2nd flotilla had moved nine hundred men out of the city. Then at 19: 30, sixty-five ships of various types started to arrive at the Libau docks and undertake evacuation operations, in spite of the raids by the Soviet assault aircraft which had started in the middle of the afternoon.
At 21: 30, as Libau was on the point of falling to the Russians, the last S-Boote left the city.
The following S-Boote participated in this operation: the 1st flotilla, with the S707, S217, S218, S225, S226; the 5th flotilla, with the S127, S67, S85, S92, S48 and S110; the 2nd training flotilla, with the S64, S69, S76, S81, S99, S117 and S135. The three flotillas alone evacuated 2000 men. Each boat was 13 tons overweight when it took to sea[1].
On May 9, the 16th and 18th German Armies, unable to break through the Soviet forces surrounding them, surrendered, and 42 generals, 8 038 officers, 181,032 enlisted men, along with 14 000 Latvian volunteers, marched off to Soviet prison camps[2]. 14 400 soldiers had been evacuated by the Kriegsmarine.

1 – To get rid of as much weight as possible, the S-Boote fired their two torpedoes once they were at sea.
2 – The last German prisoners were freed by the Russians in 1957.

1 – As a result of these mine-laying operations the Allies lost:
On April 15: the freighter *Conakrian* (4 876 tons);
On April 16: the English tanker *Gold Schell* (8 208 tons);
On April 22: the American Liberty Ship *Benjamin H. Bristow* (7 191 tons); On May 8: the American Liberty Ship *Horace Binney* (7 191 tons).
2 – Four boats of the 4th flotilla (S204, S205, S219, S304) in Den Helder; seventeen boats of the 2nd flotilla (S210, S221), 8th flotilla (S197, S701), 9th flotilla (S130, S168, S175, S206,

S207, S214), 6th flotilla (S211, S212, S213, S222, S704, S705, S706) in Rotterdam.
3 – On April 10, 1945, there were only 900 m3 of diesel fuel left in stock for the flotillas stationed in Holland.
4 – Between January and April 1945, the flotillas fighting on the western front participated in 351 operational sorties, making an average of 87 sorties per month and 3 sorties per day.
5 – Rear Admiral Breuning was Commander-in-Chief of the Kriegsmarine naval forces on the western front.

Previous page, top :
An S-Boote surrendered to the Royal Navy in 1945.
The boat has been slightly modified and is pictured
here in 1953 during a naval review off Spithead.
The general shape has not changed much, but the British
have modified the masting and added a cubicle at the back.

Previous page, centre :
An S-Boote captured by the Royal Navy,
viewed in the port of Plymouth in July, 1945.

Left:
The S206 and S127 photographed after being turned
over to the Danish Navy by the U.S. Navy in 1947.
The S206 entered service on September 19, 1944.
She was assigned to the 9th flotilla based
at Hoeck-van-Holland and was commanded up to
the end of the war by Kapitänleutnant Ulrich Roeder.
The S127, entering service in July 1943,
was first commanded by Oberleutnant zur See Jasper Osterloh.
She joined the 8th flotilla, created in December, 1942,
and participated in fighting on the western front in 1943
and 1944. At the end of 1944, she was transferred
to the 5th flotilla in the Baltic. On May 9, 1945,
under the orders of Oberleutnant zur See Hinrich
Ahrens, she participated in the evacuation of part
of the 16th and 18th German Armies surrounded
by the Russians in the port of Libau.

On May 10, 1945, the S-Bootwaffe could still muster the following units in the Baltic Sea :

1st flotilla, S208, S216, S217, S218, S225, S707, S708, S306 ;
5th flotilla, S48, S65, S67, S85, S92, S98, S127, S132 ;
10th flotilla, S110, S215, S228, S305 ;
2nd training flotilla, S64, S69, S76, S81, S83, S99, S117, S135 ;
3rd training flotilla, S19, S20, S21, S24, S25, S50, S68, S82, S95, S97, S101, S105, S107, S108, S113, S115, S118, S120, S122, S123.
Support ships :
Tanga, Tsingtau, Carl-Peters, Buea, Hermann-von-Wissmann.

mans at the South Fall buoy and escort them to their destination. At the meeting point, several British officers boarded the S205. One of them, Captain Peter Scott, left the following account of the trip :

We still had a few dozen miles to cover before arriving in Felixstowe. This was the first time I had ever sailed on an enemy boat[1] and I was immediately impressed by the size of the S-Boote. The general silhouette was hardly visible above the surface of the water, and everything seemed to have been designed to offer minimum resistance to the elements and maximum protection for the crew when the boat was travelling at full speed. In spite of the rolling, we soon reached 30 knots. The MTBs behind us couldn't keep up, and in spite of the speed we kept perfectly dry, while my comrades on our boats had to pull on their oilskins.

The Kriegsmarine put a total of 239 S-Boote into service between 1930 and 1945. Of these, 99 survived the war intact. 127 units were sunk or scuttled on the various theaters of operations where the Schnellbootwaffe was engaged[2]. Of the 99 remaining boats, 34 were surrendered to Great Britain, 30 to the US Navy, which in 1947 ceded 14 of them to the Norwegian Navy and 13 to the Navy of Denmark. The Soviets requested 28 as war reparations. In 1951, the S130 and S208 were returned to the Bundesmarine by the Royal Navy, and ended their career as training boats.

7 500 officers and men fought in the Schnell-bootwaffe between 1939 and 1945. Among them, 149 officers, 860 petty officers and 4 639 seamen participated in operations on the western front. Losses amounted to 767 dead or missing, and 620 wounded. 322 men ended the war in Allied prison camps.

On May 13, 1945, when Rear Admiral Breu-ning, accompanied by Korvettenkäpitan Fimmen and Kapitänleutnant Rebensburg, stepped off the S204 onto the Felixstowe pier, a Royal Navy detachment greeted them with an honors salute.

Below:
Refloating an S-Boote in a British port in 1945.

Bottom :
An S-Boote seized by the British in 1945
and integrated into the Royal Navy.

---

1 – Even though the Allies had managed to capture a U-Boote, they never managed to capture a complete S-Boote during the war.
2 – On May 8, the Commonwealth coastal forces were composed of 1 383 boats, including 422 MTBs, 21 SGBs, 940 MLs and HDMLs. 143 units were also sent over by the Americans. 115 MTBs, 28 MGBs, 1 SGB and 79 MLs and HDMLs were destroyed during the seven years of the war.

Korvettenkapitän Georg Christiansen while he was still leader of the 1st S-Boote flotilla. He was promoted to that rank in March, 1943, and the photograph was taken shortly later. He was named staff officer in September and remained at headquarters until 1945. On October 1, 1939 he had taken command of the S23 in the 1st flotilla with a rank of Oberleutnant zur See.

Commanding officers
of S-Boote

Leutnant zur See Klaus Feldt pictured in November of 1939 just after taking command of the brand new S30, recently delivered to the 2nd flotilla. He was named Kapitänleutnant in 1941 and took command of the 2nd flotilla between November 1941 and February 1944. From there he was promoted to Schnellbootwaffe headquarters and ended the war with the rank of Korvettenkapitän.

Kapitänleutnant Felix Zymalkowski photographed in 1942 before taking over as commander of the 8th S-Boote flotilla, a job he would keep until the end of the war.

Oberleutnant zur See Kurt Fimmen with his Knight's Iron Cross received on August 18, 1940. At that time he was commanding the S26 in the 1st S-Boote flotilla. On May 31, 1940, the S26 and Oberleutnant zur See Christiansen's S23 sank the French escort ship Cyclone. Kurt Fimmen ended the war as Korvettenkapitän at the head of the 4th flotilla.

Kapitänleutnant Siegfried Wuppermann in 1943 as commander of the 1st S-Boote division, made up of the 3rd flotilla which had been divided into three combat groups. On October 1, 1939, he had taken command of the S20 in the 1st flotilla with the rank of Oberleutnant zur See, and had participated in the fighting during May and June, 1940. In January of 1941 he changed units and took over the S60 in the 3rd flotilla. To participate in the major offensive launched against the USSR in June, he left with his unit for the Baltic Sea. At the beginning of 1942 he again changed theaters of operation: the 3rd flotilla headed for the Mediterranean and Wuppermann took command of the S58. He was named Kapitänleutnant at the end of 1942 and took over command in September 1943 of the new 21st flotilla, a job he kept until February 1944.

KL Niels Bätge

OLzs Hermann Büchting

OLzs Horst Weber

KL Karl Müller

KL Karl Ehrhard Karcher

OLzr Karl Friedrich Künzel

KL Albert Müller

OLzs Klaus Degenhard Schmidt

KL Kurt Johannsen

OLzr Heinz Haag

KL Jens Matzen

KL Werner Toniges

KK Friedrich Kemnade

KK Göte Friedrich von Mirbach

KK Hermann Opdenhoff

KL Heinz Birnbacher

KL Bernd Klug

KL Töniges

KL Klaus Feldt

OLzr Hans Schirren

Differents S-Boote series
(1930-1945)

UZ 16 W1 S1 (1932)

S2 to S5 (1932)

S6 to S13 (1935)

S14 to S25 (1936 - 1939)

S30 to S37 (1939 - 1940)

S26 to S29 (1940)

S38 to S53 (1940 - 1941)

S100 to 150 (1943)

S170 (1944)

S701 to S709 (1944 - 1945)

S-Boote produced for exportation

S1 F3 for the Bulgarian Navy

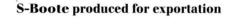

S151 to S158 for the Dutch Navy

S601 to S604 For the Yugoslavian Navy

Construction list of the S-Boote

Type	Delivered	Builder	Place	Builder	Machinery
S1 S5	1930-1932	Lürssen	Vegesack	MAN	3 X L7Z 19/30
S6 S9	1933-1934	Lürssen	Vegesack	MAN	3 X L7Z 19/30
S10 S13	1934-1935	Lürssen	Vegesack	Daimler Benz	3 X MB 502
S14 S17	1936-1938	Lürssen	Vegesack	MAN	3 X L11Z 19/30
S18 S25	1938-1939	Lürssen	Vegesack	Daimler Benz	3 X MB 501
S26	1940	Lürssen	Vegesack	Daimler Benz	3 X MB 501
S27	1940	Lürssen	Vegesack	Daimler Benz	3 X MB 501
S28 S29	1940	Lürssen	Vegesack	Daimler Benz	3 X MB 501
S30 S31	1939	Lürssen	Vegesack	Daimler Benz	3 X MB 512
S32 S33 S36	1940	Lürssen	Vegesack	Daimler Benz	3 X MB 512
S37	1940	Lürssen	Vegesack	Daimler Benz	3 X MB 512
S38	1940	Lürssen	Vegesack	Daimler Benz	3 X MB 501
S39 S40	1941	Lürssen	Vegesack	Daimler Benz	3 X MB 501
S41	1941	Lürssen	Vegesack	Daimler Benz	3 X MB 501
S42	1941	Lürssen	Vegesack	Daimler Benz	3 X MB 501
S43	1941	Lürssen	Vegesack	Daimler Benz	3 X MB 501
S44 S52	1941	Lürssen	Vegesack	Daimler Benz	3 X MB 501
S53	1941	Lürssen	Vegesack	Daimler Benz	3 X MB 501
S54 S61	1940-1941	Lürssen	Vegesack	Daimler Benz	3 X MB 512
S62 S69	1941-1943	Lürssen	Vegesack	Daimler Benz	3 X MB 501
S70 S82	1942	Lürssen	Vegesack	Daimler Benz	3 X MB 501
S83 S89	1942	Lürssen	Vegesack	Daimler Benz	3 X MB 501
S90 S91	1942	Lürssen	Vegesack	Daimler Benz	3 X MB 501
S92 S99	1943	Lürssen	Vegesack	Daimler Benz	3 X MB 501
S100	1943	Lürssen	Vegesack	Daimler Benz	3 X MB 511
S101 S105	1940-1941	Schlichting	Travemünde	Daimler Benz	3 X MB 501
S106	1941	Schlichting	Travemünde	Daimler Benz	3 X MB 501
S107 S110	1941	Schlichting	Travemünde	Daimler Benz	3 X MB 501
S111	1941	Schlichting	Travemünde	Daimler Benz	3 X MB 501
S112 S122	1942-1943	Schlichting	Travemünde	Daimler Benz	3 X MB 501
S123 S133	1943-1944	Schlichting	Travemünde	Daimler Benz	3 X MB 511
S134 S150	1943-1944	Lürssen	Vegesack	Daimler Benz	3 X MB 511
S167 S169	1943-1944	Lürssen	Vegesack	Daimler Benz	3 X MB 511
S170	1944	Lürssen	Vegesack	Daimler Benz	3 X MB 518
S171 S186	1944	Lürssen	Vegesack	Daimler Benz	3 X MB 511
S187 S194	1944	Schlichting	Travemünde	Daimler Benz	3 X MB 511
S195 S207	1944	Lürssen	Vegesack	Daimler Benz	3 X MB 511
S208	1944	Lürssen	Vegesack	Daimler Benz	3 X MB 511
S209 S218	1944-1945	Lürssen	Vegesack	Daimler Benz	3 X MB 511
S219 S228	1944-1945	Schlichting	Travemünde	Daimler Benz	3 X MB 511
S301 S306	1945	Lürssen	Vegesack	Daimler Benz	3 X MB 518
S307 S321	1945	Lürssen	Vegesack	*Not delivered*	
S701 S709	1944-1945	Waggon Fabrik	Danzig	Daimler Benz	3 X MB 511

Glossary

B-Dienst: *Funkbeobachtungsdienst:* German Navy radio-listening services.

Cavitation: formation de tiny air bubbles around a propeller when spinning rapidly in water. Cavitation is a very noisy phenomenon.

Chadburn: Engine order transmittal box connected to the machine room.

CMB: Coastal Motor Boat.

Coastal Forces: British command structure including MTB, MGB, ML and HDML units during WWII.

DSC: Distinguished Service Cross.

DSM: Distinguished Service Medal.

DSO: Distinguished Service Order.

E-Boat: Enemy Boat: the British word for the S-Boote.

EMA: *Einheitmine type A:* Standard type A mine.

EMB: *Einheitmine type B:* Standard type B mine.

EMC: *Einheitmine type C:* Standard type C mine.

Enigma: Standard type A mine.

Fährprahm: Flat-bottomed craft created by the Germans and used mostly during operations in the Mediterranean for supply and personnel transportation.

FAT.: *Flächen Absuchender Torpedo:* circular-search torpedo.

FdT: *Führer der Torpedoboote:* Torpedo-boat leader.

FdS: *Führer der Schnellboote:* Gunboat leader.

Flak: *Flugabwehrkanone:* Anti-aircraft cannon.

FMA: *Flubmine type A:* Type A floating mine.

FMB: *Flubmine type B:* Type B floating mine.

FUMB: *FunkmeBbeobachtunggerät:* Microwave radar equiping the S-Boote.

G5: Soviet torpedo-launching gunboat.

HDML: Harbour Defense Motor Launch.

Kalottenbrucke: Armored pilot's bridge: to protect the crews during fighting the S-Boote bridge was armored from the beginning of 1943 on.

Kriegsmarine: On May 21, 1935, the German fleet changed its name and became the Kriegsmarine. The old flag with the colors of the German Empire and the Maltese cross was replaced by a new flag with a swastika in November.

Lauertaktik: S-Boote attack tactic with the boats separated into two half-flotillas, each one composed of several S-Boote pairs.

LCA: Landing Craft Assault.

LCI: Landing Craft Infantry.

LCT: Landing Craft Tank.

LMA: *Luftmine type A:* type A aerial mine.

LMB: *Luftmine type B:* type B aerial mine.

LUT: *Lage Umgehung Torpedo:* Zigzag-search torpedo.

LSI: Landing Ship Infantry.

LST: Landing Ship Tank.

MAS: *Motoscafi antisommergibili:* Anti-submarine motor boat used in the Italian Navy.

Metox: Electronic radar detection device invented by the Germans.

MGB: Motor Gun Boat.

ML: Motor Launch (coastal patrol boat).

MTB: Motor Torpedo Boat.

MS: *Motosiluranti:* Torpedo gunboats similar to the MAS used by the Italian Navy.

Nautical mile: distance equivalent to 1 852 m.

OberKommando der Marine (OKM): Commander in chief of the German Naval Forces.

Opération *Barbarossa*: Code name for the German invasion of the USSR.

Opération *Dynamo*: Code name for the Allied evacuation of Dunkerque.

Opération *Husky*: Allied invasion of Sicily.

Opération *Neptune*: Allied code name for the naval phase of *Overlord*.

Opération *Overlord*: Allied code name for the invasion of Europe in June, 1944.

Opération *Seelöewe*: German project for the invasion of England.

Opération *Torch*: American invasion of North Africa.

Opération *Weserübung*: Code name for the German invasion of Norway.

Percuteur: On a torpedo the metal hammer that sets off the detonator.

PT: US Navy Patrol Torpedo Boat.

Reichsmarine: Created on May 31, 1931 by the Weimar Republic to replace the provisional navy. Its role was to protect the German territorial waters, with a small number of vessels.

RNR: Royal Naval Reserve.

RNVR: Royal Naval Volunteer Reserve.

R-Boote: *Raumboote:* mine-sweeper.

S-Boote: *Schnellboote:* armed motorboat.

S-Boot Bunker: Concrete structures built by the Germans to protect the S-Boote flotillas.

S-Bootwaffe: All S-Boote units with their command structure.

Stichttaktik: Attack tactic which replaced the Lauertaktik. The S-Boote pairs operated in a single group and launched their torpedoes simultaneously.

Tallboy: Huge British bombs invented by engineer Barnes Wallis and his team, and used from May, 1944, on by the Royal Air Force Squadron 617 Lancasters.

TMA: *Torpedomine type A:* Type A anti-ship mine.

TMB: *Torpedomine type B:* Type B anti-ship mine.

U-Boote: *Untersee-Boote:* submarines.

UMA: *U. Boot-Abwehrmine type A:* Type A anti-submarine mine.

UMB: *U. Boot-Abwehrmine type B:* Type B anti-submarine mine.

Selected Bibliography

BOOKS

Gerhard Hümmelchen: *Die deutschen Schnellboote im zweiten Weltkrieg,* verlag Mittler und Sohn 1996.

Erich Gröner: *Die deutschen Kriegsschiffe 1915-1945.* Band 2, Bernard und Graefe Verlag Bonn 1999.

Harald Fock: *Die deutschen Schnellboote 1914-1945,* Koehlers Verlagsgesellschaft Hamburg 2001.

Harald Fock: *Fast Fighting Boat, their design construction and use,* Annapolis Md Naval Institute Press 1976.

Friedrich Kemnade: *Die Afrika flottille. Der Einsatz der 3. Schnellbootflottille in Sweitten Weltkrieg* Stuttgart 1978.

Gerhard Behrens: *Die Geschichte der 1. Schnellbootflottille 1931-1945 in Bildern,* Kiel 1986.

Bryan Cooper: *E. Boat threat on London -* Mc Donald and Jane's 1976.

Schlutz Herbert Max: *Die deutsche Schnellbootwaffe in zweite Weltkrieg,* Erlangen 1987.

Paul Schmalenbach: *The genealogy of S-Boote* 1969, Warship International.

Hervieux Paul: *The S-Boote war in the West 1941 – 1942,* Paris 1967.

Kühn Volkmar: *Schellboote im Einsatz. 1939 – 1945,* Stuttgart 1978.

James Foster Tent: *E-boat alert. Defending the Normandy invasion Fleet* 1996, Air Life England.

Serge Ouvaroff: *Baroud sur mer,* Les deux sirènes 1948.

Jean Mayen: *Alerte vedettes rapides,* Presse de la cité – 1962.

Eddy Florentin: *Les rebelles de la Combattante 1939 – 1945,* Flammarion 1998.

Douglas Reeman: *Les torpilleurs feux croisés,* Plon 1983.

François Emmanuel Brezet: *Histoire de la marine allemande,* Perrin 1999.

Robert Jackson: *Kriegsmarine, the illustrated history of the german navy in W.W. II* Avro Press 2001.

L.C. Reynold - H.F. Cooper: *Mediterranean MTB's at War – Short MTB flotilla operations 1939 – 1945,* London 1994.

AJD North: *Royal Navy Coastal Forces 1939 – 1945.* Almark Publication. June 1972

Vincent Bréchignac: *Les flottes de combat 1944-1945.* Société d'édition géographique maritime et coloniale.

Eberhard Möller - Werner Brack: *Dieselmotoren für Fünf Deutshe Marinen,* Mittler Verlag 1998.

Jack P. Mallmann Showell: *German Navy Handbook 1939-1945,* Sutton Publishung 1999.

Keiten Phelan - Martin H. Brice: *Fast attack craft* Mac Donald and Jane's – London 1977.

Leonard C. Reynolds: *Dog boats at war. Royal navy D. Class MTB's and MGB's 1939-1945,* Sutton Publishing 1998.

Erminio Bagnasco - Achille Rastelli: *Navi e Marinai Italiani nella grande guerra,* Albertelli Editore. Parma 1997.

Henri Le Masson: *Guérilla sur mer,* Editions France Empire 1973.

Norman Polmar - Samuel Loring Morison: *PT-Boats at war - World war II to Vietnam,* MBI publishing company 1999.

Jackson Robert: *Kriegsmarine: the illustrated history of the German Navy in WWII* Aurun Press. London 2001.

Philipp Kaplan - Jack Currie: *Convoy Merchant Sailors at war 1939 – 1945,* Aurun Press 1998

PUBLICATIONS

1939-1945 Magazine: n° 25, 96, 99, 103, 132, Heimdal.

Militaria magazine: n° 76 – novembre 1991

Alpha encyclopédie des armes – N° 117 – Les vedettes rapides – 1939-1945

Marines magazine:
n° 15: Le débarquement de Normandie,
n° 12: PT-Boats en Méditerranée,
n° 28: Au cœur de la Kriegsmarine,
n° 11: Les combats de mai-juin 1940.
Special issue n° 1: La Kriegsmarine,
Special issue n° 5: La campagne de Norvège,
Special issue n° 7: Les vedettes au combat 1939 – 1945,
Special issue n° 6: La fin de la guerre sur mer en Europe,
Special issue n° 10: La guerre en Méditerranée 1940 – 1942.

Warship Pictoral: n° 15 Kriegsmarine Schnellboote by Steve Wiper, Tucson Arizona décembre 2001.

Warship Profile: n° 31 Schnellboote by Gerhard Hümmelchen, London 1974.

Warship Profile: n° 30 MTB Vosper 70 Ft by David Cobb.

Royal Naval Coastal Forces: by AJD North, Almark Publication London 1972.

Squadron Signal Publication 2000: Vosper MTB in action warship n° 13 by Garth Connelly.

Osprey Publishing: German E. Boats 1939-1945 by Gordon Williamson, Osprey 2002.

Osprey Publishing: German Seaman by Gordon Williamson, Osprey 2001.

Magazine Signal:
n° 3 – février 1941,
n° 19 – octobre 1943.

Yachting et Progrès technologique à Monaco 1904-1914. Canots automobiles, août 1994.